D0712739

Japan's Reshaping of American Labor Law

Other books by William B. Gould

Black Workers in White Unions: Job Discrimination in the United States. Cornell University Press, 1977.

A Primer on American Labor Law. MIT Press, 1982.

Japan's Reshaping of American Labor Law

William B. Gould

The MIT Press
Cambridge, Massachusetts
London, England

KF
3369
G64
1984

© 1984 by
The Massachusetts Institute of Technology

All rights reserved. No part of this book may be reproduced in any form
by any electronic or mechanical means (including photocopying, recording,
or information storage and retrieval) without permission in writing from
the publisher.

This book was set in Baskerville
by Achorn Graphics
and printed and bound by
Halliday Lithograph
in the United States of America

Library of Congress Cataloging in Publication Data

Gould, William B.
  Japan's reshaping of American labor law.

  Includes bibliography and index.
  1. Labor laws and legislation—United States.
2. Labor laws and legislation—Japan. I. Title.
KF3369.G64   1984   344.73'01   83-24916
ISBN 0-262-07091-X   347.3041

For Hilda, Bill, Tim, and Ed,
who braved the cold winter wind of Tokyo.

Contents

Preface

This book commenced when I disembarked in Tokyo from a long, wearying flight from Moscow on August 30, 1975, and was greeted warmly at Haneda Airport by Professor Kichiemon Ishikawa of the University of Tokyo Law Faculty. He and his graduate student Akira Okuyama took me to my hotel. That evening I joined them and Mrs. Ishikawa for my first Japanese dinner. Professor Ishikawa's generosity and solicitude led to two months of hectic and stimulating interviews and conversations in Tokyo and most of Japan's major cities and industrial areas. Professor Ishikawa also kindly arranged for me to serve my first of two stints as a visiting scholar at the University of Tokyo Law Faculty during the fall of 1975. I was assisted financially through my appointment as a Rockefeller Foundation Conflict in International Relations Fellow.

Japan's mystique and resilience, the seeming similarity of its labor law to that of the United States, and the impact of my whirlwind 1975 visit made me long to return. Return I did, first in 1976 and then on five other occasions. The most lengthy and important of these visits took place in 1978 when I was a Guggenheim Fellow and, for a second time, a visiting scholar at the University of Tokyo Law Faculty. I am grateful to the John Simon Guggenheim Memorial Foundation, the University of Tokyo, the Social Science Research Council of the Rockefeller Foundation, and the Japan Society for Promotion of Science for helping to finance my 1978 visit. The assistance arranged by Professor Ishikawa was particularly valuable, as the dollar declined rapidly against the yen and it became clear that Japanese agricultural policy had tripled the California food bill for our family's three healthy and frequently ravenous young men.

In 1978, as before, Professor Ishikawa arranged for numerous interviews and discussions with representatives of trade unions, employers, and government, as well as with academics. He gave unstintingly of his own time in answering my many questions. Among the many others who contributed through responding to my questions, identifying appropriate cases, portions of books, and articles for translation from Japanese into English, and the like were Professor Kazuo Sugeno of the University of Tokyo Law Faculty, Dean Tadashi Hanami of Sophia Law School, Professor Koichiro Yamaguchi of Sophia Law School, Professor Yasuhiko Matsuda of the Yokohama National University Study Center for American Law and Economy, and Professor Eiji Takemae of Tokyo Keizai University. Professor Matsuda even translated articles and cases for me. Rexford Coleman, formerly with Baker & McKenzie in Tokyo, arranged for that firm to assist me with my inquiries and to provide translations throughout much of 1978.

The opportunity to participate as Distinguished Lecturer in the Kyoto American Studies Seminar, with Professor Sugeno acting as interpreter and with the support of a Fulbright award, helped focus my thinking.

I am grateful to Mrs. Kiyoko Fujii and Mrs. Mitsu Kimata, both of the International Labor Affairs Division of the Ministry of Labor; Osamu Hirota of the Japan Institute of Labor; Ichiro Seto of the International Metalworkers Federation; his Assistant Director, Seigo Kojima; Robert Immerman, former Labor Attaché of the U.S. Embassy in Tokyo; and Kazuo Adachi, Managing Director of Hoechst Japan Ltd.

In order to complete a project like this, it was necessary to communicate with many who could not speak English. In 1975, Stephen Marsland, a student at the Industrial Labor Relations School at Cornell University, provided excellent interpreting service and traveled throughout Japan with me. I was able to give talks under the auspices of the U.S. International Communications Agency, and their interpreters, most particularly Kenji Nadoyama, were helpful in my interviews. I gained insights through discussions with Tomio Fukui and Katsuhiko Takaike, two knowledgeable Japanese attorneys.

For translating cases and articles I thank Beth Cary, Michael Lewis, Andrew Goble, Hitomi Tonomura, David Groth, Kent Gilbert, Donna Jean Albright, Roderick Seeman, Thomas Nevins, and Conan Grames. Mr. Grames organized the Baker & McKenzie translating team.

Research assistants who contributed to this work were Karen Snell, Betty Meshack, Thomas Duffy, Marcella Davison-Aviles, and Pamela Krop of Stanford Law School. Papers written by Bruce Hironaka of Stanford and Alvin Nagao of the University of Hawaii Law School were helpful to me. Mark Askanas of the University of California at Davis performed the very difficult task of constructing and filling in the notes. Mr. Duffy's work was financed in large part through a grant by the U.S. Department of Labor.

I am also grateful to Clarie Kuball, Toni Dakan, Nancy Cooper, and Jan Watanabe for typing the manuscript.

The book was completed by virtue of a leave of absence from Stanford Law School in the fall of 1982 and my acceptance of an offer by my former colleague Victor Li to become a Fellow at the East-West Center in Honolulu.

I am particularly indebted to Professor William Simon of the Stanford Law School, who read the entire manuscript and provided me with many valuable comments and criticisms. John K. Emmerson of Stanford's Hoover Institution and Professor Nobutaka Ike of the Stanford Political Science Department also provided helpful comments.

This is but the first of what surely will be many books in English dealing with Japanese and American labor law and drawing comparisons between America and Japan. Perhaps it will forge some breakthrough to a badly needed understanding between these two great nations, the United States and Japan.

Introduction

Ever since Commodore Perry sailed into Tokyo Bay more than a century ago and emblazoned Japan upon America's consciousness, Americans—indeed the entire West—have expressed alternately (and sometimes simultaneously) puzzlement, frustration, and anger with the Land of the Rising Sun. Of course, part of the mystery is due to cultural differences. However, Japan is not just an oriental culture. Japan is a modern nation, an industrially advanced economy possessing an economic power that permits her to denounce all slights, perceived as well as real, as attempts to deny her the first-class status to which she is properly entitled.

For most Americans, a mélange of considerations make Japan too difficult to analyze rationally. For Americans over 45, the first thoughts that Japan triggers are bitter ones of Pearl Harbor and of Guadalcanal, Tarawa, Iwo Jima, and Okinawa, the scenes of the most savage hostilities that the modern world has seen.

In the wake of World War II a special relationship evolved between Japan and the West, marked by economic assistance in the form of early accommodation of Japan's protection of her infant industries, aid in rebuilding her infrastructure, and a nuclear umbrella which has permitted her to spend less than 1 percent of her gross national product on defense. These and other factors (not the least of which has been a superior record of productivity increases[1]) have helped a defeated nation to compile a gross national product that is the third largest in the world.

However, with Japan's success have come numerous comments similar to this (from columnist William Safire of the *New York Times*): "Let us remind Japan, Inc. and others that by protecting themselves from United States products, they call into question their taken-for-granted protection by the United States."[2]

The United States and Japan face one another across the Pacific at a time of economic tension, triggered most immediately by the record trade surpluses Japan has run up against the United States in the late 1970s and the early 1980s and the declining fortunes of union-organized industries in the United States, such as automobiles and steel. It does not seem to matter that there have been ebbs and flows in the trade balance in the past decade alone, and that the world economy and its failures may be the principal villains in this piece rather than Japanese protectionism or any erosion of the work ethic among American employees or employers. Japan's relations with the United States (and Europe) have deteriorated at an alarming rate these past few years. Expressions of tension and hostility are to be heard on both sides of the Pacific. It may well be that Americans continue to possess attitudes similar to those they held before World War II. During World War II and today, Americans have regarded the Japanese as inferiors—a people whom, out of the goodness of our hearts, we endowed with democratic government and modern industrial power. The undying myth of "cheap labor" as the cause of Japan's success—a proposition so tenaciously held by American unions and companies in industries assaulted by Japanese competition—is vivid testimony for this point.

In any event, if the very real barriers of language, race, and culture are to be hurdled in an attempt to find a more inviting road than the one that was followed during Japan's desperate scramble for raw materials in the 1930s, some knowledge of each society and its cultural underpinnings seems essential. In all major aspects, Japan and the United States remain fundamentally different cultures. What makes Japan so elusive for the outside observer (an elusiveness deliberately and assiduously promoted by the Japanese) is her insularity and other dominant features that predate both Commodore Perry and the Meiji Restoration: paternalism, a desire for harmony, and informal consensus. However, because this is a book that attempts to use the law to explain and compare industrial-relations systems rather than to provide a detailed analysis of Japanese law as such, a preliminary sketch of the Japanese legal terrain and its relationships to the industrial-relations system is in order before all else. The relationship between law and industrial relations is important because Japan and the United States have labor laws that resemble one another and, in some respects, appear identical. Are the same questions posed to the adjudicating bodies? Are the same answers provided when the same questions are posed? Frequently, the answer to these questions sheds light on societal and cultural differences between the two countries.

In some respects, the Japanese legal system seems almost "Dickensish," with its protracted delays that spawn litigation covering decades—a deficiency which is enormous even by American standards. A primary reason for this situation is that Japan has only 15,000 lawyers in a country with half the population of the United States—and there are more than 500,000 American lawyers. But this reflects Japan's preference for a society in which law is subordinate to human considerations. As Jiro Tokuyama has pointed out: "The very precision of the law is alien to the Japanese. . . . If a Japanese is involved in an automobile accident, his first reaction is often to send apologies and perhaps a gift to the victim. But such gestures should in no way be interpreted as an admission of guilt; it is simply a matter of form."[3]

In this connection, it is interesting to note that the Japanese unions do not have the same deep-rooted distrust of the judiciary that has long characterized their American and British brethren. This is so even though before World War II the judiciary applied statutes that were obviously injurious to the basic existence of organized labor, and even though since the war, to the consternation of the contemporary militant left, it has set limitations on the rights of public-employee unions. Toru Arizumi has the following to say about this matter:

The attitude of judges that "living law" meet the requirements of actual social living is common in most areas of the law. In the case of labor laws, the use of this doctrine constitutes one of the major reasons labor unions, despite the verbal denunciations of reactionary court attitudes, do not actually distrust the court strongly, as has been the case in American and British history. Moreover, because it has been almost impossible in the Diet to revise or abolish laws that suppress the labor movement or to improve laws that protect and encourage organized labor, workers attempt to obtain from the courts as favorable interpretations as possible under the existing legal system.

Still another point is that Japanese judges do not hesitate to step into any area of the people's lives when they think it necessary to do so to provide legal protection. Thus, they take up family problems, dispute problems in local assemblies and, in some cases, the validity of student expulsions from schools or universities. Likewise, when there are controversies over sanctions exacted by unions, such as suspensions or expulsions of members, the cases may be tried in the courts. It is not rare for a person expelled from a union for disobeying a union decision regarding political action to appeal to a court to invalidate the expulsion.[4]

The Japanese judiciary and administrative agencies that mirror those of the United States are in the mainstream of labor-management conflict resolution. Of course, many of the functions engaged in by the Japanese judges are grist for their American counterparts' mill. Nevertheless, the general observation seems an accurate one. The paradox is that this is so despite the potentially (and in many cases actually) paralytic effect of the scarcity of lawyers on the operation of the judicial system. However, as I have hinted, this scarcity may in some instances be something other than the hindrance that Americans would readily assume it to be; indeed, it may promote the conciliation and negotiation for which the Japanese are properly renowned.

In the Japanese industrial-relations system itself, paradoxes abound. The system discourages interfirm mobility for employees, but encourages certain kinds of job mobility inside a company. Security and wages are provided for older workers, but in times of economic crisis workers 45 or older are more likely to be the object of pressures (both subtle and direct) to leave a company so that younger and more vigorous workers may be continuously employed. The idea of government intervention in wages (and thus the collective bargaining process itself) is alien to Japan, yet no other government so effectively insinuates itself into labor negotiations (through both behind-the-scenes maneuvering and discussions and budgetary allocations for public employees' wages) and thus dictates the parameters of negotiated settlements. Finally, I have never been in a country where so many people complained about employment conditions and future job prospects as in Japan;[5] however, according to Japan's Ministry of Labor, although most Japanese are allotted 20 days of vacation they take only 61.4 percent of that time. (If one considers the days accumulated from the previous year, the percentage is 37.5.) Counting national and special holidays, weekends, and vacations, the average Japanese worker takes off 92 days in a year—36 fewer than his American counterpart. A "work ethic" is still dominant, yet boredom and discontent are voiced by some workers.

But now we are moving ahead of our story. First we must look at the historical evolution of modern industrial relations and labor law in Japan, and then we must focus on the ways in which apparently similar legislation has operated quite differently in Japan and the United States. Although historically Japanese law and judges are influenced by the civil-law traditions of Germany and France, the American labor-law administrative agency—the National Labor Relations Board—has spawned seemingly similar institutions in Japan. If ever there was living proof that the law cannot function in a vacuum, it is to be found in this tale of two nations with contrasting philosophies, cultures, and conduct. The lesson of a comparison of labor law in Japan and the United States is a lesson in the limits of law itself.

Japan's Reshaping of American Labor Law

1

Overview

... group solidarity remains in Japan because people work at it. Whether in villages, towns, urban neighborhoods, or work places, leaders exert themselves to retain the loyalty of group members by responding to their needs. Children are taught the virtue of cooperation for everyone's benefit, and, however annoying they may find group pressures, adults remain responsive to group attitudes for they are convinced that everyone gains from restraining egoism.

Ezra F. Vogel[1]

Today we are aware of a Japanese system of industrial relations that differs in fundamental respects from the American system. The battle cry of American trade unions has been "Take labor out of competition between companies and plants." The extent to which this philosophy has translated itself into a demand for rigid wage parity (or closely comparable wages and conditions) was witnessed in the United Auto Workers' 1983 negotiations with the Chrysler Corporation in the United States and Canada. In Japan this attitude has never taken root. The unions have not focused on uniform rates and conditions of employment and have not sought to eliminate differentials among industries and job classifications. Despite such slogans as "Equal wages for equal work," Japanese unions have not affected existing wage structures.[2] Rather, the principal concern has been "base-up" or percentage wage increases. Japanese negotiators do not concern themselves with comparability as it relates to the actual rate of pay; therefore, individual companies have broad latitude and discretion. A company's unique situation and the economic peculiarities of the individual enterprise are recognized. To the Westerner, this appears to be an inward-looking attitude that does not promote worker solidarity. It is in substantial part attributable to the Japanese system of enterprise or company unions.

This system of union organization not only reflects traditional Japanese paternalism but also is "largely a product of the structure of industry and the structure of labor markets."[3] In the primary sector of the Japanese economy—an environment of large companies that can provide benefits such as permanent employment in an internal labor market—company unions have flourished; they constitute 94.2 percent of all Japan's unions. Employees in the secondary labor and industrial market of multilayered subcontractors and in many small enterprises have more difficulty. So do unions that seek to represent them.[4]

The significance of the dual economy is considerable. Twenty-three percent of Japanese workers are employed in businesses with more than 500 employees. In addition, 12 million workers are in companies with 30 to 500 workers and 13,750,000 work with even smaller companies. H. Scott-Stokes writes: "Since the slowdown after the 1973 oil-price rise, average pay in concerns with fewer than 30 employees has fallen behind from 63 percent to only 58 percent of wages in companies with more than 500 employees. Cash handouts and bonuses average close to $1,666 a month in the big companies, but are little more than half that at small factories."[5] The enterprise union is generally a union of regular full-time workers, although many major corporations have employed only full-time employees since the labor scarcity of the late 1960s forced them to do so. This means the exclusion of so-called temporary workers, a disproportionate number of whom are women. According to the Ministry of Labor, in 1976 there were four times as many permanent employees as temporary workers. Among newly hired employees the ratio was almost 5 to 1. However, among female workers there are 1.5 times as many "temporaries" as permanent workers.

Although unions comprise a larger percentage of the eligible workers in Japan than in the United States, union coverage does not extend to such temporaries, and frequently not to the employees of subcontractor firms that are in the corporate family. These employees are part of the second tier of Japan's dual economy and receive inferior wages and working conditions, although some of the cultural characteristics described below have a measure of applicability to them as well. Japanese unions are reluctant to organize workers in the second tier of the economy. As the *New York Times* has noted,

. . . in Japan, far more than in the West, bonuses and fringe benefits, and especially job security and union protection, produce entirely different environments in the two tiers. The big companies find this "dual structure" profitable. It provides a cheap, flexible pool of unorganized workers at their subcontractors for which the "mother" company is not legally responsible. Japanese companies such as Toyota and Nippon Steel have many more subcontractors than General Motors or United States Steel. In hard times, these workers can be laid off at a distance.[6]

In any country where unions exist, the structure and scope of their membership coverage have enormous implications.

Management, Labor, and "Community of Interest"

American unions are generally organized on an industrial or craft (or occupational) basis. Even members of industrial unions (such as the United Auto Workers, the United Rubber Workers, and the United Steelworkers, which organize production workers and skilled workers together) are much more job-conscious than company-conscious, because American union representation is based on particular job categories in which workers in an appropriate unit or group of employees have a "community of interest" with one another.[7] In Japan, the essence of enterprise unionism precludes such analytical rigidity. The lack of job consciousness makes it possible to have a more flexible transfer system inside a company, which undercuts strict job categorization. Jurisdictional disputes between contending unions are unknown in Japan. Although the American problem is not so difficult as that in multi-union Britain, the regulation of jurisdictional disputes and stoppages has been a major concern of American labor law,[8] and of labor and management as well.

The lack of job consciousness and the flexibility of Japan's enterprise unions are also manifest in the way in which management is distinguished from labor. Part and parcel of enterprise unionism are employees' solidarity with and loyalty to the firm. Essential to an understanding of Japanese employees' loyalty is the relationship between the foreman and the worker, which has been characterized as *in loco parentis*. The contact between foreman and worker is the lineal descendant of the "labor boss" system that developed with industrialization. Cooperation has its origins in homogeneity and cohesiveness and in the *oyakata-kokata* (master-apprentice) relationship practiced by craftsmen of the Tokugawa period. This relationship, co-opted by management with the advent of industrialization, connotes a familial or parental bond. In a sense, the concept of *amae* (a desire to be dependent) is related to this same theme. This dependency, most frequently associated with the need of the infant to be near the mother, manifests itself in the industrial-relations system through employees' reliance on companies for housing, transportation allowances, and leisure activities—features that are generally alien to the Western system. This may also explain why Japanese employees comply with company discipline to an extent unparalleled in the United States.

This may be all the more puzzling to Westerners because, although Japanese labor law excludes so-called supervisors from union membership by excluding them from the definition of "employee," unions do represent workers who are labeled supervisors but who are regarded as working foremen and are responsible to section chiefs or *kacho* (who are excluded from the union) on personnel matters. The considerable number of supervisory ranks has blurred the demarcation line between supervisors and employees. Robert Clark states that in Japan "the actual work of supervisor, which in a Western company would have been done by a single set of foremen, was shared by employees in a number of ranks."[9]

The overlap or slight blurring of hierarchy and of blue collar and white collar is reflected even among company directors. One out of six Japanese company directors was once a union leader. Clark writes: "Of 313 major Japanese companies . . . 74.1 percent had at least one executive director who once served as a labor union leader. The figure was 66.8 percent in 1978. In Japanese management, executive directors are the top day-to-day decision makers."[10] This means that Japanese unions have an abundance of white-collar and supervisory members, from among whom come a disproportionate number of the leaders. Not only have managerial personnel held positions of leadership in company unions; in some instances they have climbed the ladder to a position from the national federation itself. For instance, the international-affairs secretary for the Japan Auto Workers (*Jidoshasoren*), whom I first met in 1975, was in charge of sales for Nissan when I returned to Japan in 1978.

The Japanese pattern of mobility between labor and management means that union presidents and other high officials are sometimes (though not often) graduates of the University of Tokyo and other leading Japanese universities. It also means that almost anyone who has worked for a Japanese company has been a member of a union at some point. It affects the style and attitude of trade unions in Japan by inhibiting militance, providing expertise, and creating more contact and perhaps some egalitarianism between blue-collar and white-collar employees. The fact that the salaries of Japanese corporate executives are considerably lower than those of their American counterparts may have some bearing on all of this. The announcement of new bonuses for General Motors executives before the ink was dry on the 1982 UAW-GM "concession agreement" makes the point vividly. The relatively narrow differential between blue-collar and white-collar salaries in Japan does the same.[11] Vogel states:

Those with higher positions continue to dress like others, often in company uniforms, and peers retain informal terms of address and joking relationships. Top officials reserve less salary and fewer stock options than American top executives, and they live more modestly. It is easier to maintain lower pay for Japanese top executives, because with loyalty so highly valued, they will not be lured to another company. This self-denial by top executives was designed to keep the devotion of the worker, and it undoubtedly succeeds.[12]

All of this is in stark contrast with the United States, where, for example, the exclusion of supervisors from the provisions of the National Labor Relations Act (NLRA) is predicated on the assumption that the supervisor-employee relationship is necessarily adversarial because supervisors represent management. In a dissenting opinion that appears to form the rationale for the exclusion of supervisors under the 1947 Taft-Hartley amendments to the NLRA, Justice William O. Douglas said

We know from the history of [the 1930s] that the frustrated efforts of workingmen, of laborers, to organize led to strikes, strife, and unrest. But we are pointed to no instances where foremen were striking; nor are we advised that managers, superintendents, or vice-presidents were doing so. . . . If foremen were to be included as employees under the [NLRA], special problems would be raised—important problems relating to the unit in which the foremen might be represented. Foremen are also under the Act as employers. That dual status creates serious problems. An act of a foreman, if attributed to the management, constitutes an unfair labor practice; the same act may be part of the foreman's activity as an employee. In that event the employer can only interfere at his peril.[13]

In the United States, supervisors are not generally organized into trade unions, although occasionally there are supervisory unions. American employers are not obliged under law to bargain with such unions in the private sector, because supervisors are excluded from the definition of "employee" under the NLRA and under much of the state labor legislation that affects public employees.[14] (However, to a limited extent which the U.S. Supreme Court has not defined, supervisors are protected from discharge and discipline under the NLRA when employer-imposed discipline has a coercive impact on employees.[15]) Additionally, American unions have had great difficulty organizing nonsupervisory white-collar employees in the major industrial unions, which are overwhelmingly blue-collar in membership. Although the 1981–82 recession created such difficulties for white-collar employees that some may yet turn to the unions, the distinction between blue collar and white collar is still felt and may be a defining feature of American industrial relations.

Locals and Nationals

The differences between American and Japanese unionism are reflected in the relationships between the national federations and the local unions (in the United States) and enterprise unions (in Japan). So company-conscious are the Japanese that, according to a Ministry of Labor survey conducted in 1974, out of 1,362 unions examined, only 5 percent engaged in negotiations with the participation of union officials from outside the company. This contrasts sharply with the involvement of the

Detroit, Akron, and Pittsburgh offices (and regional offices as well) of the United Auto Workers, the United Rubber Workers, and the United Steelworkers in negotiations of their local unions.

At the same time, particularly since the 1960s, Japan has seen the emergence of *shunto* (spring offensive), a form of centralized wage bargaining organized by the relatively weak national federations with which Japan's companywide or enterprise unions are affiliated. (Approximately 72 percent of Japan's unions are affiliated with federations.) *Shunto* involves a coordination of bargaining efforts between weak and strong unions for wage bargaining on a national basis, and its preservation was facilitated by the substantial economic growth Japan enjoyed in the 1960s and the early 1970s. Most important, *shunto* involves coordination between the public-sector unions (which have been more militant, left-wing, and sometimes Marxist in their rhetoric) and the private-sector unions (which have tended to be more like business unions, and have been conservative even by the standards of American trade unionists). The wage negotiations are actually conducted at the plant or company level. *Shunto* is simply the coordination of uniform wage demands coupled with a strategic decision to apply nationwide pressure to a particular industry or company. The wages that are negotiated in the spring are only about 65 percent of the total wage payments; the other portions consist of bonuses (negotiated later in the year) and overtime. Paid on the basis of the particular firm's financial well-being, the bonus can amount to 6 months' wages in a good year and considerably less[16] in a bad year. Thus, "concession bargaining" is built into the bargaining system; wages can swing up or down as much as 30 percent a year.

Japanese federations generally transcend company plants throughout the country and are organized along industry lines. However, the staffs of these national federations are usually small, reflecting their inferior status with respect to the company unions. The national centers—*Sohyo* (the General Council of Trade Unions of Japan) and *Domei* (the Japanese Confederation of Labor) are the two principal ones—are the equivalent of the American national federation, the AFL-CIO. [Out of a national union membership of 12,369,000, 36.6 percent are members of unions affiliated with *Sohyo*, 17.8 percent are members of unions affiliated with *Domei*, and 10.7 percent are members of unions affiliated with a third center, *Churitsuro-ren* (the Federation of Independent Unions of Japan).] A fourth and smaller center is *Shinsambetsu* (the National Federation of Industrial Organizations). The International Metalworkers Federation–Japan Council, the Japanese branch of the international trade secretariat for various metalworkers' unions throughout the world, has both *Sohyo* and *Domei* affiliates and has played an increasingly prominent role in *shunto* during the past few years.

Until the oil crisis of 1973–74, *Shitetsuroren* (the General Federation of Private Railway Workers' Unions of Japan) was the leader, or, as the Japanese say, "first batter." Often *Gokaroren* (the Japanese Federation of Synthetic Chemical Workers' Unions) vied for the position of leadership. However, *Tekkororen* (the Japanese Federation of Iron and Steel Workers' Unions) became the pattern setter until steel's recent decline in international markets. Even today, steel continues to establish the framework for wage settlements in *shunto*. In 1978, the steel offer and settlement (the two are usually identical) had more of an impact than that in any other industry. The major difference was that other federations, such as *Jidoshasoren* (the auto workers) and *Denkiroren* (the electrical workers), roared ahead with percentage increases twice as high as that in steel.[17] These federations have been able to escape the full impact of the "first batter's" wage negotiations.

Although the AFL-CIO is not directly involved in collective bargaining, one might take a look at the American federation's prominent role in combating the efforts of the Nixon and Carter administrations to establish wage and income policies[18] and its efforts to have government reconsider them. In fact, at this political level, one apparent difference between the American and Japanese federations prevails over such a tangential similarity and runs to the fundamental difference between American and Japanese unionism: genuine political involvement. Although Japanese federations have a reputation for involvement in politics (particularly left-wing or Marxist politics; *Sohyo* supports the Japan Socialist Party and *Domei* the more moderate Democratic Socialist Party), a majority of the JSP's members are *Sohyo* members and the party is dependent upon the unions financially. Although the involvement is more institutional and substantial than that which exists between the AFL-CIO and the Democratic Party in the United States, these political commitments do not penetrate the heart of the union movement at the enterprise level. No significant element in the labor movement supports the dominant Liberal Democratic Party.

Enterprise unionism has both strengths and weaknesses. Among its strengths is that the union is aware of the peculiar needs of the company or the enterprise. For example, unions have engaged in promotional and sales efforts that originated with management. In 1978, leaders of the electrical workers' union flew to the United States to explain the industry's position and to argue against barriers to imports from Japan. The president of the auto workers, Ichiro Sioji, has engaged in sales efforts on Nissan's behalf in the Soviet Union and Mexico. The iron and steel workers have used their affiliation with left-wing *Sohyo* to good advantage in promotional efforts in the People's Republic of China. Perhaps a measure of convergence is taking place as the United Auto Workers and other American unions join ranks with management to protect themselves against foreign competition, which imperils them both.

Another strength of enterprise unionism is that resistance to work-force reduction can easily be mobilized because members are employees of the company. Also, the union membership not only has a strong financial involvement with the company (and thus enterprise consciousness) but also has a strong bond with the rank and file because they work for the same company and have contact with one another. In this sense, one finds what Americans would understand as solidarity.

The weaknesses are these: It is easy for the company to manipulate the union and the leadership, the union is inevitably dependent on the company, and the white-collar employees (particularly the leaders) are more likely to support the company than the workers in many areas of dispute.[19]

Job Security and Wages

If the structure of enterprise unionism is the first pillar of the Japanese industrial-relations system, the second and the third are permanent employment (*shushin koyo*) and the method of wage payment (*nenko*).

Some Japanese and American observers disagree with this assessment because approximately 80 percent of Japanese workers are not permanent employees. Koji Taira and Robert Cole[20] have estimated that approximately 20 percent of Japan's wage earners are covered by *shushin koyo,* which guarantees employment until an age somewhere between 55 and 60. Employers with more than 500 workers on their payroll employ 23 percent of the work force, and it is generally the larger companies that provide permanent employment. (According to a 1974 Ministry of Labor retirement study, approximately 85 percent of these workers are able to find some kind of employment after reaching retirement age.)

Considerable strains are being placed on the system and the way in which wages are paid in Japan. *Nenko,* the seniority wage system, is based on the length of an employee's service with a company. This system is coming under strain because of the larger number of older workers in Japan[21] and an upward push in the retirement age from 55 to 60,[22] but there is still a substantial difference in the attitudes of Japanese and American employers toward layoffs.

In the United States dismissals and layoffs are ordinary (if regrettable) events, and there has not been much of a search for alternatives in times of economic stress, but in Japan extraordinary efforts have been undertaken by employers to provide alternatives to unemployment. For instance, employers often institute *kikyu* (which means to return home for a rest)—the plant is shut down one, two, or three days a month and the employees receive 90 or 95 percent pay. Another method formulated as an alternative to dismissal is *shukko* (the detachment or farming out of workers to subsidiaries or subcontractors of major companies). This is the method that is resorted to by the more established companies. The employees of subcontractors or subsidiaries may be bumped from their positions, much as junior employees in basic manufacturing are bumped by senior co-workers at a time of layoffs (the "last hired, first fired" seniority system in the United States). In Japan, the displaced employee may not be a junior worker. Indeed, it is more likely that he will be an older employee. Whereas younger workers are the victims of an economic downturn in the United States and Europe (a phenomenon that is furthered by age-discrimination legislation in the United States[23]), the older worker is more vulnerable under the Japanese system. *Katatataki* (tap on the shoulder) is subtle pressure by management for early "voluntary" retirement for workers over 45. This practice contradicts American policies opposed to age discrimination which assume that older workers can be as productive as younger ones.

Shushin koyo (permanent employment) has been a special privilege enjoyed by employees of large corporations. No reference to the subject is found in any collective bargaining agreement or in the Rules of Employment. It is not the product of either law (Japan's Labor Standard Law provides a worker with 30 days' notice) or collective bargaining but rather a unilateral decision of the employer. Nonetheless, a departure from the practice where it is in effect would run up against deeply ingrained expectations of the workers. (Women, who now constitute approximately 40 percent of the work force, are not generally the system's beneficiaries.)

Despite the fact that *shushin koyo* is by no means universal in Japan, employment security—more accurately, a reluctance to dismiss in contrast with other measures, such as holidays, shorter work weeks, and transfers—is more prevalent in Japan than in the United States. Accordingly, even though the lifetime-employment system may not be universal, it affects the thinking and the policies of most employers in Japan.[24]

Two developments in the United States may serve to narrow some of the differences between the two countries. The first is agreements, particularly in the automobile industry, that have established 60 percent income guarantees for employees with 10 or 15 years' seniority, placed limits on plant closures, contracting out of work, and layoffs, and actually provided permanent employment for 80 percent of the workers in six plants. The second is that a number of jurisdictions (California and Michigan are among the leaders[25]) have placed legal limits on the ability of employees to dismiss workers.

Dealing with Industrial Conflict

In light of the differences between the American and Japanese industrial-relations systems outlined so far, it is not surprising that American unions and management have been more conflict-oriented and less given to the Japanese style of cooperation between labor and management. This is true whether it comes to resolving differences by industrial strife or through peaceful methods such as arbitration. Though Japanese labor agreements contain grievance-arbitration clauses that resemble in language and form the comparable contract provisions contained in American collective bargaining agreements, and though Japanese law makes arbitration available to unions and employers that request it under the auspices of the central (*Chuo Rodo Inkaii* or *Churoi*) and local (*Chiroi*) Labor Relations Commissions, arbitration is rarely used in Japan, whereas in the United States it has become the generally accepted method for resolving most disputes that arise during the term of a collective bargaining agreement. Moreover, individual grievances, which are integral to the American grievance-arbitration process, appear to be regarded as inconsistent with the Japanese penchant for group consensus.[26] As a general proposition, the arbitration process appears to be inconsistent with the Japanese desire to avoid confrontation or open conflict. To the extent that parties are disputatious, the controversy will generally focus on the Rules of Employment. These rules are fairly voluminous documents which the Labor Standards Law requires management to promulgate in consultation with the union, where there is one, or with a majority of the workers where no union is on the scene.[27] They cover a wide variety of matters, including dismissal, discipline, and transfer—matters that Americans usually deal with through the arbitration process and the collective agreement will often address elsewhere in the West. In Japan, the collective bargaining agreement is apt to be in the appendix to the Rules of Employment.

It is just as peculiar from the Western perspective that different agreements may address different subjects. For instance, the parties may negotiate a separate wage agreement and separate agreements relating to fringe benefits such as transportation or housing allowances, and the wage agreement may constitute a separate document.

In treating dispute resolution, one cannot ignore the machinery for joint consultation (*roshikyogiseido*) that exists in 63 percent of the labor-management relationships where there are more than 100 employees. This machinery, which many Japanese brand as an attack on collective bargaining rather than an adjunct to it, deals with matters ranging from transfers necessitated by technological innovation to the providing of information by management relating to sales and even profitability. It prizes informality and behind-the-scenes discussions—characteristics deeply ingrained in Japanese behavior. This penchant for informality is consistent with the Japanese aversion to confrontation.

It is of interest that the 1982 collective bargaining agreements negotiated between the United Auto Workers and General Motors and Ford provide for joint union-employer committees which are designed to provide advance information to the union and discussion on business decisions.[28] Similar machinery is provided for by law in Germany and, to some extent, at the European Economic Community level.[29]

Equally important to any assessment of dispute-resolution procedures are the statistics relating to strikes. In 1976 the United States, with twice Japan's population, lost almost 12 times as many working days because of strikes or lockouts as Japan. Specifically, the United States lost 38,000,000 working days because of disputes in 1976, whereas Japan lost 3,253,715. Of course, these statistics are hardly a conclusive test for determining industrial-relations maturity or even industrial peace. Great Britain, where industrial relations are far more chaotic and inefficient than in either the United States or Japan,[30] had a smaller number of disputes than either of those two countries (2,016, as compared with 2,720 for Japan and 5,600 for the United States) and approximately the same number of working days lost as Japan (3,284,000). However, in many of Japan's major firms—in the automobile industry (Toyota, Nissan, Mitsubishi, Toyo Kogyo), in steel (Nippon Steel, Kawasaki), in shipbuilding (Kawasaki, Mitsubishi, Ishikawajima, Harima, Sumitomo), and in rubber (Sumitomo, Bridgestone)—no kind of strike or industrial action has been heard of since at least the 1950s. When strikes do occur, they are of relatively brief duration. The number of disputes in relationship to union membership has increased substantially in recent years (prompting Levine and Taira to argue that "Japan resembles France closely in important strike characteristics" and that this "belies Japan's reputation as a country of 'consensus culture,' "[31]), but, as Levine and Taira have noted, more than strike statistics are required to reflect the extent to which relationships are harmonious:

The Japanese appear to be more at peace with their working conditions than workers in some other countries. But the individual expression of conflict may be substituted by the collective expression. For example, Sweden has a lower strike volume than Japan, but its absenteeism is much higher than Japan's. One could say that Swedish workers, instead of collectively expressing their dissatisfaction through strikes, individually "strike" by not showing up for work. By contrast, Japanese workers do not individually "strike" but collectively do so more frequently than Swedish workers.[32]

However, the attachment to the firm on the part of loyal Japanese workers makes it less likely that they will "vote with their feet" and express their grievances through resignations. To this extent, conflict that might manifest itself through quits in an American company must be contained in the workplace. Moreover, Japanese unions frequently use other methods ("acts of dispute," as the Japanese call them) as an alternative to the strike. This reflects what Tadashi Hanami has characterized as the "competition and class conflict," which, along with "fundamental paternalism," is part of the Japanese system in his view.[33] With regard to the strike itself, Hanami writes

If you look at the Japanese union movement from the viewpoint of the Western unions, the Japanese way of striking looks like a stupid act of suicide. But the meaning and function of the strike is completely different in Japan. Most of the Japanese strikes are not strikes in the Western sense. Strike is a means of protest, or more precisely, it is the only means of showing their will. When they go on strike, they do not mean that they will never return to their jobs until they are satisfied or completely defeated. Rather, sometimes they first go on strike and then start to bargain. Employers also start to bargain seriously only after the union carries out some short-term strikes and shows how serious they are. Members of labor relations commissions often complain that both of the parties to the dispute bring them the case for conciliation or mediation without bargaining for themselves at all.[34]

Not much of Japan's industrial strife turns violent, but when it does the bitterness can run deep. Generally, such disputes arise in situations where one of two striking unions has returned to work. When there is violence, it seems to be tolerated by the law to a greater extent in Japan than in the United States.

The two countries' differing approaches to labor conflicts are illustrated even more graphically by the different attitudes toward litigation and law to which I have alluded above. Both Japan and the United States have unfair-labor-practice machinery and administrative agencies that have responsibility for implementation of the law. In the United States, the case load of the National Labor Relations Board (NLRB), which has responsibility for unfair labor practices, has become a major labor-law problem. The approximately 40,000 cases involving unfair-labor-practice charges coming before the NLRB have contributed to the delay and to pressure for labor-law reform. Japan is confronted with a similar problem, and it may well be that labor-law reform will soon become a major part of the labor-policy debate in that country (particularly if reform should ever be enacted in America). However, the number of cases filed with Japan's administrative agencies—the central Labor Relations Commission, which sits in Tokyo, and the local Labor Relations Commissions, one of which exists in each of Japan's 47 prefectures—is minuscule when one considers the case load of the NLRB. In Japan, over 1,000 cases were filed in 1975, and 828 were filed in 1976.[35]

The fundamental reason for these differences (and indeed most others I shall discuss) lies in the attitudes of workers and unions. In the United States, particularly since the mid-1960s and the 1966 rejection of the negotiated pact between the International Association of Machinists and American Airlines, numerous commentators have noted the rebelliousness of the rank and file and the frequent unwillingness to accept agreements negotiated by the leadership. There is hardly an industry that has been immune from "blue collar blues" or discontent, which has manifested itself in refusals to ratify negotiated agreements of wildcat strikes and in similar ways. In Japan, it is likely to be the other way around: The rank and file are likely to be tugging at the sleeves of the union leaders in Tokyo, advising them that they (the leaders), who are far away from the economic problems of individual firms, should exercise more restraint. Japanese workers, being company-oriented as their unions are, are more concerned about the real prospect of job losses if the union become too strident or undisciplined. That most certainly is a lesson of the 1978 negotiations in which Japanese workers in the private sector (with the exception of the auto workers' union, which is in the most profitable and export-oriented segment of Japanese manufacturing) knowingly accepted an actual reduction in their standard of living.[36] The contrast with the 1982 American auto negotiations in which 48 percent of union members in General Motors withheld their approval of an agreement is vivid.

Finally, Japanese workers may lodge suits in courts of general jurisdiction on their own initiative even though the subject matter is covered by labor law, whereas in the United States the doctrines of preemption and exclusive jurisdiction and the exclusive nature of the grievance-arbitration machinery remove a large number of cases from the courts.[37]

These, then, are some of the basic differences between the Japanese and American industrial-relations systems. It is difficult to imagine two systems more dissimilar (especially when one looks at the cultural attitudes), yet Japan and the United States have, to a great extent, shared the same labor-law framework since the conclusion of World War II. The details of the laws, and their interpretation and application, help us to see that the laws of the two countries, like the industrial-relations systems, are identical only when observed from the most superficial of vantage points. This book attempts to focus on administrative and judicial procedure and substantive law and to identify problems that have arisen in both systems as a vehicle for demonstrating how the Japanese and American legal and industrial-relations systems function differently. Although a fairly large number of issues have been chosen, this book does not attempt to present a comprehensive, treatiselike picture of the Japanese and American systems. What it does is highlight some of the basic assumptions that exist in both countries through an examination of administrative processes and the handling of unfair labor practices. To begin, we must look back to the conclusion of World War II and the beginning of the MacArthur occupation.

2

The Historical Framework

We insist that a new order of peace, security and justice will be impossible until irresponsible militarism is driven from the world. . . . we do not intend that the Japanese shall be enslaved as a race or destroyed as a nation. . . . the Japanese government shall remove all obstacles to the revival and strengthening of democratic tendencies amongst the Japanese people. Freedom of speech, of religion and of thought, as well as respect for the fundamental human rights, shall be established.
Potsdam Declaration, July 26, 1945

On September 22, 1945, a document entitled *U.S. Post-Surrender Policy for Japan*, prepared by the Department of State, the War Department, and the Navy Department, was released to the press by the White House. (It was actually dated August 29, 1945.) Part IV contained a provision entitled Promotion of Democratic Forces, and it stated: "Encouragement shall be given and favor shown to the development of organizations in labor, industry and agriculture, organized on a democratic basis." On October 11, 1945, General Douglas MacArthur, when called upon by the new Japanese prime minister, Baron Shidehara (the foreign minister during Japan's "liberal 1920s"), addressed the issue of trade unions.[1] According to the press release published that day by the general headquarters of the U.S. Army forces in Tokyo, General MacArthur stated to the prime minister that he expected among the "reforms in the social order of Japan" the "encouragement of the unionization of labor—that it may be clothed with such dignity as will permit it an influential voice in safeguarding the working man from exploitation and abuse and raising his living standard to a higher level. . . ."[2]

As Theodore Cohen has pointed out, this represented a sharp shift in American policy.[3] Until November 1944, the Department of State's position was that no reform or reorganization of the Japanese economy should be undertaken by any American or Allied occupation. However, by June 11, 1945, the Department of State overrode the president's advisors (including a former ambassador to Japan, Joseph Grew, who had stated "Experience [shows] . . . that democracy in Japan would never work") and opted for political and economic democracy. Thus, trade unions were promoted in Japan by the Supreme Commander for the Allied Powers (SCAP), General MacArthur, and by the SCAP's Labor Division (part of the Economic and Scientific Section), which had specific responsibility for the formulation of labor policy. (Under the September 2 instrument of surrender, the authority of the Japanese government was "subject to the Supreme Commander for the Allied Powers.") Moreover, the Department of State's decision led to Japanese labor legislation—major portions of which resemble American labor law, although the resemblance is one of form rather than substance and although the similarities must be seen in light of Japan's historical and continued adherence to the civil-law tradition, particularly that of Germany and France.[4]

The labor legislation was to be drafted by the Japanese and subject to American approval. The authors were members of a Labor Legislation Committee established by Premier Shidehoro after General MacArthur advised him to encourage trade unionism. Suehiro Izutaro was the principal draftsman.[5]

General MacArthur, a right-wing Republican who was prominently mentioned as a presidential aspirant in 1944, 1948, and 1952, was hardly a pro-union New Dealer, but he was convinced that Japanese unions were necessary to counterbalance the influence of the *zaibatsu* (the large intraindustry commercial interests that had so expertly fueled Japan's war machine). In essence, MacArthur, while neither sympathetic to nor knowledgeable about unions,[6] believed that they were important in the infusion of democratic principles necessary to Japan's well-being.[7]

Nevertheless, the materials and records of the MacArthur occupation in Japan indicate frustration with Japanese labor policy, particularly as it related to the formulation of labor law. The SCAP was supreme as the result of the surrender terms, but his authority was not unbridled. The Far Eastern Commission (FEC), established as a result of the foreign ministers' conference held in Moscow in December 1945, was designed to be the policy-making body for the Allies in Japan. As a practical matter, its authority was soon superseded by that of the SCAP, who was soon on the scene with a full staff. However, the *FEC 16 Principles for Japanese Trade Unions*, devised on December 12, 1946, established policy, and section 6 of the Principles eventually produced what came to be regarded by the Americans as mischief by encouraging union involvement in political activities. Iwao Ayusawa has said: "We know that SCAP was more embarrassed than helped, for instance, by Principle No. 6, which stressed the importance of participation of trade unions in political activities. SCAP had begun to sense increasing Communist influence among the unions of government workers. The Communist leaders were pleased with the Principle and used it to their advantage."[8]

Some of the legislation enunciated in 1945 and 1946 (at the very time of the FEC principles) bore a resemblance to American labor law of that time. As the occupation progressed, amendments and new legislation that were drafted made the similarity more pronounced. Thus, to an extent unknown in the case of any two other industrialized countries in the world, a similar legal framework provides us with the opportunity to see how institutions offer different answers to the same legal questions in dissimilar cultural settings. For the Americans, who were in step with the switch in the American attitude toward reform of Japan and saw the Japanese worker as an ally on the road to democratic reform in Japan, the seven years of occupation were full of surprises and frustration.

As noted above, the initial legislation passed in 1945 and 1946 was formulated by the Japanese, obviously with some knowledge of American as well as other foreign labor-law systems. (It has been said that the 1945 legislation was based on drafts of legislation first proposed in 1921 but not enacted by the Japanese Diet at that time.[9]) A number of other American reforms devised during the occupation with a view toward promoting democratization were adopted—for instance, women's political rights were expanded, the *zaibatsu* were dismantled, and land reform was pursued. In labor and in other fields, these efforts produced results which were quite different from the American phenomena that had inspired them.

When the Japanese surrendered, in August 1945, modern labor legislation in the United States (most specifically the National Labor Relations Act) had been in existence for 10 years. As James Gross has demonstrated, the National Labor Relations Board had a profound impact on the structure of trade unions (and thus on the entire tenor of labor-management relations) through its fashioning of appropriate units or groupings of employees for the purpose of collective bargaining.[10] Frequently, the NLRB had a hand in promoting industrial unions by including production and skilled workers in the same unit where craft unions found it difficult to obtain a majority of the vote.

To be sure, there had been labor legislation before the NLRA. It is important to recount briefly the problems relating to union organization in the United States and the way in which such legislation addressed them, for contemporary American law can be seen at least partially as a response to history.

Before the National Labor Relations Act, a variety of judicial techniques had been employed to suppress union organizational activity. After the 1890 enactment of the Sherman Antitrust Act (aimed at the major trusts, which had suppressed competition), congressional concern about trade-union activities was not in evidence. The U.S. Supreme Court had held in the *Danbury Hatters* case[11] that secondary economic pressure engaged in by unions against those who did business with another employer involved in a labor dispute could subject the union to the treble damage liability contained in the Sherman Act. In 1914, when Congress passed the Clayton Antitrust Act (which stated that the labor of human beings was not a commodity and sought to specifically immunize labor disputes from antitrust liability), Samuel Gompers, the first president of the American Federation of Labor, proclaimed the statute "labor's Magna Carta." This view proved to be short-sighted; the supreme court soon concluded that economic pressure for "unlawful objectives"[12] was not within the protection of the Clayton Act. Moreover, in the 1920s an equally ominous phenomenon emerged on the horizon: the more frequent use of the labor injunction to restrain strikes and picketing, particularly when those activities were carried out for the purpose of organizing workers into unions. The abuses associated with this technique [*ex parte* proceedings, trials based on affidavits (which were often form affidavits used for a number of proceedings), and contempt penalties imposed for disobedience by the same judge who had heard the injunction case, without the presence of a jury], and the fact that a temporary or preliminary injunction made a hearing on a permanent injunction irrelevant because of the importance of expeditious relief to both sides,[13] prompted Congress in 1932 to pass the Norris-LaGuardia Act, which was aimed at limiting the issuance of injunctions in labor disputes by federal courts.

The Norris-LaGuardia Act was important in American labor history for two basic reasons. The first is that Congress had learned some lessons from the Clayton Antitrust Act. Rather than give the courts the opportunity to distinguish between appropriate and inappropriate union activity, Congress sought to deprive the federal courts of jurisdiction over injunctions in practically all instances. Second, the supreme court concluded in *United States* v. *Hutcheson*[14] that, although the Norris-LaGuardia Act did not specifically address the question of union liability in antitrust cases, that legislation must be harmonized with other laws such as the Clayton Act. This led Justice Felix Frankfurter (who authored the court's opinion) to conclude that the judicial precedent that had rendered union economic pressure vulnerable to the strictures of antitrust legislation on the grounds that it was improper and inappropriate when engaged in for unlawful objectives was overruled or modified by the Norris-LaGuardia Act, and that so long as a union acted in its "self-interest," without conspiring with an employer to suppress competition in a product market, the union's activity was beyond the reach of antitrust legislation.

The most important element in modern legislation was, however, the National Labor Relations Act of 1935. Congress enacted this law under the commerce clause of the U.S. constitution on the grounds that the "denial by some employers of the right of some employees to organize and refusal by some employers to accept the procedure of collective bargaining" produced strikes and "other forms of industrial strife or unrest," which often interfered with interstate commerce. Congress, in its Findings and Policies of the NLRA, alluded to the "inequality of bargaining power between employees who do not possess full freedom of association or actual liberty of contract" in comparison with the power of employers. To deal with the "substantial obstructions to the free flow of commerce" that were related to these problems and to assure workers their "full freedom of association, self organization, and [the right of] designation of representatives of their own choosing for the purpose of negotiating the terms and conditions of their employment or other mutual aid or protection," Congress sought to protect the right of employees to select their own representatives and to engage in collective bargaining. In defining employers and employees for the purpose of coverage by the National Labor Relations Act, Congress specifically excluded all those in the public sector at the federal, state, and local levels, as well as independent contractors, supervisors, and agricultural laborers. A National Labor Relations Board was created.

The National Labor Relations Board was given two methods through which to implement the freedom of association and other rights of employees protected by the statute. First, secret-ballot elections for representation were guaranteed to employees who petitioned the NLRB for collective bargaining. If a majority of employees voting cast their ballots for the union, then an employer would have an obligation to bargain with the union as the exclusive bargaining representative for all employees, union and nonunion, or members of another union, in an appropriate unit or grouping of employees.[15] Sometimes the unit would involve a group of companies in a multi-employer association,[16] although such bargaining structures have never gained the popularity in the United States that they enjoy in Europe. Second, unfair-labor-practice machinery was established through which the NLRB could protect the same rights of employees. Specifically, it was made an unfair labor practice for an employer to interfere with, restrain, or coerce employees in the exercise of their rights to engage in collective bargaining or to band together for the purpose of "mutual aid and protection." It was also an unfair labor practice for an employer to "dominate or interfere with the formation or administration of any labor organization or contribute financial or other support to it."[17] Moreover, employers were forbidden to engage in discrimination "in regard to hire or tenure of employment or any term or condition of employment to encourage or discourage membership in any labor organization,"[18] to retaliate against workers who cooperated with the NLRB,[19] and to refuse to bargain collectively with a labor organization that had been designated by the employees as their exclusive bargaining representative.[20]

The NLRB was authorized to conduct hearings and to issue "cease and desist" orders against unfair labor practices, and also to require "such affirmative action including reinstatement of employees with or without back pay as will effectuate the policies of this act." Thus, the NLRB's order, being the product of an administrative hearing, was not self-enforcing. If an employer resisted, an obligation to seek enforcement of the order was placed upon the NLRB, and the method of enforcement was through a petition to the circuit court of appeals.

On the Japanese situation, Kichiemon Ishikawa has said the following:

Until 1946, Japanese labor law did not exist at all in any meaningful sense. . . . in a burst that may well be likened to an eruption, labor-relations law emerged as a major component of Japan's social and economic structure. Within 20 months of the beginning of Japan's occupation, more than 5 million men and women have been enrolled as members in 17,000 unions whose formation have been encouraged, and whose protection have been assured, by the occupying forces. . . . thus in Japan unlike America . . . modern labor law may [not] be justly regarded as a consequence rather than as the generator of organized labor activity.[21]

In Japan, labor law took a very different form in 1945 when the Trade Union Law was enacted. (It became effective in 1946.) Chapter I of the Trade Union Law contained certain general principles. Article 1 of chapter I said "The aim of the present act shall be to raise the status of workers and thereby contribute to economic development through the guarantee of the right of organization and encouragement of collective bargaining." Article 2 of chapter I further stated that the provisions of article 35 of the criminal code "shall apply to collective bargaining and other acts of the trade unions which are appropriate, being performed for the attainment of the objects of the preceding paragraph." In the 1949 amendments to the law, this language was followed by a proviso that "in no event shall acts of violence be construed as appropriate acts of trade unions." Thus, the way was open for the courts to determine what was appropriate or inappropriate for the purpose of protection under the Trade Union Law.

Soon after the passage of the Trade Union Law, Chairman Suehiro of the central Labor Relations Commission expressed the view that "vague expressions" such as "appropriate or proper acts" were ill suited to Japan inasmuch as "neither practices of labor relations or ethics governing those relations have sufficiently developed in this country." Accordingly, Suehiro took the view that criminal law was not to be utilized in connection with labor-union activity, provided that "this shall not apply to a case where undue damage has been caused either to the employers or third parties who have no direct relationship to the labor dispute, trespassing the bounds of necessity for attaining the objectives of the union." Although subsequent amendments have articulated the view that violence cannot be regarded as "appropriate" activity within the meaning of the law, scholars have attempted to immunize minor or nonserious crimes or various forms of interference with the entry and exit of employees or others to or from plant premises. It is doubtful that this approach has more precision than that put forth by Tadashi Hanami, who has set forth a "compromise interpretation" that would take the following approach: "A typical case might be when trade unionists enter the offices of the management, shouting, threatening and demanding to bargain, successfully force a meeting and eventually refuse to leave in spite of management requests to do so. In such cases, as long as their attitude was not too violent or excessively threatening, they will not be punished for crimes such as threatening behavior, coercion, or trespass."[22]

Article 12 further stated that "no employer shall claim indemnity from a trade union or members or officers of the same for damages received through a strike or other acts of dispute which are proper acts." Thus, in connection with articles 1, 2, and 12, the object was to immunize so-called proper or appropriate conduct or acts of dispute of trade unions from both criminal and civil liability. In this respect, the Trade Union Law covered much the same ground as the Clayton Antitrust Act and the Norris-LaGuardia Act, which were also aimed at protecting the unions against litigation for strikes and other trade-union activities. However, in contrast with the Norris-LaGuardia Act, Japan had no clear policy declaration against judicial interference in labor disputes.

The Trade Union Law did much more than this. Article 2 defined trade unions, for the purpose of the act, as organizations "formed autonomously by the workers, with the workers as the main constituents, for the main purpose of maintaining or improving the conditions of work and for raising the economic status of the workers." The definition of a trade union was not to include organizations that admitted to membership those who represented the interests of the employer, those that depended on the employer's aid for "major expenses," those whose objects were "confined" to "mutual aid work" or "other welfare work," or those that "principally were aimed at carrying on political or social movements." Article 3 defined the workers as those who "lived by wages, salaries or other remuneration assimilable thereto regardless of the kind of occupation," but article 4 specifically denied police, firemen, and employees of penal institutions the right to organize or join trade unions. (The last of these problems has always been handled in the United States as a matter of state law; some states have taken the position of article 4.[23])

With regard to the definition of trade unions, section 2(5) of the NLRA defines a labor organization as any organization in which "employees participate" and "which exists for the purpose, in whole or in part, in dealing with employers concerning grievances, labor disputes, wages, rates of pay, hours of employment or conditions of work."[24] The approach is quite different from that of article 2 of Japan's Trade Union Law, particularly insofar as the latter provision excludes certain organizations that are involved in non-trade-union activities. Finally, excluded from the Japanese definition of employees were supervisors who have the authority, "in the interest of the employer," to "hire, transfer, suspend, lay off, recall, promote, discharge, assign, reward or discipline, other employees or responsibility to direct them, or to adjust their grievances or effectively to recommend such action . . . in a manner which requires the use of 'independent judgment.' "

Chapter II of Japan's Trade Union Law, entitled Trade Unions, imposed on unions procedural requirements that not only have no counterpart in American labor law but probably would have been regarded as unconstitutional under the first amendment.[25] Representatives of a union were required to submit to "administrative authorities," who would then determine whether the union was in "conformity" with the requirements of article 2. A union was also obligated to submit a "statute" that provided for rules, containing (among other things) regulations relating to meetings, expenditures, and how the representatives of the union were to be selected. The United States had no analog to this kind of national regulation until the Labor-Management Reporting and Disclosure Act of 1959, better known as the Landrum-Griffin Act.[26]

Only in article 10 of chapter II was there reference to principles vaguely similar to those of American labor law. Under article 10, union representatives were to have the "power" to negotiate with an employer "for conclusion of a trade agreement or on other matters." Article 11 provided that no employer should discharge a worker or "inflict disadvantages" on him because of his union membership. Here the provisions were vaguely analogous to those of the NLRA that forbade discrimination because of union membership and required collective bargaining. However, none of the Japanese provisions imposed any kind of compulsion upon employers to bargain.

Chapter III of the Trade Union Law was entitled Treaty Trade Agreements. It stated that, when trade agreements (the frequently used European term for what Americans would refer to as collective bargaining agreements) were negotiated between unions and employers, they had to be submitted to the administrative authorities "within the week after the signing." No trade agreement was to exceed 3 years, and the parties were required to assume an obligation "in all sincerity" to promote the "efficiency and maintenance of industrial peace." Further, when three-fourths or more of the workers in an establishment came under a trade agreement, the remaining workers were to be bound by the same agreement. This contrasted with the American situation, in which, once the majority has selected an exclusive bargaining representative to represent all workers within an appropriate unit, all of them (and their individual contracts, if any are in existence) are bound by the collective bargaining agreement. Under the 1945 Trade Union Law, where a "major part" of the workers in a locality come under a particular agreement the "administrative authority" was to request one of the parties to the contract to extend the agreement for workers of "the same kind in the same locality."

American labor law provides that workers must become "members" of the union to the extent of paying the equivalent of dues and initiation fees as a condition of employment where the exclusive agent has negotiated a union security clause in the agreement, but the Taft-Hartley amendment that required a vote on such provisions was repealed in 1951. In Japan a union shop may be negotiated if a majority of the workers support the union. The provisions of Japanese law that allow for the extension of agreements for other workers in the same locality owe their origins to Germany, not the United States. (The British have similar legislation.)

Under chapter IV of the Trade Union Law, so-called Labor-Relations Committees or Commissions consisting of equal numbers of representatives of employers and workers and of "central members" or neutral, public third parties (*daisansha* or *churitsuiin*) were established. Administrative authorities were to appoint representatives of the employers and the workers with recommendations of organizations on both sides and central members with the agreement of the representatives of employers and workers. The Labor Relations Committees consisted of a national Labor Relations Committee and prefectural Labor Relations Committees. The functions of the committees were to be the compilation of statistics on labor disputes and investigations of conditions of labor, mediation, arbitration, and conciliation.

Violations of chapter II relating to trade unions' obligations and rights—including discharge on account of union membership as well as the right of workers to engage in collective bargaining—were punishable through criminal penalties: imprisonment not to exceed 6 months or a fine not to exceed 500 yen. These provisions were to be invoked at the request of the Labor Relations Committee. This, of course, was in sharp contrast with American labor law, which provides for administrative orders of the National Labor Relations Board to be enforceable in the courts. (Contempt penalties, possibly invoking criminal as well as civil law, are involved only where disobedience of an existing order is presented.[27])

The Trade Union Law as initially written in 1946 caused a good deal of concern to the MacArthur occupation, because of its divergence from American precedent, its detailed regulation of unions, and its presumed unworkability in many other respects. The concern of the Americans surfaced in a memorandum, entitled Critique of the Trade Union Law and Ordinances, written by Leonard Appel of the Labor Advisory Committee in July 1946. This document, while reiterating a desire to "refrain from interfering in the legislative process and suggesting a tailor-made law,"[28] complained of "serious defects of both omission and commission from the point of view even of the minimum objectives which this legislation may properly be expected to achieve."[29] The LAC noted that the Trade

Union Law failed to "fully and properly implement" a policy that would require an employer to adopt a "strict hands-off policy" on the question of self-organization of his workers and to accept "in good faith" the collective bargaining process. The LAC also stated that the law provided no opportunity for a full and fair hearing for all parties concerned, and that the only procedure mentioned was the "criminal type sanctions"[30] alluded to above. The LAC's statement that "majority rule principle is essential to effective collective bargaining"[31] was to be echoed continuously during the occupation (at least by the Americans). Also, the LAC stated that the Trade Union Law permitted a result contrary to the American practice in the latter respect. Finally, the LAC voiced its concern over the establishment of government supervision and controls over trade unions on the part of so-called administrative authorities and the consequent creation of a bureaucracy that might meddle in internal union affairs without any specific justification for this approach either at the time or in the future.[32]

Specifically, the LAC was critical of the fact that the Trade Union Law did not prohibit unions dominated or financially assisted by companies and addressed itself to this issue only to the extent of prohibiting "major" assistance to a labor organization by an employer.[33] Moreover, the LAC noted that apart from financial assistance there were a variety of other methods through which companies could control or dominate labor organizations, and that these methods (for example, selecting representatives either directly or on a *sub rosa* basis) were not prohibited by the statute.[34] The LAC recommended a statutory provision similar to that in the National Labor Relations Act.[35] In connection with this matter and with the criticism about excessive administrative regulation of union affairs, no doubt the Americans were concerned not only about the general absence of bona fide unions but also about the potential of *Sanpo* (or *Sangyo Hokoku Kai*), the Industrial Patriotic Society that had been created by Japan during World War II. The concern was that with a revival of *Sanpo* or a similar organization employers could subordinate and control workers and their organizations much as they had during the war.[36] (References to this did not appear in the committee's report.)

A second concern of the Labor Advisory Committee was that the Trade Union Law did not invoke any obligation on an employer to bargain in good faith with a union, but merely empowered union representatives to negotiate with the employer. Unless such obligation was thrust upon management, said the LAC, "the door is open to complete frustration of trade union goals and the friction and strikes which may result where the parties are left to their own devices insofar as the bargaining process is concerned."[37]

As noted above, the LAC also criticized the absence of the majority-rule principle. The committee said that the majority-rule principle "has been proven . . . by many years of successful and practical application in all segments of American industry," and that "there would appear to be no factors which would make it any less applicable to the situation that exists in Japan."[38]

The LAC noted that, although an agreement could become binding upon workers if three-fourths of the workers were covered by it, the employer would be free to undercut the union's authority in the interim. Said the committee: "Thus, rather than a standardization of employment conditions within an enterprise, an anarchal system is promoted. And because of the patent inequality of bargaining power as between an individual or small groups of workers on the one hand, and the employer on the other, such a system interferes with and can well be the negation of collective bargaining. An employer, if he so wished, could keep the employees divided into rival groups indefinitely."[39]

The Labor Advisory Committee recommended that the Labor Relations Commission have authority to make recommendations in the form of a "cease and desist order"[40] and to order an employer to take affirmative steps to alter his unlawful conduct, rather than rely on the criminal law as the Trade Union Law of 1946 provided.[41] The committee recommended that the Labor Relations Commission have the authority to reinstate a worker with back pay, so that an employer could not rid himself of union organizers and sympathizers. Also, the committee thought it was important that the employer be required to post notices as well as to file reports from time to time showing whether he had complied with the order.

Finally, the Labor Advisory Committee focused on the "firm" regulation and supervision of trade-union activities by the government. The committee took the position that the question of whether unions were involved in politics was a matter for the unions and their members.[42]

For these and other reasons, the Labor Advisory Committee came to the conclusion that revision of the Trade Union Law was more than warranted in light of its "unduly restrictive features." Said the committee:

The Trade Union Law as it now stands gives to observers abroad a distinctly unfavorable and unfair impression in view of the otherwise salutatory progress since the surrender toward the evolution of a sound, democratically inspired trade union movement. . . . The techniques of adroitly bringing about a speedy revision of the law can best be determined by the Labor Division with its fund of working knowledge derived from months of experience in handling similar legislative matters. It is believed that informal suggestions to Japanese government officials, to the Japanese labor experts who are devoting their talents to serve us with the Labor Legislation Drafting Committee, to leading trade unions, and to enlightened employers will at least serve as a springboard for achieving the desired changes.[43]

The Trade Union Law was eventually amended in 1949 and has been amended in minor respects since then. Before we examine the amendments, it is important to fill out the picture of labor legislation in Japan. First, and perhaps most important, the Japanese constitution, unlike the American, directly protects trade-union activity. The first Trade Union Law was passed before the promulgation of the constitution, but the amendments and much of the other labor legislation came after the constitution's effective date in 1947 and therefore must be interpreted in light of constitutional provisions.

Three provisions of Japan's constitution must be considered with regard to labor law. Article 28 states that "the right of workers to organize and to bargain and act collectively is guaranteed."[44] It is generally thought that the words "act collectively" were designed to protect the right to resort to acts or economic pressure, which includes the right to strike. There is no comparable constitutional provision in the United States, although the first amendment has been interpreted to protect workers and the freedom of association and also to protect the right to organize and band together for purposes of collective bargaining when the state interferes with such.[45] Article 27 states: "All people shall have the right and the obligation to work. Standards for wages, hours, rest and other working con-

ditions shall be fixed by law. Children shall not be exploited."
Article 25 also has some bearing on labor. That provision
states: "All people shall have the right to maintain the
minimum standards of wholesome and cultured living in all
spheres of life. The state shall use its endeavors for the promotion and extension of social welfare and security and of public
health."

The Trade Union Law is only one area in the basic legal
terrain of labor-management relations. The Labor Relations
Adjustment Law, passed on September 27, 1946, and amended
in 1949 and 1952, is also important. This statute is designed to
promote the adjustment and settlement of labor disputes so as
to "contribute to the maintenance of industrial peace and economic development." The central Labor Relations Commission
and the prefectural Labor Relations Commissions were cast in
the role of mediating and arbitrating bodies, and a Special Adjustment Committee was established under article 8 of this law
for the purpose of performing such functions. Moreover, the
commissions were obliged to appoint and keep a panel of con-
ciliators, who were to be "men of knowledge and experience or
capable of rendering assistance for the settlement of the labor
dispute." Thus, the commissions, in addition to making recommendations to the prosecutor about employers' discrimination
against union members, had an extremely important task
thrust upon them by the Labor Relations Adjustment Law. In
cases where conciliation was involved, the chairman of the commission could appoint a conciliator on the request of both or
one of the parties to a dispute or "on his own initiative." Mediation could be obtained from the Special Adjustment Committee; it could "draft a proposal for settlement, present it to and
recommend the parties concerned to accept it and to publish
the proposal for settlement together with a statement of the
reasons therefore" in any one of three situations: where requested, where the parties' "trade agreement" provided for it,
or where the case involved "public welfare work." Article 8 of
the statute defined public welfare work as work that provides
services "essential to daily life of the general public," including
transportation, postal, telegraph, and telephone work, water,
gas, or electricity supply, medical treatment, and public health
work. It seems clear that the Japanese call "mediation" what
Americans characterize as "fact finding," that is, recommendations by a third party.

Finally, arbitration would be provided by the commission upon request of both sides, where the trade agreement provided for it, but in no other situation. From the beginning, the Japanese, while providing for arbitration, treated it with caution and, in contrast with the cases of mediation and conciliation, made certain that the process rested on the consent of the parties. Although Americans have promoted voluntarily negotiated arbitration machinery, the same caution that the Japanese displayed toward arbitration generally has been adopted by them toward interest arbitration [arbitration over new contract terms, as opposed to rights arbitration (the interpretation of an existing collective bargaining agreement)]. (Japanese law and practice do not appear to acknowledge the American distinction between rights arbitration and interest arbitration.)

Under article 2 of chapter IV, where the prime minister deemed that in the case of public welfare work the suspension of operations arising from an act of dispute "seriously threatened national economic activities or daily life of the nation" a process of "emergency adjustment" could be utilized. In such circumstances, the central Labor Relations Commission could engage in conciliation, mediation, or arbitration (without a request or a trade agreement providing for such), or new undefined measures could be taken if they were deemed necessary for the settlement of the dispute. Where emergency adjustment was used, the parties were obligated not to resort to any act of dispute for 50 days from the publication of the process.

The Labor Relations Adjustment Act has no real parallel in American labor law. It (and, to some extent, the Trade Union Law) involves the Labor Relations Commissions in the business of performing two sets of functions: not only those that are analogous to the tasks of the National Labor Relations Board, but also those of the Federal Mediation and Conciliation Service. In American labor law, the Japanese emergency adjustment process is paralleled by the 80-day injunction enacted by Congress in the Taft-Hartley amendments of 1947 in the case of disputes affecting the health or safety of the nation and by the 60-day "cooling off" period provided for by the Railway Labor Act for disputes arising in the railroad and airline industries.[46] However, because of technological innovation in the case of telephones, because the public sector is involved in the case of the postal service, and because of the local nature of other industries with emergency potential (gas, water, and electricity), the Taft-Hartley amendments have had a considerably narrower scope than article 8. That is, as a practical matter, technological progress has facilitated the replacement of strikers by supervisors and managers. As a matter of law, states' control of public utilities under their own labor law is unconstitutional by virtue of the preemption doctrine, under which state jurisdiction is displaced by federal.[47]

The third of the triumvirate of Japanese labor legislation is the Labor Standards Law, which has no real analog in American labor law at the federal level. The Labor Standards Law provides that wages must be paid in cash and "in full directly to the workers," although payment in other forms may be permitted where provided for by law or collective agreement. Moreover, wages must be paid at least once a month at a definite date. Additionally, chapter IV obliges employers not to employ workers more than 8 hours per day or 48 hours per week and to provide a recess. These provisions are somewhat similar to those of the Fair Labor Standards Act of 1938 in the United States.[48] The Labor Standards Law also established employers' obligations in connection with holidays and annual vacation with pay, set up safety requirements, and established regulations on the employment of minors and women. However, the most important part of the Labor Standards Law insofar as this book is concerned is chapter II, which obliges employers to clarify the rules on wages, hours, and other conditions of work. Clarification may be articulated in the form of an individual contract of employment or through employment rules applicable to all workers. These are the so-called Rules of Employment.

The Labor Standards Law, from whence the Rules of Employment emerge, is one of the major bases for judicial activity in connection with employment security for workers. Article 2 specifically states that "worker and employer must abide by the collective agreement, the rules of employment, and the labor contract, and must discharge their respective duties faithfully." Article 20 obligates the employer to give any worker 30 days' notice of dismissal. If 30 days' notice is not provided, wages equivalent to 30 days must be paid in most situations.[49]

At the inception of the MacArthur occupation, all three of the above-mentioned statutes protected public as well as private employees. The Japanese constitutional provisions dealing with labor make no distinction between the public and private sectors. However, since the attempted general strike of 1947 and 1948 these groups have been treated differently under law—first by the occupation and later by the Japanese government. Ordinance 201 was issued by the occupation shortly after General MacArthur stated to the Japanese government his intention to deal differently with the rights of private-sector and public-sector employees. General MacArthur quoted President Roosevelt (whom he characterized sardonically as a great "exponent" of labor's rights) to the effect that there is no right to strike against the state. Ordinance 201 prohibited use of the strike weapon by public employees.

In 1948 the Public Corporation and National Enterprise Labor Relations Law (*Koroho*) was enacted. The railroads, the tobacco monopoly, and later the telephone and telegraph industries—all of which were operated by the government—were designated as public corporations and placed under this statute and under the jurisdiction of a separate Public Corporation and Labor Relations Commission (*Koroi*). For workers in these industries, striking was prohibited by this statute although they were able (within the confines of management's prerogatives on the scope of collective bargaining) to negotiate collectively with the employer. Other, more "pristine" public employees had been denied the right to bargain as well as the right to strike under government ordinance 201. This policy of division between the public and the private sector was applied to both local corporation and government employees under the Public Enterprise Labor Relations Law of 1952. Although there has been much controversy in Japan about this U.S.-imposed dichotomy between the private and public sectors since the early 1960s, the different treatment has persisted.

The 1949 amendments to the Trade Union Law are central to any discussion of Japanese labor law today. First, the preamble was broadened so as to provide more in the way of affirmative rights for workers. Article 1 states that the purposes of the Trade Union Law are to "elevate the status of the workers," to promote policies that will place them on an "equal standing with their employer in their bargaining," and to protect "autonomous self-organization and association" in unions for the purpose of carrying out collective action which includes the "selection of representatives of their own choosing for the purpose of negotiations." Second, because of militant Japanese

trade-union activity in the postwar period—"production control" (a tactic similar to sit-down strikes), mass picketing, and
violence—the statute attempted to make clear that "appropriate acts" of trade unions which were immune from criminal
prosecution were not to include in any instance "acts of violence." Article 8 maintained immunity for appropriate acts, but
(in contrast with British[50] and Australian[51] labor law) provided
immunity for members of unions as well as the unions themselves. In Britain, where the Trades Disputes Act of 1906
(amended by the Trade Union and Labor Relations Act of
1974[52]) and now the Employment Acts of 1980 and 1982 have
provided immunity to the unions in case of labor disputes,
individual workers are theoretically liable to suits for breach of
the individual contract of employment in connection with suspensions of work undertaken at the initiative of the employee,
including strikes. In the United States, suits against unions (but
not members) can be maintained in the case of secondary boycotts or violations of collective agreements by the unions, under
the antitrust legislation, or under state law in the form of criminal prosecution or civil cases where the subject matter is not
preempted by the National Labor Relations Act.[53] Third, the
unions that had access to the Trade Union Law were those
whose "main purpose" was improving conditions of employment. In response to occupation concerns, article 2 excluded
from this definition unions that admitted supervisory or managerial employees to membership—that is, employees whose
official duties and obligations "directly conflict with their loyal-
ties and obligations as members of the trade union concerned."
Moreover, financial assistance by employers to labor organizations was prohibited, with the exceptions of permitting union
members who are employees to confer and negotiate during
working hours without loss of time, employer contributions to
welfare funds, and "furnishing of minimum office space."[54]
Eliminated was the 1945 statute's reference to prohibition of
"major" contributions. Under American labor law, the test of
what constitutes lawful support of a union by an employer is
whether the financial contribution is "allowable" cooperation,
designed to foster good will, or whether it is inducement to
support a particular organization or management policy.[55]
Though American employers may or may not ordinarily provide financial support for union officials attending union meetings, they may under certain circumstances pay union officials

for time spent in negotiating with management.[56] The courts will look to the facts and circumstances of each case. A basic difference between the two statutes is that the National Labor Relations Act contains no proviso relating to office space. Indeed, in the overwhelming number of cases where such facilities are provided in the United States, a statutory violation is established.[57]

Article 7(4) of the Trade Union Law prohibited retaliation for filing complaints with new Labor Relations Commissions or for cooperation through the presentation of evidence or testimony in an unfair-labor-practice case or in connection with an adjustment of a labor dispute under the Labor Relations Adjustment Law. This was also borrowed in large part from the unfair-labor-practice provisions of the National Labor Relations Act.

Moreover, rather than allow for governmental administrative supervision of union activities by requiring reports, article 5 of the statute as amended simply required that any union seeking to utilize the Trade Union Law must have a constitution including the union's name, the address of the main office, a provision affording members the right to participate in all affairs of the union and to be given equal treatment, an assurance that there will be no disqualification because of race, religion, sex, social status, or family origin, machinery for the election of union leaders by secret ballot by the members, a provision for a general meeting at least once a year, financial reports showing revenues, expenses, names of main contributors, and other information, a requirement that no strike action be undertaken without the approval of a secret-ballot majority of members, and the same kind of majority-vote requirement in connection with revisions of the constitution itself.

Most important was the change in the statutory approach to prohibitions against discrimination on account of union membership. Unfair labor practices, along the lines of those contained in the National Labor Relations Act, were established in article 7. Article 7(1) stated that an employer would be prohibited from discharging or discriminatorily treating workers because of union membership or for performing "proper acts" of a union. A proviso in article 7(1) stated that membership could be required as a condition of employment in an agreement between the union and the employer where the union represented a majority of the workers in a particular plant. Although the NLRA provides that union security agreements can be negotiated, today there is no requirement that a majority of the workers vote for it. (However, as noted previously, the Taft-Hartley amendments, passed 2 years before the Trade Union Law of 1949, contained the requirement that a secret-ballot election be conducted wherever a union sought a union security agreement obligating workers to become members as a condition of employment. This provision was repealed in 1951.[58])

Article 7(1) of the Trade Union Law highlights a basic difference between the two statutory schemes. It states that the union must represent the majority of workers in order to have a union security agreement. Although the "right to work" proviso in the Taft-Hartley amendments[59] allows states to prohibit union security agreements entirely, American labor law has always utilized the majority-rule approach in connection with union representation of workers. That is, under the NLRA a majority of workers in an appropriate unit or grouping of employees can designate a union to bargain for them through a secret-ballot election under the auspices of the NLRB or through other methods, such as the signing of union authorization cards.[60] Once a union is selected by a majority of workers, it is the exclusive bargaining representative for all of the employees in the appropriate unit. The employer has an obligation to bargain with the union and with no others for all employees, whether they are union members, non-unionists, or members of a rival union.

None of these features exist in Japanese labor law. There is no method for selection of a representative provided by the Trade Union Law, and no concept of exclusivity. The appropriate unit is unknown. American labor officials on the SCAP staff discussed and in some instances urged the adoption of some or all characteristics of the American representation system. Theodore Cohen apparently took the position that the determination of appropriate units by the central Labor Relations Commission would be too complicated and cumbersome a task; nevertheless he urged that elections be "arranged" by the commission.[61] However, both labor and management—for different reasons—resisted such proposals. The employers saw a system of elections and exclusivity as giving one union too much power and authority to speak for the workers. Japanese employers were particularly uneasy about any labor-law reform that would enhance the power of the unions, having been confronted with militant union behavior in the postwar period when traditional management leadership was eliminated or ostracized. The unions did not support this approach because the labor movement was and is so divided. Each major labor center feared that its influence and membership would be decimated wherever an election and the dictates of exclusivity worked against it. There were legal obstacles as well. Many Japanese scholars today take the position that the doctrine of exclusivity is inconsistent with article 28, which guarantees the right to bargain to all workers. Since exclusivity was denied workers who wished to bargain through a minority union, the argument was that article 28 would be undermined in the process.[62]

Finally, in the initial stages of the occupation, votes for exclusive representatives seemed wildly impractical to the Americans. As Cohen has written, such procedures might have been a "dead letter," inasmuch as "plant workers were never asked which federation they preferred; that was decided by their union offices."

Then and now it would be difficult indeed to establish demarcation lines for appropriate units, inasmuch as the sense of job classification is not nearly as well developed in Japan as in the West. Job classifications are more blurred than in the West because, to some extent, payments are based on considerations other than the job (subjective evaluations and the like),[63] and also because Japanese employers have greater flexibility in connection with job assignments across classifications. In essence, the mobility that exists in the employer's own internal labor market—in contrast with the relative immobility in the external market—makes it difficult to shape appropriate units with clarity. Accordingly, though the majority-rule concept applies to union security agreements, neither majority rule as it relates to union representation, nor exclusivity, nor the appropriate unit, nor the ballot-box election is embodied in Japanese labor law.

The result of these differences is that Japanese labor law has had a peripheral impact on the contours of the trade-union movement. In contrast, in the United States the NLRB played a decisive role in determining the existence of industrial units and thus the place of industrial unions in labor-management relationships. The dissatisfaction of the American Federation of Labor with the treatment accorded craft unions in unit determinations was a vital factor in that organization's decision to join with management in support of the 1947 Taft-Hartley amendments.

Article 7(2), like American labor law, establishes an employer's obligation to bargain collectively with "the representative of workers," whereas the 1946 statute had only empowered union representatives to bargain with the employer rather than requiring the employer to bargain with the union.

In addition to what has been alluded to previously, there are three basic differences in the statutory schemes. The first is that American law obliged an employer to bargain only in the event that the workers had selected a union as their exclusive representative. Obviously, this is not the case in Japan. Moreover, an employer in Japan may refuse to bargain where he has "fair and appropriate reasons" for so doing. On the surface, this would appear to be different than in the United States, and many Americans thought so during the occupation. In part, however, this statutory language appears to be the rough analog to determinations under the National Labor Relations Act as to whether subject matter is mandatory—that is, whether it involves wages, hours, or conditions of employment, over which either party is required to bargain to the point of impasse. The one difference between the two systems is that, apparently, Japanese employers may refuse to discuss a subject altogether where fair and appropriate reasons exist, whereas under American labor law (in connection with nonmandatory subject matter, at least) there is still an obligation to bargain, but not to the point of impasse between the parties. As a practical matter, it would seem that there is little difference between the two countries.

A more subtle and important difference between the American and Japanese statutes has been articulated by T. Hanami:

... the wording of the Trade Union Law of 1949 suggests that the concept of "unfairness" has been superseded by the concept of "impropriety." The 1945 Trade Union Law, which introduced the American system into the Japanese law, referred to *fukosei rodo koi,* a literal translation of the English words "unfair labor practices." The reason for the change in the present laws is more or less accidental. The person who drafted the text chose *futo rodo koi* (improper labor practices) simply because the earlier phrase did not sound natural in Japanese. However, there is no general agreement that it is so. Actually, *fukosei* (unfair) is perfectly appropriate when the criticism is addressed to the government or to other authorities. When it comes to the attitude or behavior of private persons, *kohei* and *fukohei*, equivalents of impartiality and partiality, are more suitable. It seems that the Japanese language lacks an appropriate word to express the concept of fairness or unfairness in personal relations. . . .[64]

This becomes particularly clear when we consider the administrative process and the manner in which the unfair-labor-practice prohibitions are enforced in each country. This important theme cuts through any discussion of Japanese resistance to the American adjudicative approach.

A third difference is that the Trade Union Law retains the 1945 statute's condemnation of illegal conduct by employers but does not condemn similar activity by unions. This is particularly remarkable because the Taft-Hartley amendments had been law for 2 years and because a reaction against perceived abuses of power by trade unions was present in both countries. Moreover, General MacArthur was undoubtedly sympathetic to the Taft-Hartley approach. Again, however, the law was shaped to the peculiarities of Japan. Restraints similar to those accepted in the United States were ruled out by the protections afforded unions by article 28 of the Japanese constitution. (Besides, the practical upshot has been that unfair-labor-practice standards have been imposed on unions by the courts in both criminal and civil proceedings where union conduct is not "appropriate" or "proper.")

In Japan, prohibitions against inappropriate conduct or unfairness are implemented the central and local Labor Relations Commissions. The number of members on the central Labor Relations Commission was 24 until 1978, when it was increased to 27. The Tokyo Labor Relations Commission has 39 members, the Osaka commission 33, and the Hokkaido, Kanagawa, Aichi, Hyogo, and Fukuoka commissions 27 each. All the other local commissions have 15 members each, inasmuch as their case loads are not heavy. Under the Trade Union Law of 1945, the Labor Relations Commissions had the authority to recommend criminal prosecution to a prosecutor where violations were thought to exist. Under the 1949 amendments, the commissions have the authority to subpoena documents, to require testimony, and to hold hearings in connection with unfair-labor-practice cases. (Public members who do not come from the ranks of labor and management have exclusive jurisdiction to decide such cases.) Like the National Labor Relations Board, the Commissions now issue orders. Decisions of the local and central Labor Relations Commissions and requests for review of these decisions may be filed with the district courts. In the United States, review is a step higher, at the intermediate judicial level (the circuit courts of appeals). In Japan, the central commission reviews the decisions of local commissions, except in matters of obvious interprefectural importance (in which cases the central commission has original jurisdiction). The central commission is under the jurisdiction of the Ministry of Labor, and the local commissions are under the jurisdiction of the prefectural governors. However, both the labor minister and the prefectural governors appoint union and management representatives to the central and local commissions in accordance with the recommendations of the unions, and employers and public members with the "agreement" of employer and labor members of the commission. In contrast with the United States, in Japan the members or commissioners are part-time appointees. Political interference is avoided through the statutory provisions that permit the appointment of only three of the seven public members of the central commission (there are also seven union and seven employer members, respectively) from the same political party. Similar provisions apply in connection with the local Labor Relations Commissions. In the United States, the National Labor Relations Board has five members, and, although there is no statutory requirement, under all presidents there have generally been three from one of the major parties and two from the other, depending upon which party is in power.

Although Japan's Labor Relations Commissions are independent agencies, their staff members (especially those of the central commission) are likely to have come from the Ministry of Labor or some other governmental entity. In the United States there seems to be a greater tradition of a career in one agency rather than in government. Although Secretary of Labor Frances Perkins appears to have regretted the NLRB's independence considerably,[65] the Department of Labor staffers do not have as much influence in the NLRB as the Japanese staffers have in the labor commissions.

Although the role of Japan's Labor Relations Commissions is to perform mediation, arbitration, and conciliation and to resolve unfair labor practices, only the public members participate in the adjudication of unfair labor practices. Labor and employer members may participate in the hearings, but they appear to do so infrequently.

Under article 27, when a complaint is filed alleging that an employer has violated article 7, the Labor Relations Commission (generally the local one) is to make an "immediate investigation" and to hold a hearing unless the unfair labor practice arose more than a year before the filing of the complaint. Like the National Labor Relations Board, the commission is to make findings of fact and issue an order subsequent to the hearing if that proves necessary. The language of the Trade Union Law relating to relief contained in article 27(4) is that the order is to grant "in full or in part the relief sought by the complaints" or to dismiss the complaint. The National Labor Relations Act in section 10(c) makes no reference to the relief being "sought." Appeals in Japan or "request for review" may be filed by the parties with the district court, and decisions of the district court may be appealed to the high court and the supreme court of Japan, whereas in the United States appeals of an NLRB decision are taken to the circuit court of appeals and a review may be subsequently sought before the Supreme Court.

There are both similarities and dissimilarities in the origins of American and Japanese labor law, and some of them are useful in considering the impact of labor law in each country.

In both nations, the enactment of basic laws related to labor-management relations precipitated rapid union growth and galvanized organized labor into action. The 1930s American union slogan "President Roosevelt wants you to join the union" could well have been changed to "General MacArthur wants you to join the union" in postwar Japan.

Japan became the first industrialized country outside of the United States to adopt an unfair-labor-practice system. Moreover, the Trade Union Law created an administrative agency to interpret it, just as the National Labor Relations Act established the NLRB. Further, just as the NLRA led to a battle between the Congress of Industrial Organizations and the American Federation of Labor, the Trade Union Law led to one between the *Sohyo* and the *Domei*. (However, in Japan the stakes were not so high, given the absence of a ballot box and exclusivity.)

Both countries reacted toward public-employee unionism with caution and outright hostility. Both countries prohibited strikes by public employees in a blanket fashion.

Here the formal distinctions end. When one probes more deeply, basic differences become clear.

The right to join unions and to engage in union activity has a firmer constitutional foundation in Japan. If Japan were to enact its own "Taft-Hartley amendments," constitutional questions not presented in the United States would be involved.

Not only are the representation procedure and unfair-labor-practice provisions for the unions absent from the Japanese scene, but the entire concept of unfair labor practices as it has evolved in the United States is less precise and different in its meaning. It suggests that there are not public rights or wrongs, but rather problems that need third-party assistance so that harmony and compatibility may be facilitated. Though portions of American labor law seem similarly motivated, the problems encountered in the Japanese translation of unfair labor practices were hardly the same ones found in America.

Finally, Japan's small number of lawyers tended to promote an administrative process that has functioned differently. Superficially, the Japanese commissions look the same as the American NLRB. The contrasts, however, are dramatic. That is the matter to which we now turn.

3

The Administrative Process

Basic to any understanding of the way Japan's Labor Relations Commissions (referred to hereafter as LRCs) function is an assessment of their role in arbitration, mediation, and conciliation. The adjustment department of the central LRC, which handles these processes, has three sections: one that determines jurisdiction, one that specializes in hospitals, railways, and airlines, and one that conducts research.

In the last several years, only 4 out of 110 cases have gone to mediation, and none to arbitration. Of arbitration, mediation, and conciliation, the last is the most popular, because of its informality, its speed, and its success ratio. Only the public members are involved in conciliation, and often the dispute will go to an outside part-timer. This is the speediest method, generally taking 14 days. It relies heavily upon *sakusen,* or informality. Mediation, on the other hand, must be tripartite and generally takes 35–40 days. The procedure is more formalized and legalistic. Recommendations by the third party may be issued under either conciliation (*assen*) or mediation (*chotei*), and the recommendations may be verbal or written. However, under mediation there are very few verbal recommendations; as one might expect, there are many more recommendations of this kind under conciliation. Most cases are resolved successfully with the central LRC's assistance. The success rate reached 77 percent in 1973. (Since then, the annual success rates of the commission have been 62.3, 66.1, 60.9, 62.6, and 59.6 percent.)

There is close coordination between the adjustment and unfair-labor-practice sections of the local LRCs, but the same does not appear to be the case at the central level. This inclines the handling of unfair-labor-practice cases more toward practicality and dispute resolution. The reason for this coordination at the local level is that the local LRC is more likely to be close to the parties involved, being responsible for the investigation (*chosa*) as well as the actual trial in unfair-labor-practice cases. (A second hearing or trial in unfair-labor-practice cases takes place before the central LRC in Tokyo.) However, there is contact between the unfair-labor-practice and adjustment sections at the central LRC. Each Monday there is a secretariat meeting at which reports are provided on all cases, and thus the potential for contact exists.

It is important to consider these additional dispute-resolution functions not possessed by the National Labor Relations Board when examining the very different ways in which Japan and the United States handle unfair-labor-practice cases (figures 3.1 and 3.2).

Complaints or charges are filed by private parties in both countries, but after that there are always basic differences. In the first place, the number of cases coming before Japan's local and central LRCs is much smaller than the number coming before the NLRB (table 3.1). Moreover, the NLRB's case load increases more relentlessly.

On the average, there have been 30 times as many cases filed in the United States as in Japan. However, in Japan there is no doctrine of preemption applicable to labor-law cases that would deprive the courts of jurisdiction over subject matter addressed by the Trade Union Law and the LRCs. The U.S. Supreme Court held in *San Diego Building Trades* v. *Garmon*[1] that all unfair labor practices "arguably" protected or prohibited by sections 7 and 8 of the National Labor Relations Act are within the exclusive jurisdiction of the NLRB, and this doctrine remains intact (with some significant limitations[2]). In Japan, however, there is no doctrine of exclusive jurisdiction for either the local or the central LRC. Cases that involve unfair labor practices as well as discipline or dismissals can go directly to the district courts, and in Tokyo and Osaka such cases are assigned to the court's special labor bench. It is not clear to what extent the courts duplicate the jurisdiction of the LRCs, but the overlap appears to be considerable.

Statistics of the Tokyo labor bench show that 36 cases involving alleged breach of individual contract of employment were received by the Tokyo court in 1976 and 56 in 1977. All of this means that the Japanese statistics are somewhat understated if one looks solely at the LRCs. On the other hand, many suits

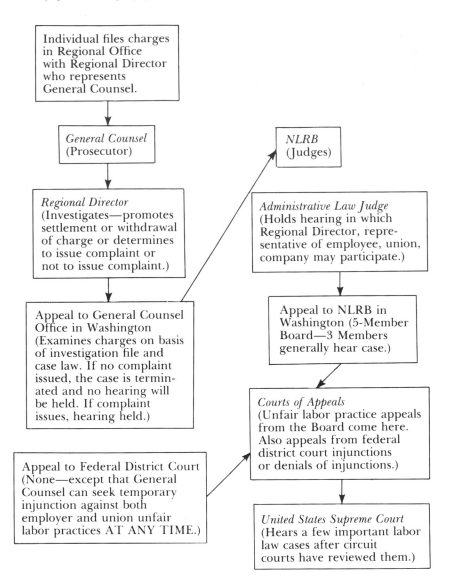

Figure 3.1

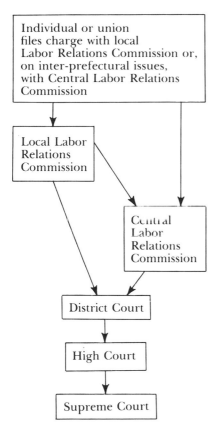

Figure 3.2

filed in the United States alleging breaches of collective bargaining agreements can be heard in the federal district courts as well as the state courts under section 301 of the National Labor Relations Act, which permits parties to sue for "violations" of collective bargaining agreements.[3] Yet the role of the judiciary in Japan is a larger one when it comes to hearing cases involving both the individual contract of employment and an unfair-labor-practice issue. The cases often involve both discharges and alleged refusals to bargain. Japanese courts are apparently not the least bit reluctant to decide issues involving interpretation of article 7 of the Trade Union Law when cases are presented to them directly. The unions do not appear to object or to allege usurpation, perhaps because they do not distrust the judiciary and perhaps because sometimes the

Table 3.1
Number of unfair-labor-practice cases filed.

| | Japan[a] | | |
	Local commission	Central commission	U.S. (NLRB)[b]
1975	929	93	31,253
1976	730	98	34,509
1977	729	95	37,828
1978	685	64	39,652
1979	563	83	41,259
1980	778	84	44,063

a. Source: Annual report of central Labor Relations Commission.
b. Source: NLRB annual reports.

courts may move more expeditiously than the administrative process.

In the United States, the NLRB is presumed to have discretion as the expert agency in connection with law as well as fact[4] (the test for review is whether substantial evidence on the record as a whole supports the NLRB's findings) when the case is reviewed by the court of appeals. In Japan, possession of original jurisdiction over unfair-labor-practice cases undoubtedly contributes to duplication and an undermining of the role of the LRCs as expert agencies, but resort to the judiciary has become critical in cases where expeditious relief is needed because of the nature of many unfair-labor-practice cases, the slowness of the administrative machinery, and the fact that the same procedure (including a hearing) is invoked at both the local and the central level. Moreover, the lack of any well-defined or articulated standard for judicial review in Japan may well erode the agencies' authority and claim to expertise.

When a case is filed with one of the LRCs, a staff member is assigned who will hold meetings with the parties to attempt to investigate and find facts. However, even before this, a written complaint must have been filed by the individual worker in order to trigger the process. Some LRCs require as many as 20 copies.[5] Oral complaints are permitted, but the LRCs are not set up to receive them and there is no standardized form for filing a charge.[6] As Ishikawa has noted, this may discourage the filing of charges in some instances, and thus it may be a minor factor in Japan's relatively small case load. In America, a written charge is required, but the NLRB has a standard form and will assist an individual worker in preparing it.

In Japan, subsequent to the filing of the charge and at the above-mentioned meeting, if one party refuses to answer questions or does not wish to reveal information that is within its possession, article 22 of the Trade Union Law makes the LRC anything but impotent. That provision states that, whenever the commission "deems it necessary for carrying out its work," it "may require the attendance or presentation of reports of the employer . . . or the trade union or others concerned, or it may require the presentation of necessary books and documents, or it may also have its members of staff . . . inspect factories and other working places concerned or inspect the conditions of business, books and papers, and other objects." However, article 22 is rarely invoked by either the central or the local LRC.

The NLRB is unlikely to subpoena evidence in the course of an investigation, but it will do so before or during a hearing. The major difference is that the LRCs in Japan will rarely do so because it upsets the consensus between labor and management. The view is that, if necessary, doubts will be resolved against the party that has possession of the evidence but refuses to produce it at the hearings. (This approach closely resembles that employed by American arbitrators.) It is at the hearing that the facts come out, and the greatest potential for settlement exists during and after the hearing. The Japanese investigation is additionally handicapped by the fact that on-the-spot field investigations are undertaken infrequently, on the grounds that "a fair judgment may not be possible when [one is] engulfed by the atmosphere of the place of the dispute" and that "there is a hazy notion that it is too hard on part-time officials to require them to travel to the place of the dispute."[7] Moreover, it appears to be assumed that full-time staffers do not have the authority or prestige to elicit information during on-the-spot interviews or other forms of investigation. In the United States, field investigations are the rule and not the exception, and NLRB agents in the field are expected to ask questions and obtain information.

In sharp contrast with the procedures in Japan, a very thorough investigation is engaged in by the NLRB when a charge is filed at one of its regional offices throughout the United States. Traditionally, most settlements (NLRB-approved or not) have taken place at this stage of the proceeding (table 3.2). Often the

Table 3.2
NLRB settlements of unfair-labor-practice cases, fiscal year 1980.

Method and stage of disposition	Number	Percentage of total cases closed	Percentage of total method
Agreement of parties	11,531	27.5	100.0
Informal settlement	11,357	27.0	98.5
Before issuance of complaint	7,424	17.7	64.4
After issuance of complaint, before opening of hearing	3,848	9.2	33.4
After opening of hearing, before issuance of administrative law judge's decision	85	0.2	0.7
Formal settlement	174	0.5	1.5
After issuance of complaint, before opening of hearing	118	0.3	1.0
Stipulated decision	60	0.2	0.5
Consent decree	58	0.1	0.5
After opening of hearing	56	0.2	0.5
Stipulated decision	17	0.1	0.2
Consent decree	39	0.1	0.3
Total number of cases closed	42,047	100.0	0.0

Source: NLRB annual report, 1980, table 7, p. 256.

NLRB urges a compromise or solicits a withdrawal, although in recent years (particularly in the San Francisco office) a larger number of settlements are taking place after this stage, apparently because of the pressure for prompt resolution of whether a complaint should be issued.

In Japan, there is an adversary proceeding between the union and the employer, with the Labor Relations Commission acting as judge. It is the union that comes forward with the evidence, and this helps explain the LRC's relatively diffident attitude toward fact finding. Nonetheless, the Study Group on Labor-Management Relations Law, appointed by the Ministry of Labor, criticized the present mode of investigation in a report issued in 1982.[8] The study group recommended that commissions "make the most" of field investigations and that investigations be conducted by staffers.

In contrast, the NLRB is divided into two parts. The general counsel is a presidential appointee who acts as a kind of civil prosecutor and has agents for unfair-labor-practice cases in regional offices throughout the country. The other, judicial side of the NLRB is made up of administrative law judges (formerly known as trial examiners), who operate at the trial level, and the five presidentially appointed board members who sit in Washington and review decisions of the administrative law judges just as in Japan the central LRC reviews decisions of the local LRCs. Once a complaint issues, the line between the general counsel and the respondent begins to harden. The administrative law judge, unlike the LRCs in Japan, is not really in a position to facilitate a settlement. A formalized judicial process is at work at this stage, and the likelihood of settlement diminishes appreciably. The Taft-Hartley amendments, which created a rigid line between the administrative law judge and the general counsel on the ground that employers' due-process rights had been ignored or abused under the NLRA, shape the settlement possibilities (or lack of them) once the judge and the prosecutor are both involved.

NLRB statistics shed some light on this. In 1980, the NLRB closed 11,721 cases pursuant to agreement between the parties. The NLRB can enter into an agreement with the respondent over the objection of the charging party, but if a complaint has been issued the general counsel's exercise of discretion may be attacked by the charging party in the federal courts.[9] Informal settlement resolved 11,547 cases (either non-NLRB-adjusted cases where a private agreement resulted in a withdrawal of the charge or cases where the informal agreement has been reduced to writing and approved by the regional director). One hundred seventy-four cases were the products of formal settlements where the agreement was in the nature of a consent decree, the future violation of which could result in contempt penalties.

A majority of the small number of formal agreements are entered into either after a complaint has issued or after a hearing has commenced. However, the same is true of only about one-third of the informal settlements.[10] This seems to indicate that the complaint and the hearing produce a considerably more adversarial and confrontational atmosphere. Where the prospect of liability is great, this is often apparent only after a complaint or hearing has brought the cold light of day to bear upon the case. Otherwise, the more formal procedure reduces the prospect for settlement.

In Japan, a far greater percentage of settlements take place after a hearing has been concluded. (American statistics do not

Table 3.3
Stages of establishment of amicable settlements in 1977 (7 local Labor Relations Commissions).

		Number of cases	Percentage
Withdrawn	After charges filed	9	24.3
	After start of investigation	17	46.0
	After start of hearing	8	21.6
	After end of hearing	3	8.1
	Total	37	100.0
Amicable settlement by parties	After charges filed	21	24.1
	After start of investigation	20	23.0
	After start of hearing	31	35.6
	After end of hearing	15	17.3
	Total	87	100.0
Amicable settlement with commission intervention	After charges filed	75	35.6
	After start of investigation	53	25.1
	After start of hearing	58	27.5
	After end of hearing	25	11.8
	Total	211	100.0
Total	After charges filed	105	31.3
	After start of investigation	90	26.9
	After start of hearing	97	29.0
	After end of hearing	43	12.8
	Total	335	100.0

even take into account settlements after a hearing is closed; they simply reflect what has happened once a hearing before an administrative law judge has begun. See tables 3.3–3.5.)

In Japan, a very different pattern is manifested after a hearing. The facts have emerged and the parties tend to cool off. Of course, a hearing before the central LRC is a reexamination or second hearing inasmuch as it duplicates the fact-finding process that already has taken place before the local LRC. The startling difference between the United States and Japan is that in Japan the number of cases in which there is a settlement or a withdrawal rivals the number of cases in which the LRCs are

Table 3.4
Unfair-labor-practice cases settled in Japan in fiscal year 1976.

	Number	Percentage of total closed	Percentage of total method
Agreement of parties	432	63.7	100.0
Informal settlement	195	28.8	45.1
Formal settlement (with commission intervention)	237	35.0	54.9
Total number of cases closed	864	100.0	0

Source: Central Labor Relations Commission, Annual Report, Fiscal Year 1976 (Tokyo, 1977), p. 2.

Table 3.5
Unfair-labor-practice cases settled in Japan in fiscal year 1977.

	Number	Percentage of total closed	Percentage of total method
Agreement of parties	482	53.8	100.0
Informal settlement	149	16.6	30.9
Formal settlement (with commission intervention)	333	37.2	69.1
Total number of cases closed	964	100.0	0

Source: Ministry of Labor.

required to issue a decision. At no point is the former as low as half of the latter.

In any event, after the hearing has concluded, the commission will begin to work actively on settlement possibilities with labor and management representatives. Sometimes the public member will meet with the deputy director and the section chief to discuss these possibilities. It is the section chief and/or the deputy director who are likely to make contact with the parties. Two staff members of the LRC generally will have taken evidence, and they may also take soundings with the parties to discuss a settlement. The rules and regulations of the LRC allow the public member to propose a settlement at the conclusion of the hearing, or just before the issuance of an order. Article 38 contemplates the possibility of written recommendations. This is a rare procedure, however, and fewer than 10 percent of the cases are resolved this way. Verbal recommendations may be provided, although they are usually based upon the decision of the local LRC itself. Finally, as with the NLRB, the parties may settle on their own initiative without the involvement of the LRC (although the LRC must be notified).

In Japan negotiations can take place after the verbal recommendations, but not after the written recommendations. However, the LRC will sanction any settlement or withdrawal that takes place, whereas the NLRB will scrutinize the contents of the settlement or withdrawal to determine whether public rights have been adequately protected. In sum, the Japanese LRC has no veto. Moreover, the success of the Japanese at the time of the hearing may reflect a natural incentive to settle (prompted, at least in part, by the poor quality of non-hearing settlement procedures).

The NLRB has no procedure providing for recommendations of any kind during or after the hearing. Indeed, the tendency of the general counsel and the board to torpedo agreements that are acceptable to labor and management—a practice never countenanced in Japan—has sparked considerable controversy in the United States. In *Community Medical Services of Clearfield, Inc.*[11] a majority of the board reiterated its view that the public rights at stake in unfair-labor-practice proceedings override private agreements in a wide variety of circumstances. In *Clearfield,* a non-board settlement approved by the administrative law judge provided for the execution of a collective bargaining agreement and the future reinstatement of a number of strikers, although some of them did not return to the same or equivalent jobs. The settlement agreement did not provide for back pay for employees who, it was alleged by the general counsel, had been discriminatorily denied reinstatement, nor did it provide for the posting of a notice in the plant advising that the employer would not violate the law in the future. Castigating the view that "labor relations harmony between the parties would be fostered by rubber stamping inadequate settlement agreements," the NLRB attacked the failure of the settlement to provide for back pay or the posting of a notice at the plant advising the employees of the employer's wrongdoing: ". . . we are at a loss to understand how a settlement agreement that surrenders employees' entitlement to back pay can be said to protect their interests. . . . there is an overriding public interest in the effectuation of statutory rights which cannot be cut off or circumvented at the whim of individual discriminatees."[12]

However, in *Clearfield* a collective agreement had been negotiated in lieu of back pay. American labor law (and Japanese also) does not obligate labor or management to consummate a collective bargaining agreement. Since a contract (particularly with wage increases, as in the *Clearfield* case) is the most important asset a union can possess, since the employer was not legally obligated to negotiate a contract with the union, since a contract may be difficult to obtain, and since the employees supported the settlement, most of the factors appear to militate against the NLRB's decision. Said the NLRB: ". . . we think it is clear that we would encourage wrongdoers to subvert the collective bargaining process by flouting their obligation to bargain in good faith if we approved settlements whereby they could wipe the slate clean by offering to execute a contract on condition that employees be denied full remedial relief."[13]

The NLRB has distinguished *Clearfield* from subsequent decisions, on the ground that "massive violations" had been committed and that back pay was relinquished.[14] Yet the position of the dissenters, former members Penello and Murphy, seems to be the better one. Their denunciation of the majority opinion as "litigation for litigation's sake" rings true. The dissenters stressed the fact that the contract was negotiated with back-pay liability in mind and that the union gained more through settlement than through litigation. Indeed, the NLRB Task Force, recognizing that settlements have reached a plateau and that the NLRB's resources have been stretched to the limit in recent years, has recommended that the NLRB accept private settlements unless individual discriminatees have "reasonable objections."[15]

In part, the Japanese pattern of settlement rather than litigation is attributable to the types of unfair labor practices that come before the Labor Relations Commissions. In the United States, the overwhelming number of cases that come before the NLRB involve organizational campaigns or union-employer relationships that are new or shaky. These cases invariably involve discharges and dismissals that are allegedly due to union activity. In such cases, the unions are generally concerned with obtaining speedy hearings and relief. In a large number of cases, there simply is no opportunity or scope for settlement inasmuch as the parties do not acknowledge a bilateral relationship. The number of such cases seems to be increasing in Japan also, particularly in the context of two-union discrimination. Straightforward union organizational struggles, so prominent on the American litigation landscape, simply do not occur with frequency in Japan. As in Europe, employer resistance to unions is less severe, for without the doctrines of exclusivity and majority rule it becomes virtually impossible to avoid unions altogether. However, with Japan's divided union movement, cases of two-union discrimination are plentiful. In the early 1950s, the phenomenon of the so-called second union meant that a moderate, cooperative union was formed in response to a more militant and confrontationist stance on the part of the collective bargaining representative for the workers. Quite often such a union was promoted and encouraged by supervisory personnel, both in and outside the union's area of representation. These cases appear to have revived in the late 1960s and the 1970s in much the same form as their predecessors.

It is not entirely clear why the two-union cases have become so important again, but it is thought that there are a number of factors. The first is the rapid economic growth Japan experienced in the 1960s and the increased rationalization and job dislocation that went with it. It appears as though new conflicts arose out of such problems and that with them emerged schism and an increased number of breakaway unions. A union that is at the center of conflict and in disfavor with the employer finds it increasingly difficult to bargain with the employer; thus, it brings a large number of charges alleging discrimination against its members in connection with wage payments, merit and job evaluations, and so on.

One of the most difficult cases involving two-union discrimination was *Japan Mail Order Inc.* v. *Tokyo Labor Relations Commission*,[16] decided by the Tokyo High Court. In this case, the first union had entered into collective bargaining with the company demanding a lump-sum bonus payment of 5 months' base pay plus a uniform amount for all workers. The company responded by stating that the union should "cooperate with an increase in productivity" as a *quid pro quo* for the payment. Meanwhile, it offered the second union a similar payment with the same conditions, and that union signed the agreement. (The second union, as one might suspect, had the allegiance of a majority of the workers.) The first union resisted, alleging that the phrase "cooperation with an increase in productivity" would inevitably lead to rationalization accompanied by a "reduction of employees, intensification of labor, real wage decrease, elimination of the labor union and converting the union into a company union [*goyo kumiai*]." The company disputed this characterization. The union charged that the failure to provide the workers with a lump-sum payment that had been provided the other union was an unfair labor practice inasmuch as it constituted discrimination on the basis of union membership. The Tokyo High Court rejected this argument, saying: ". . . the company decided that in order to increase the payment it would have to pay in advance the amount received for the next year's increase in productivity to be attained on the basis of harder work by the employees. Therefore it is with good reason that the company added the condition of 'cooperation with increase in productivity,' making it difficult to accept the view of the relief order [formulated by the Labor Relations Commission] that there is no rationale."[17] The court noted that if the union obtained the payments without signing the productivity agreement, this might constitute discrimination against the union that had signed the agreement. This, then, is one kind of difficult case that is made more visible by the absence of an exclusivity doctrine, which might eliminate continuous or extreme bargaining and jockeying between rival unions.

However, in many cases where a union is unable to assert itself as an effective collective bargaining representative, the Labor Relations Commission becomes a kind of substitute for the bargaining table. In such cases, the union may not be very concerned about speedy relief. To the contrary, the union may want to keep the employer at the hearing and involved in the procedure as long as is possible. Only in such situations can any form of collective bargaining take place. Such behavior is not unknown to the United States, but it is far more pronounced on the other side of the Pacific. This sort of situation leads to a very different kind of hearing from that which takes place in the United States before an administrative law judge. Particularly at the prefectural or the local level, the hearing can be very informal. Even though lawyers are present, union members will interrupt questions and answers provided by the other side as well as their own witnesses' testimony during cross-examination. There will be a good deal of shouting and sometimes applause by the union side, particularly when a witness has finished testifying and the union members believe that the testimony has helped their case. Union members will also not hesitate to excoriate the management representatives and to attack them for their alleged misdeeds. In short, this is a forum for the union and its members to show solidarity and to rally in response to the employer's campaign against them. Because the procedures take on these characteristics, it is fair to say that the aims of the parties (in this case the unions) will be quite different from those of their American counterparts in many instances. When one considers that anti-union animosity in discrimination cases is always difficult to show and that the LRCs rarely use their discovery authority, one can see that the objective of a union may be not a formal order but rather a compromise or settlement that will enhance the union's ability to engage in the collective bargaining process to some limited extent in the future.

It is therefore not surprising that Japan, like the United States, has suffered from a heavy backlog of cases. (See tables 3.6 and 3.7.) The records of the administrative processes in both countries are horrendous. (See tables 3.8 and 3.9.) This becomes more graphic when one considers that the Japanese statistics (which include some cases that have been to both the central and the local LRC) fail to take into account the time involved in the increasing number of cases that proceed to all three levels of the Japanese judiciary. As Ishikawa has noted about the delays built into the Japanese statutory scheme, "Those who contemplate pursuing justice through all the labyrinthian paths along which it totters are generally believed to be millionaires' sons or psychopathic personalities with a passion for litigation."[18]

Other factors are at work in Japan. The scheduling of hearings is sporadic, and the result may be that hearings are held for one or two days every month or so. The reason given is that the lawyers' calendar is full. In the United States, although private labor arbitration hearings are frequently scheduled in this manner, the rule is that those of the NLRB are held on consecutive days. The only Japanese Labor Relations Commission that appears to have attempted to take a stand and regulate this problem is that of Fukuoka. The Fukuoka commission, which at one time excluded lawyers altogether on the ground that their presence fostered delay, sets a firm timetable for

Table 3.6
Unfair-labor-practice cases pending at beginning of fiscal year.

	Japan[a]	U.S.[b]
1975	1,173	9,711
1976	1,417	11,156[c]
July–September 1976[d]		13,259
1977	1,469	14,256
1978	1,302	14,482
1979	1,358	16,942
1980	1,357	16,657

a. Source: Japan Ministry of Labor.
b. Source: Annual reports of NLRB, table 1.
c. Fiscal year had ended in June and was changed to end in September.
d. Transition quarter.

Table 3.7
Unfair-labor-practice charges against employers pending at beginning of fiscal year in United States.

1981	15,083
1980	13,213
1979	12,957
1978	11,227
1977	10,570
July–September 1976[a]	9,853
1976	8,119

Source: Annual reports of NLRB, table 1A.
a. Transition quarter.

hearings to which lawyers are required to adhere as a condition of being admitted to practice before the agency. Another factor responsible for delay is that many of the commissioners fail to apply evidentiary standards and thus allow the parties to control the hearing. The study group recommended that the presiding commissioner "take the initiative" in questioning witnesses and in obtaining information. Moreover, the study group recommended that more skilled staffers assist in this process.

In order to put this problem of delay in perspective, the study group also noted that some of the statistics look worse than they should because a disproportionate amount of the backlog is at the Tokyo and Osaka Labor Relations Commis-

Table 3.8
Average days for settlement of unfair-labor-practice case in Japan.

	Local Labor Relations Commission			Central Labor Relations Commission		
	Order	Withdrawn	Average	Order	Withdrawn	Average
1975	544	387	425	626	401	489
1976	624	366	429	679	619	637
1977	700	893	865	563	552	555
1978	777	477	535	565	563	563
1979	650	393	457	670	592	609
1980	758	653	679	821	717	746

Source: Annual reports, central Labor Relations Commission.

Table 3.9
Median days elapsed in processing of unfair-labor-practice cases in United States.

	1975	1976	1977	1978	1979	1980
Issuance of complaint to close of hearing	55	75	90	116	142	15
Close of hearing to ALJ decision	72	89	113	140	157	158
ALJ decision to NLRB decision	134	120	134	128	123	13
NLRB decision to regional office referral for enforcement	39	37	39	40	38	36
Referral for enforcement to filing of petition for enforcement in court of appeals	34	38	29	29	29	30
Filing of petition to issuance of court of appeals opinion	292	317	330	331	365	391

Source: Joseph E. DeSio, Associate General Counsel, NLRB.

sions. Nevertheless, the study group noted that there had been a rapid increase in charges filed between 1965 and 1974, and also an increase in complicated allegations of promotions and salary discrimination. Accordingly, it made recommendations beyond that set forth above. One recommendation was that the central Labor Relations Commission make the most of "on the spot" investigations by its secretariat. Another was that refusal-to-bargain cases be handled rapidly. Other recommendations, along with proposals put forward in the United States to deal with the backlog, are more appropriately discussed in chapter 4, but certain comparative themes cut through the present chapter too. The first is that, in both countries, employers appear to be taking more administrative decisions to the courts with a better prospect for reversal or modification than existed previously. The administrative process is deferred to less and less. Another is that the American process, which is more adversarial and confrontationist than its Japanese counterpart, responds in different ways to the greater number of charges with which it is confronted. Once the general counsel determines that a complaint must be issued, he has an incentive for both disclosure through discovery (rarely invoked by the NLRB) and, more important, an expeditious process. These incentives are simply absent from the Japanese administrative environment. In part, the reasons are institutional. There is no general counsel in Japan. The labor unions must initiate proceedings. The small number of lawyers, the crowded calendar, the need for a new forum for collective bargaining through the administrative process, and the fact that discovery powers are in the hands of the Labor Relations Commission rather than the unions often make the pursuit of remedies desultory.

The fact that the United States was not afflicted with the same kinds of problems before the general counsel was separated from the board by virtue of the 1947 Taft-Hartley amendments (and authority for pursuing complaints was placed in the hands of a review section) suggests that the differences between the two countries are more cultural than institutional. Accordingly, whatever the recommendations of the study group, it may be that the process in Japan cannot be expedited appreciably. However, it may also be that some of the delay may enhance the potential for settlement. Part of the reason may be more opportunity for dialogue and ultimate compromise. Americans, despite their legitimate concern with the speeding up of the administrative process, may find much that is useful in the post-hearing settlement procedures described above. The culture on this side of the Pacific is more likely to inhibit conciliation at this point, the gauntlet having been thrown down, so to speak. However, the principal difficulty is that responsibility would fall in the hands of the administrative law judge—where delays are growing most alarmingly because of an ever-increasing case load and an inadequate staff. When these problems are resolved, the Japanese experience will bear closer scrutiny by American labor lawyers and scholars. Even at that juncture, the attempt to devise effective remedies, so closely related to the number of cases and the agency's ability to process them rapidly, must still be addressed. That is a matter to which we turn next.

4

Remedies

The problem of remedies lies at the heart of any discussion of law—particularly labor law, which deals with complex and practical problems in the establishment and administration of the collective bargaining process. Both American and Japanese labor statutes have specific sections that address this subject.

Section 10(c) of the National Labor Relations Act authorizes the National Labor Relations Board to order parties who have violated the unfair-labor-practice provisions of the statute to "take affirmative action including reinstatement of employees with or without back pay as will effectuate the policies of [this] Act."[1] Article 27(4) of the Trade Union Law states that the Labor Relations Commission "shall make the finding of fact and issue its order in accordance therewith either granting in full or in part the relief sought in the complaints or dismissing the complaint."[2]

The NLRB must base its findings on a preponderance of evidence, and under the *Universal Camera* test[3] the court of appeals must enforce the resulting order if there is "substantial evidence" in the record to support the facts on which the NLRB relied. (Of course, although the NLRB is the expert administrative agency to which deference is to be paid by the judiciary in matters of interpretations of law,[4] the courts have not hesitated to reverse the NLRB when, in their view, the agency had strayed from the statutory mandate.[5]) Orders of Japan's Labor

Relations Commissions are also enforceable in the courts (although the appeal is to the district court), and no substantial evidence test or standard of review is to be found in the law or in the decisions of the courts. Americans find the absence of any statutory standard puzzling and perplexing.

Ever since 1938, the U.S. Supreme Court has expressed the view that the relief provisions of the National Labor Relations Act are designed only to authorize orders that are "remedial" rather than "punitive," even though the latter may be designed to deter future violations of the statute.[6] This distinction has hobbled the NLRB in its administration of the statute and is largely responsible for the promotion of and debate about the Labor Reform Bill of 1977,[7] which was designed to not only expedite the NLRB's administrative process but also to provide more effective remedies (such as double damages or double back pay in the case of unfair dismissals of workers in organizational struggles and "make whole" remedies, which would provide workers with damages in lieu of wages that they would have received through an unlawfully thwarted collective bargaining process[8]). Yet the distinction between remedial and punitive is found neither in the language of section 10(c) nor in the legislative history.[9] Indeed, Justice Frankfurter referred to the debate about what is remedial and what is punitive as a "bog of logomachy."[10] Both American and Japanese labor-law cases speak of the purpose of remedies as one of preserving the *status quo ante* or creating that which would have been had no unlawful activity been engaged in by the respondent. However, both American and Japanese decisions recognize that remedies must involve more than recreating the *status quo ante* or creating what would have been, and in both countries it is recognized that remedies play a critical role in deterring violations in the future and in establishing a healthy environment for labor-management relations. These themes run through many of the problems relating to remedies that have been faced by both countries.[11]

The Breadth of Administrative Orders

In *NLRB* v. *Express Publishing Co.*[12] the U.S. Supreme Court struck down a broad blanket order of the NLRB that contained general language ordering an employer not to violate the NLRA in any manner whatsoever. Said the court:

[It] is obvious that the order of the board, which when judicially confirmed, the courts may be called on to enforce by contempt proceedings, must, like the injunction order of a court, state with reasonable specificity the acts which the respondent is to do or refrain from doing. It would seem equally clear that the authority conferred on the board to restrain the practice which it has found the employer to have committed is not an authority to restrain generally all other unlawful practices which it has neither found to have been pursued nor persuasively to be related to the proven unlawful conduct.[13]

The Supreme Court further stated that a court, when affirming an NLRB order, has broader authority and power to restrain conduct that has been committed or that may be "fairly . . . anticipated from the defendant's conduct in the past."[14] The court noted that it was "salutary" that when one unlawful act had been committed a defendant might be prohibited from committing others. Said the court:

The breadth of the order, like the injunction of the court, must depend upon the circumstances of each case, the purpose being to prevent violations, the threat of which in the future is indicated because of their similarity or relation to those unlawful acts which the board has found to have been committed by the employer in the past. . . . to justify an order restraining other violations, it must appear that they bear some resemblance of that which the employer has committed or that danger of their commission in the future is to be anticipated from the course of his conduct in the past.[15]

The court noted that the subtleties of labor relations might lead the NLRB to conclude that discriminatory discharges of union members might be anticipated from an unlawful refusal to bargain in the past, inasmuch as the former could undermine the collective bargaining process. Jaffee has pointed out that the decision has two "equally significant facets": Where a violation is "isolated," the order must be restricted to repetition of the particular type of illegal conduct; where the violation is not isolated, the prohibition should be explicitly directed at future violations, which may go beyond those established in the record.[16] Under the authority of the *Express Publishing* decision, the NLRB (in a reversal of precedent) has held that "automatic adoption of broad orders in every discharge case is not warranted, but rather a narrow order, responsive to the particular actions of a violation of the [NLRA], would usually be more appropriate."[17]

In Japan, the position is that article 27 of the Trade Union Law does not authorize cease-and-desist orders (*chusoteki fusakui meirei*), which are broad and "abstract" orders of "forebearance" of the kind condemned in *Express Publishing*. The accepted view is that remedies are to be aimed at the conduct that is occurring. However, the Supreme Court of Japan held in the 1961 *Tochigi Kasai* decision[18]—for reasons similar to those put forward in *Express Publishing*—that where there is a likelihood that particular unfair labor practices will be repeated the Labor Relations Commission may, in its discretion, issue so-called orders of forebearance prohibiting practices that are the same as or similar to those that have occurred in the past even though the conduct may have been eliminated.

The reason for caution in Japan is similar to that expressed by the American courts. If a broad order containing prohibitions of unrelated practices is issued, an employer who violated it could be subject under article 28 of the Trade Union Law to both a "correctional fine" (*karyo*) and imprisonment (*bakkin* or *kinko*). Under such circumstances the law would be buttressed by punitive sanctions without prior resort to the administrative process.

The practices of the NLRB and the Labor Relations Commissions differ even more substantially than the cases indicate. The normal practice in the United States is for the NLRB and its administrative law judges to issue an order that contains fairly broad language (although the language is tempered by the dictates of *Express Publishing*). In Japan, the situation is antithetical. The normal practice is to issue carefully tailored orders prohibiting the specific conduct that was found to be unlawful in the proceeding. Perhaps the explanation can be found when one examines the penalties involved—probably the most appropriate area of inquiry, inasmuch as both the American and Japanese courts rely on the potential for penalties as a justification for limiting the administrative agency's authority to issue an order.

In the United States, both civil and criminal contempt penalties may be imposed on a contumacious defendant if the NLRB initiates a proceeding before the court of appeals that has enforced its order. However, even where the NLRB initiates a proceeding—and it appears as though the agency has been somewhat conservative in engaging in such efforts[19]—the proof that is necessary in connection with civil contempt is "clear and convincing" evidence. Where criminal sanctions are sought, the normal criminal standard applies: The violation must be established beyond all reasonable doubt. Both standards contrast with the standard that applies to NLRB administrative proceedings: The violation must be established by a preponderance of evidence. Moreover, the courts will refuse to impose contempt sanctions where defendants have acted in "good faith" even though their conduct violates the terms of the decree. And because the courts of appeals, being appellate courts and not trial courts, are not used in contempt proceedings, quite often the appellate judges are uninitiated and appoint masters who may file reports and recommendations to the court. In many instances, this has tended to complicate and delay the proceedings.

Contempt is alien to Japanese law. Article 28 operates with a fair degree of automaticity. Recall that article 28 states that where there is a violation of an order and where the order has been "sustained by the fixed judgment of the court in accordance with the provision of article 27," those who commit violations are "liable to imprisonment not exceeding one year or to a fine not exceeding 100,000 yen, or to both." Thus, the penalties are established in the statute. Rather than requiring a more exacting standard of proof, as the American courts do, under the circumstances of article 28 the Japanese courts require a less demanding standard of proof once the question of a violation of a court decree arises. This helps explain why the Labor Relations Commissions are more careful about providing broad orders, and why they generally limit an order to the specific violation involved, but by no means is it the only factor. One other is a preference for leaving the parties to their own resources to the extent practicable. To the extent that an order is narrow, that objective is more likely to be realized.

Posting of Notices

The two countries differ considerably in their approaches to posting of notices as a remedy through which employees (and sometimes members of the public) who venture onto plant premises are advised that a respondent has violated the law and has been ordered not to engage in similar misbehavior in the future. In the United States, employers (and today labor organizations as well) are invariably subjected to notice posting. This has been required as a remedy with automaticity under the provisions of section 10 of the NLRA, which permits the NLRB to order "affirmative action." In its Second Annual Report, however, the NLRB appears to have understated the matter when it stated the following:

In most of the cases in which it was found that an employer had engaged in an unfair labor practice, the board ordered the employer to post notices to his employees in conspicuous places in his plant, or place of business, stating that he would cease and desist as required by order of the board. In some cases, the board has desired to make certain that a particularly important fact will be brought to the attention of the employees, and has ordered the respondent to state specifically that it will cease and desist from committing the particular unfair labor practice, or that it will take the necessary affirmative action to remedy the situation.[20]

Some American courts have concluded that an employer should not be required to confess to an illegal act or to make an implied admission of guilt.[21] The NLRB, on the other hand, has sometimes insisted on oral admissions or apologies to assembled employees when the employer's conduct is egregious.[22]

As might be expected, the Japanese are more cautious. Though the percentage of cases in which notice posting is required is increasing (table 4.1), the remedy is by no means automatic. As representatives of the Hiroshima Labor Relations Commission advised me, frequent use of this remedy would make employers "lose face." Many American employers are extremely unhappy about notice posting, but it is doubtful that their feelings are as strong as those of their Japanese counterparts. The increasing percentage of Japanese cases in which posting is required, coupled with the caution recently

Table 4.1
Number of relief orders for unfair labor practices and number of notice postings by local Labor Relations Commissions.

	Relief orders	Relief orders with notice postings	Notice-posting percentage
1950	34	1	2.9
1955	23	2	8.6
1956	23	7	30.4
1960	71	9	12.6
1970	84	14	16.6
1975	128	32	25.0
1976	123	35	28.5
1977	101	36	35.6
1978	90	32	35.5
1979	107	36	33.6

Source: secretariat of central Labor Relations Commission.

demonstrated in this area by the American judiciary, suggests a mild degree of convergence between practices in the two countries.

Reinstatement of Employees

Under Japanese labor law, both the courts and the Labor Relations Commissions have jurisdiction over dismissals. The judiciary deals with individual contracts of employment (often interpreting unfair-labor-practice law in the process), and the LRCs decide unfair-labor-practice matters. When dealing with the above-mentioned matters as a matter of original jurisdiction, the Japanese courts have the authority to determine whether a dismissal has validity. Although the LRC will use relief orders containing provisions to the effect that "dismissal is nullified,"[23] the effect of the order is simply to provide for reinstatement and not to conclude that the dismissal is without legal effect. This is why the courts order back pay as a remedy and do not specifically provide for reinstatement, although the practical effect of the order is to provide for reinstatement. The LRC's order simply provides for reinstatement (*genshoku fukki*) with back pay.

In the United States, although under common law reinstatement was regarded as an inappropriate remedy because it would compel the performance of personal services, the National Labor Relations Act—specifically section 10(c)—reversed this rule in labor-management relations, at least where the protection of section 7 rights to protest working conditions and to join unions and engage in union activity are involved. Even before the NLRA, under the Railway Labor Act,[24] where no specific mandate from Congress was provided, the Supreme Court compelled reinstatement of workers who had been discriminated against so as to implement the legislative policy against such discrimination contained in the Railway Labor Act.[25] Moreover, in *Phelps-Dodge Corporation* v. *NLRB*[26] the Supreme Court held that reinstatement was an appropriate remedy where workers had obtained "regular and substantially equivalent employment" despite the fact that section 2(3) excludes such persons as "employees."[27]

Although Japanese law provides for reinstatement, it does not extend to workers who are discriminated against in connection with hiring. The Labor Relations Commissions cannot order their hiring or reinstatement. However, there are situations where a refusal to rehire has been deemed to have the same practical effect as a dismissal, and in such cases reinstatement has been regarded as appropriate.[28] Perhaps Japanese labor law on this subject can best be explained with reference to *shushin koyo*. Since large Japanese employers provide permanent employment and thus a greater measure of job security than is present in the United States, it is generally assumed that the courts and the Labor Relations Commissions have been cautious in interfering with their right to hire or select employees. In this area, Japanese management must exercise careful judgment and discretion—factors with which the LRCs and the courts are loath to tamper. Only where rehiring is involved—frequently when the courts find the termination of a business to be "dissolution camouflage" (*giso kaisan*)—will there be a departure from this approach.

The U.S. Supreme Court took the position in the *Phelps-Dodge* case that, inasmuch as reinstatement is a "conventional correction for discriminatory discharge," "it would indeed be surprising if Congress gave a remedy for one [firing] which it denied for the other [hiring]." Further, "to differentiate between discrimination in denying employment and terminating it, would be a differentiation not only without substance but in defiance of that against which the prohibition of discrimination is directed."[29]

Both countries' rules of law may well reflect societal practices. *Phelps-Dodge* represents an interventionist posture the Japanese are unwilling to accept for reasons previously stated—even though the price is tolerance of discrimination.

The Adequacy of Reinstatement and Back Pay

Since the early 1960s there has been a continuous debate about the adequacy of back pay and reinstatement, which began with the report of a federal commission chaired by Archibald Cox of Harvard Law School. The principal problem is delay in the administrative process. Today approximately 40,000 unfair-labor-practice charges are filed with the NLRB each year, in comparison with 11,325 in 1960. The number of complaints issued by the regional directors and the general counsel went from 2,141 in 1960 to 3,793 in 1976. From the filing of a charge through the decision of the administrative law judge and finally on to a decision by the NLRB it takes approximately a year for a case to be processed. But, as we have seen, the average is well in excess of a year if the case goes beyond the administrative process to the court of appeals.

The statistics for the Japanese Labor Relations Commissions seem to be even worse. On average it took more than 4 years (without any kind of appeal to the courts) for the Tokyo LRC to complete a case and issue a "partial remedy" in 1976. For cases in which complete remedies were fashioned, the LRC took 613 days. It took 592 days where there was formal settlement and 256 days where there was an informal settlement.

The difficulty with delay for the worker who has been unlawfully dismissed is not only loss of wages. In the first place, as the Pucinski Report of the U.S. House Labor Committee demonstrated,[30] some employers have often used the tactic of dismissing employees who have identified with the union as a kind of "license fee." That is to say, it is much cheaper to provide back pay than to negotiate a collective bargaining agreement with a union. Also, it is more unlikely that an agreement will be negotiated where workers are dismissed, because their fellow workers will get the message very quickly (particularly if those who are discharged remain unemployed), and the victims of dis-

crimination may become demoralized. Delay obviously harms
those who have been discharged. In addition to possible loss of
income, it may be that a worker cannot make payments. Furniture, household goods, and appliances may be repossessed and
mortgages may be foreclosed. A worker may suffer "humilia-
tion and embarrassment . . . in the eyes of his wife and children."[31] Thus, the collective interest in unionization on the part
of workers may be effectively undermined even though a remedy is provided.

Damage awards beyond back pay, however, have not been
provided in either American or Japanese labor law. In Japan,
orders to pay damage awards (*isharyo*) have sometimes been
requested by petitioners because of property damage or personal injury (physical or emotional) suffered as a result of unfair labor practices, but the Labor Relations Commissions have
uniformly taken the view that such orders are not within their
discretion and are therefore invalid.[32] Under American labor
law, though it seems clear that the reference to reinstatement
with back pay in section 10(c) of the NLRA is merely illustrative
of affirmative action and does not exhaust all remedial possibilities, damage awards have been rejected by the NLRB ever
since its decision in *National Maritime Union*.[33] In truth, the basis
for the rejection of damage awards as a remedy has not been
articulated clearly in the United States or Japan. In Japan, it is
not clear why damage awards lie beyond the language "relief
sought" contained in article 27.

An American judge (Wade McCree) has stated within the
context of a duty-of-fair-representation suit (*St. Clair* v. *Local
Union No. 515*[34]) the following: "Generally in contract law con-
sequential damages will not be awarded unless the consequences were clearly contemplated by the parties as being at the
heart of the contract. Accordingly, the usual monetary measure
of damages for wrongful discharge at common law under the
National Labor Relations Act, and arbitration and under the
Equal Employment Opportunity Act, is back pay less interim
earnings. . . ." This leads to a second problem: the limitations
that are placed on back pay in American labor law. Under
Anglo-American law there is a duty to mitigate damages. Although that concept is not specifically written into section 10(c)
of the NLRA, the U.S. Supreme Court accepted the mitigation
approach in *Phelps-Dodge*. The court found that the rule
fulfilled "the healthy policy of promoting production in em-

ployment" and that it advanced the remedial purposes of the statute. Said Justice Frankfurter, speaking for the court: "Making the workers whole for losses suffered on account of an unfair labor practice is part of the vindication of the public policy which the board enforces. Since only actual losses should be made good, it seems fair that deductions should be made not only for actual earnings but also for losses which he willfully incurred."[35] Thus, there is a duty to mitigate through reasonable diligence, and interim income that should have been obtained is deducted from back wages. The *Phelps-Dodge* rule is based in part on the view that, unless such deductions were made, the remedy would be punitive. However, it would be equally plausible to examine the question from the standpoint of the employer. "Thus," Justice Frankfurter wrote, "it could be argued that a back pay award is not punitive unless an employer is required to pay out a sum greater than he would have paid if he had never committed the violation."[36] Curiously, under American law, unemployment compensation, unlike wages, is not deducted,[37] although it is difficult to articulate a clean, logical demarcation line between the two situations.

The consequences of the *Phelps-Dodge* rule are unfortunate in two respects. First, the worker, already unable to claim recompense for losses in addition to wages, is also saddled with the loss of interim or potential income. The employer (who is, in many instances, able to undermine the workers' collective interest in unionism through unlawful dismissals and thus to profit in other areas not directly related to the individual discrimination) may be seen to get something of a windfall. Moreover, the effect of the rule is to necessitate hearings subsequent to the unfair-labor-practice case on the question of what should constitute back pay. This is not a mere question of examining the employer's records. The inquiry must focus on what kind of jobs were available that the worker might reasonably have obtained during the interim period. An additional complication is created by the rule that the worker, though initially obligated to seek employment that is substantially equivalent, must seek jobs beneath his qualifications after a reasonable period of time. This means more delay and a further frustration of the NLRA's policies. In Japan, the rule is now quite different. In the *Dai Ni Hato Taxi* decision of the supreme court, issued by the grand bench in early 1977,[38] all of the justices, in three different opinions, took the position that at least under certain circumstances interim income could not be deducted from an award of back pay. The court said that when an employer is able to remove the worker from the workshop, "all workers' general union activities are subject to oppression and restriction." "For this reason," the decision continued, "the relief order is considered not only from the perspective of offering remedy for individual damages wrought by the encroachment on the discharges, but also is considered together with the obstruction to overall union activities. The conditions of obstruction are thus removed and corrected and restoration of normal order in the industrial relations between the collective groups which was the intent of the law takes place."[39] In the majority view, the initial focus of attention must be on the individual worker and the kind of job through which he obtained his interim income. If the job involved heavier "psychological or physical requirements" that made it undesirable and unpleasant, this would be an argument against deducting interim income.

In *Dai Ni Hato Taxi* the majority found that the interim work obtained by taxi drivers—driving for other companies—was not so difficult as to warrant a remedy. This precluded the deduction of interim income. The court stated that there would need to be a tight relationship between the individual harm and the impact on the collective interest in order for interim earnings not to be deducted. The court also said that the "ultimate effect of restrictions on general union activities" has "a close relationship to the severity of the harm actually done to the worker in question who was discharged." In assessing the harm done, the court stated that such factors as the differences in the "ease or difficulty" in finding other jobs, the nature and content of the interim job, the working conditions at the interim place of work, and the kind of wages and allowances offered are all to be taken into account. The court specifically stated that the question of whether the worker has earned interim income "will make a difference in fashioning the back pay remedy."

At the other extreme is the separate dissenting opinion of Justice Seiichi Kishi. Justice Kishi's view was that interim income can never be deducted from back pay. In essence, Justice Kishi's view was that the appropriate vantage point for assessing the remedy is that of the employer rather than the employee. The interim income, in Justice Kishi's view, "has nothing to do with the employer and is something which is purely coincidental."[40] The objective here is to establish industrial-relations "order." Though it is important to note that deducting interim income involves considerations that are purely from the employee's side and have nothing to do with the employer who has committed the statutory violation, all attempts to fashion effective monetary remedies cannot be viewed as mere attempts to restore the *status quo ante* but must be seen as attempts to order and structure good industrial relations for the future as well as to provide compensation. Justice Kishi stated that the objective is to restore and secure "normal labor relations order between labor and management," and in this respect the opinion seems sound. One cannot say the same about the portion of the opinion that states that the unfair-labor-practice system is designed to "obligate and require the employer to restore conditions to what would have been without the unfair labor practice."[41] What "would have been" is arguably more speculative than the restoration of good industrial relations.

The dissenting opinion of Justice Shigemitsu Dando, joined in by three other justices, points out that article 7 of the Trade Union Law is not designed "primarily" to protect the rights and interests of individual workers in the employer-employee relationship, but rather is meant to prevent managerial interference in organized activities. A paper entitled "Why Back Pay?"[42] points out that a union incurs organizational and financial expenses in connection with protesting an unfair labor practice, for which it should be compensated. This may be putting it a bit differently than the opinions of Justices Dando and Kishi do, but it highlights the same collective interests, which are paramount to individual compensation. A focus on collective interests cuts in favor of an expansive interpretation of statutory remedies and reflects Japan's concern with the group.

The dissent of Justice Dando differed with the majority in its conclusion that consideration of the working environment in the company where interim income was obtained was so substantially different as to properly preclude the deduction. Equally important, Justice Dando's opinion stressed the amount of discretion given the Labor Relations Commission by the Trade Union Law and stated that the judiciary should defer to the commission's order as appropriate unless it could be said that the order was "unmistakably and clearly irrational." This view comports with the broad discretion the U.S. Supreme

Court has generally accorded the NLRB in the remedial sphere.[43] However, the Japanese approach to this matter remains vague and undefined.

The "Make Whole" Case

Another area of labor law relating to remedies in the United States raises some of the same points discussed in connection with the *Dai Ni Hato Taxi* case. In these cases the employer, after losing an NLRB election, refuses to bargain with the union that has been certified as the exclusive bargaining representative. The composition of the appropriate unit that has been approved is very often the issue. Because unit certifications cannot be directly enforced or appealed to the courts (in contrast with unfair-labor-practice cases),[44] the employer may seek a review of the dispute by refusing to bargain. This, in turn, triggers an unfair-labor-practice proceeding alleging a refusal to bargain which must go through the administrative law judge and the NLRB and then on to the circuit court of appeals. The difficulty here is that by the time the employer is finally obliged to bargain with the union, many of the workers may have lost interest in pursuing the matter—just as workers may have lost interest where dismissals occurred for reasons prohibited by the National Labor Relations Act or the Trade Union Law. Where no bargaining has taken place for a period of time, an NLRB order simply requiring the employer to negotiate with the union, though it is not insignificant as a remedy,[45] does not make the workers whole for the losses suffered because of the unfair labor practice. However, in the *Ex-Cello* decision[46] the NLRB held that damage awards in lieu of wages that would have been received under a collective bargaining agreement are an inappropriate remedy under the National Labor Relations Act, inasmuch as they involve (in the NLRB's view) the imposition of collective-bargaining-agreement terms—something that is prohibited by the NLRA as interpreted by the Supreme Court.[47] Subsequent to *Ex-Cello*, however, the court has accepted the view that a union can be recompensed for litigation and organizational expenses attributable to an employer's unfair labor practice where the employer's refusal to bargain and the consequent appellate litigation are based on "frivolous" grounds.

The Labor Reform Bill, which was passed by the U.S. House of Representatives in October 1977 and did not receive consideration on its merits before the Senate because of the inability of its supporters to obtain cloture against a filibuster, would have revised the law in a number of relevant respects. It would have eliminated the *Phelps-Dodge* rule on the deduction of interim earnings and the mitigation of damages. Double damage awards would have been made in cases of dismissals arising in organizational and first-contract situations. Moreover, the *Ex-Cello* rule would have been overruled so as to provide workers with income lost during the period of time that an employer refused to bargain with a certified collective bargaining representative. As an additional sanction, the secretary of labor would have been required to bar from bidding for future government contracts employers designated by the NLRB as guilty of recidivist behavior in unfair-labor-practice litigation. The bill would also have dealt with the problem of administrative delay by permitting the decisions of the administrative law judge to be summarily affirmed by the NLRB where, in its judgment, the issues presented did not involve an unresolved question of law. Most of the cases coming before the NLRB involve factual issues presenting questions of the credibility of dismissals and disciplinary actions. Moreover, the NLRB's orders would have been self-enforcing in the sense that unless the respondent moved in the circuit court of appeals within 15 days to reverse the NLRB's order, the order would be summarily enforced without argument on law or fact.

The Labor Reform Bill would provide effective remedies that might deter wrongdoers and that would get at the heart of the delay problem.[48] Opponents of the bill have argued that the prospect of double damage awards would make unions and workers more litigious and that the employers, whose backs would be more to the wall, would be similarly less inclined to settle and more prone to adjudication, but recent years have seen increasing recidivism as well as court appeals of NLRB orders.[49] If anything, the major deficiency with the Labor Reform Bill is that its remedies may not be effective enough. One appropriate addition might be to impose contracts in first-contract situations where employers have unlawfully refused to bargain or have in some other way substantially interfered with the collective bargaining process. In any event, if one can judge by the back-pay litigation, Japan seems to be considerably in advance of America in its refusal to become bogged down in the remedial-punitive "logomachy" and its willingness to see the tight relationship between so-called individual discrimination and the collective interest.

Two lines of authority demonstrate some of the difficulties Americans have had with remedies and with the fashioning of orders that would have a meaningful impact on labor-management relations. The first area is reflected in former NLRB member Peter Walther's perceptive dissent in the *Atlas Tack Corporation* case, in which a majority of members followed the traditional approach and ordered that employees be reimbursed for benefits unilaterally and unlawfully discontinued by the employer. As the dissent noted, the majority's traditional remedy required the employer to "restore the *status quo ante* with respect to the changed terms and conditions of employment should the employees, through their union, so desire," to "make the employees whole for any loss of pay they may have suffered due to the unilateral changes," and to "bargain collectively with the union, upon request, and embody any understanding reached in a signed agreement."[50]

Member Walther's dissenting opinion noted that the unfair labor practices in this case "struck at the heart of the collective bargaining process," inasmuch as bargaining had been delayed for more than 2 years before the unilateral changes and it had been 4 years since the parties had negotiated a collective agreement. Said the dissent: "The effect of such conduct is predictable—a long standing collective bargaining relationship is destroyed, and the employees' respect for the union is so totally undermined that when respondent chooses—or is ordered—to return to the bargaining table, the union does not have the support necessary to bargain effectively." The focus of the remedy therefore must be, in Walther's words, to make "every effort" to provide unions in such circumstances with "economic clout" and to "create an environment in which it is economically advantageous for the employer to engage in meaningful collective bargaining." Walther's imaginative response to the violations in *Atlas Tack* was to provide the union with authority to bargain the back-pay award in exchange for other management concessions. Such a "remedy," in the dissent's view, would more effectively protect the collective interest of all workers in self-organization and collective bargaining.

Said Walther: ". . . I view restoration of the union's ability to engage in meaningful collective bargaining to have a higher priority than direct economic restoration of theoretical employees' losses."[51]

The majority of the NLRB in the *Atlas Tack* case expressed the view that empirical data supporting the conclusions that the union would obtain more economic muscle under the dissent's scenario was a prerequisite to acceptance of the dissenting opinion. However, the dissent takes better account of the prospects for a working collective bargaining process in the future. The fact that the relationship was a "long standing one," in contrast with union organizational campaigns or a first-contract situation, makes a remedy aimed at the injury to the collective interest, like that advocated by member Walther, particularly appropriate. The union needs to function as a credible bargaining agent that is likely to deliver a contract. Despite the NLRB's inability to impose a contract, the establishment of a harmonious labor-management environment—a theme articulated in some of the opinions in the *Dai Ni Hato Taxi* case as well as by the dissenters in *Clearfield* (where the significance of contractual and established relationships was stressed in relation to a settlement's adequacy)—is an important element in the remedial statutory scheme.

A second area has been referred to above: the NLRB's involvement in back-pay-computation hearings. The Japanese Labor Relations Commissions, aside from the mitigation of damages, do not fashion specific rules on back pay. They do not involve themselves, even though their position might be properly characterized as adversarial subsequent to the establishment of liability. The underlying assumption appears to be that their involvement would be inconsistent with the role of conciliator and with the harmony that is more likely to guide unions and employers if they resolve such difficulties themselves.

However, though the Japanese approach to remedies is in some respects imaginative and foresighted, in other respects it may be regarded as entirely lacking or deficient. It may be that the back-pay cases represent something of an aberration when one considers the Japanese refusal to even consider, let alone use, their applicability to other crisis areas in Japanese labor law. It may be that Justice Kishi's explanation of the rule against mitigation of damages explains best the differences between the American and Japanese approaches. Said Justice Kishi:

The system of remedial orders against unfair labor practices as provided in article 27 of the Trade Union Law is derived from America's Wagner Act [NLRA] and the Taft-Hartley Act. In America, in the cases where both reinstatement and back pay are ordered as a remedy against discharges arising from an unfair labor practice, it seems that the general treatment in the back pay order issued is to deduct interim income earned during the period of discharge from the amount of wages which would have been earned (in the old job) during that period. However, in America and in Japan, the labor market and conditions along with the legal system are completely different. The handling of this matter as it is in America, cannot be automatically considered in connection with a legal interpretation of back pay orders in Japan. That is to say, that American labor unions, unlike those of Japan, which are organized on an individual enterprise basis, are horizontally organized, with a single union of bonds and solidarity going beyond a single company into industry-wide unions. Workers seek work places that best suit their interests and are to their advantage. It is comparatively easy and job change is frequent. Because it is often said that rather than work in a given company, one is working or attached to the union, in the case of a worker who has been discharged by virtue of an unfair labor practice and makes interim income through his work during the period of his discharge, it can be considered that that interim income represents in essence wages continuously paid in return for work done in the previous workplace before the discharge. In this background of labor practice and working conditions, the legal principle of actual loss as it relates to reparation for damages in common law is thought to influence and be applicable to the back pay question in the American context. In contrast to this, in Japan, a nation where lifetime employment is the general rule, even if a worker who is discharged gets another job and earns income, that normally is something to sustain one's daily living and the interim income earned in this way cannot at all be thought of in the same terms as the wages earned in the previous job. That is not all, in terms of the procedures themselves for unfair labor practice remedial orders. In America, after the order for remedy is issued, there still must be a procedural decision on the amount of back pay including whether or not interim income is deducted. While there is security of a procedural nature for the consideration of deduction of interim income, in contrast to this in Japan, there is no such procedural decision apparatus.[52]

Justice Kishi goes on to note the Japanese assumption that dismissal is invalid under private civil law. In the United States, not only is this not so, but the judiciary is involved (mainly through review of administrative decisions).

Two-Union Discrimination

In the United States, there are numerous problems relating to alleged and real discrimination practiced by employers in favor of one union's members over those of another union (whom they may regard as less cooperative or more militant). To some extent, these problems are made less troublesome by the system of secret-ballot election in appropriate units and by the doctrine of exclusivity. To some extent, there is a period of stability for the term of the exclusive bargaining representative or the collective bargaining agreement. The matter is hardly uncomplicated, however, where two competing unions demand recognition from the same employer for the same group of employees and the representation issue has not been resolved by the NLRB through a secret-ballot election. From 1945 until 1982 the NLRB adhered to its *Midwest Piping*[53] doctrine and precluded an employer from recognizing and bargaining with either union until the representation issue had been resolved by the NLRB. The principal rationales appeared to be that the union enjoying the benefits of the bargaining relationship would have an unfair advantage in any further contest for the workers' allegiance and that any method other than the ballot box (e.g., authorization cards) was demonstrably inferior where two unions were demanding recognition because peer pressure might bring employees to sign authorization cards for more than one union.

Although the bargaining relationship would appear to give the union enjoying it considerable advantages in Japan, the same result is not likely to be present as often in the United States. A contest between an industrial union and a craft union may make an agreement negotiated by the former union the minimum for future demands by the latter. However, a kind of job consciousness not present in Japan may account for this American phenomenon.

In any event, the NLRB has now retreated from its *Midwest Piping* decision by refusing to find a statutory violation where resort is not made to the ballot procedures by one union seeking certification.[54] The reasoning is that a competing union could immobilize an employer even though it had only *de minimus* support among the workers. If a representation petition invoking ballot procedures is filed with the NLRB, a 30 percent showing of interest in the appropriate unit must be obtained if the petition is not to be dismissed. This means that employers will be precluded from recognizing or bargaining with one union only where there is a serious rivalry.

Moreover, where an employer has a relationship with an incumbent union, it may continue to bargain and sign a contract though a representation petition has been filed by an outside union. This rule should be followed, said the NLRB, because the filing of a representation petition by an outside union, "in and of itself, should not overcome the strong presumption in favor of the continuing majority status of the incumbent and should not serve to strip it of the advantages and authority it could otherwise legitimately claim."[55]

The most unassailable portion of the NLRB's rationale—and that which is surely in line with the Japanese experience—is that neutrality simply cannot be ensured where a bargaining relationship has existed and where it is under challenge. The continuation of the relationship could mean unfair advantage, and its discontinuation could mean unfair disadvantage.

In the United States and Japan, with contrasting statutory schemes relating to union recognition, it would seem as though the major focus must be on remedies rather than on determining the circumstances under which statutory violations can be found.

Japan's different statutory scheme, and (perhaps even more important) the largely ideological rivalry between the major federations, have made this problem more pressing in that country. Although the expulsion of the International Brotherhood of Teamsters (the largest American union) from the AFL-CIO contributes substantially to union rivalry in the United States, the AFL-CIO's "no-raiding agreement" takes most union recognition disputes away from the NLRB. No comparable mechanism exists in Japan.

Ever since the late 1960s, the number of "two-union discrimination" cases has increased substantially in Japan. Generally, these cases arise where an employer is providing better wages or fringe benefits to one union than to another. These cases are difficult. The criteria (as one might expect) are subjective, and sometimes the employers refuse to disclose records and relevant evidence. The Labor Relations Commissions have dealt reasonably effectively with these problems, however, by simply resolving all doubts against those who refuse to provide evidence as well as by ruling discrimination to be evidenced on the basis of statistics.[56] However, the problem of remedy has been much more elusive. The difficulty is that the commissions only consider the question of whether individual workers have been discriminated against in connection with wage and fringe-benefit payments. If the answer is in the affirmative, back pay or restitution is provided, but meanwhile, in most cases, the employer's basic objective—the elimination of the troublesome first union, which has led him to promote or cooperate in the creation of the friendly "second union"—has been achieved. When the hearing has been concluded and appeals have been taken, the first union has no or few members. It is not able to function as a collective bargaining representative. One would think that the Japanese commissions and courts, accustomed to dealing with the collective interest in back-pay cases, would devise effective remedies to deter employers from avoiding the prospect of bargaining with first unions through such tactics, but they have not. Discretion has prompted the Japanese to steer away from interunion rivalry and employer manipulations of such—something the NLRB could not avoid, by virtue of its involvement in certification and recognition proceedings.

The United States has had these problems as well. In both countries, unions dominated or assisted by companies are prohibited under law, although the Japanese do not draw negative inferences from the words "company union." However, in the United States, when an unlawful company union has been found to have been formed and dominated by the company, the remedy has been disestablishment of the union. At one point, before the Taft-Hartley amendments, disestablishment orders were used only in connection with unions that were not affiliated with the American Federation of Labor or the Congress of Industrial Organizations.[57] The Supreme Court specifically approved of such a remedy as an appropriate vehicle through which all vestiges of company control could be eradicated in the *Pennsylvania Greyhound Lines* and *Pacific Greyhound Lines* decisions.[58]

The very same debate about disestablishment that took place in the United States has evolved in Japan. In the United States the essential question has not been whether the NLRB has the power to devise disestablishment or dissolution remedies under section 10(c); it has been whether such a remedy is practicable. In Japan, the Labor Relations Commissions appear to have the authority to dissolve "company-dominated" unions; however, the prevailing view is that such an order would be ineffective (*muko*) and impracticable inasmuch as the existence of the union is a matter to be decided by the union itself. Therefore, the reasoning goes, the matter cannot be effectively addressed by outsiders. The matter has been litigated, but not successfully.[59]

Again, the law cannot be comprehended without reference to societal factors. It is more than arguable that the deep divisiveness of the Japanese trade-union movement and the lack of solidarity are responsible for the commission's attitude. Just as exclusivity has never taken root in Japan (in part because of the conflicts between *Sohyo* and *Domei*), so also the dissolution remedy founders on the reef. Under legislation similar to that of the United States, the Labor Relations Commission has reacted quite differently. Since the reasoning is bottomed upon practicalities, the approach then must be viewed as a reaction to social conditions.

Preliminary Injunctions and Kinkyu Meirei

Under the National Labor Relations Act, the NLRB may obtain temporary or preliminary injunctive relief. Where certain kinds of unfair practices by unions (such as secondary boycotts, jurisdictional disputes, and various kinds of picketing) are involved, the statute mandates the NLRB to proceed immediately into federal district court to obtain such relief. The view is that a remedy at a later date would be academic because of the importance of speed in connection with economic pressure of this kind. However, the same is not true of certain kinds of unfair labor practices by employers, which gave rise to the demand for the Labor Reform Bill. For instance, dismissals during organizational campaigns must be remedied speedily because of the likelihood that workers will be so intimidated that they will be unable or unwilling to express their free choice. Under the Labor Reform Bill, the NLRB would be mandated to proceed in federal district court to obtain temporary or preliminary relief under such circumstances. The bill would have provided for temporary relief with the NLRB on the basis of the following criteria (among others):

whether the unfair labor practice was committed during an organizing campaign,

whether the alleged violations are reasonably apparent and are widespread or repetitious,

the likelihood that the efficacy of the NLRB's final order may be nullified in the absence of such interim relief,

the brevity of the career opportunities or the seasonal nature of the employment relationship when measured against the normal time span of the administrative processes, and

the impact of the unfair labor practices on the charging party, on other persons seeking to exercise rights guaranteed by this Act, or on the public interest.[60]

These criteria are considerably more specific than those used under the NLRA as presently written. The first requirement is now that there be "reasonable cause" to believe that a violation has been committed—a factor generally satisfied so long as the NLRB's theories on fact and law are not insubstantial or frivolous.[61] The second is more troublesome. Under section 10(j) of the NLRA, injunctive relief must be "just and proper."[62] The courts have applied five standards in determining what is "just and proper": irreparable harm, the public interest, extraordinary circumstances, legislative purpose, and the *status quo.* The standards are vague, and thus their application creates unpredictable results. Although some courts have taken the position that injury to the collective interest[63] or dissipation of majority status[64] before the administrative process is exhausted constitutes "extraordinary circumstances," there is confusion about what such an open-ended term means. Similarly, the courts are divided about how the term *status quo* is to be defined: Is it the situation that existed before the onset of the unfair labor practices,[65] or the last uncontested status before the litigated controversy arose?[66] "Irreparable harm" itself is difficult because it involves estimation of a union's support in the work force and assessment of continuing unfair labor practices and of the impact of continuing unfair labor practices upon the union's support. None of these factors is readily discernible as a general proposition.

However, a number of the courts have seemed willing to

impose bargaining orders where majority status was clearly demonstrated through union authorization cards.[67] They have been similarly activist when an incumbent union has been recognized unlawfully. Yet the elusiveness of standards—a matter not yet resolved by the supreme court—has been an obstacle to the utilization of temporary relief under the National Labor Relations Act.

The difficulties in this area are also related to a lack of will on the part of the NLRB in seeking injunctions and to the board's own internal processes. With regard to the latter point, before the general counsel or a regional director can move in court for injunctive relief, he must obtain the advice and consent of the five-member board in Washington. This is a cumbersome and time-consuming procedure and has handicapped the NLRB in its efforts.

The best analog to temporary or preliminary injunctive relief in Japanese law is *kinkyu meirei,* which is unique and has no true American analogs. The English translation for *kinkyu meirei* given by the Japanese is "emergency order," but that does not really describe what is meant. A more meaningful translation would be "interim order." *Kinkyu meirei* is designed to preserve the Labor Relations Commission's order while the appellate process is being pursued. In contrast with its American counterpart (preliminary injunctions), it has virtually nothing to do with an emergency of any kind. The statutory basis is article 27(8) of the Trade Union Law, which states that when an employer files an appeal of a decision from the Labor Relations Commission with the court, the court may, at the request of the LRC concerned, "issue [an] order in the form of a decision to require the employer concerned to comply in full or in part with the order of the said Labor Relations Commission pending final judgment by the court" or "reverse or modify the decision on application from the parties concerned or ex-officio." Article 27(9) states that if no petition is filed by the employer (subsection 6 provides a period of 30 days in which to appeal) the order of the commission shall become final; in the event that compliance does not ensue, an obligation is placed on the commission to inform the court of this.

In the United States, preliminary relief can be obtained against unions and against employers. *Kinkyu meirei* is applicable to employers only.[68] However, in the United States most of the problems arise under section 10(j) of the NLRA, which is used against employers more than against unions. The principal statutory basis for temporary or preliminary injunctions against unions provides for their imposition with relative automaticity.

Kinkyu meirei has been utilized in connection with back pay, reinstatement, orders to bargain, cease-and-desist orders, and the posting of notices. Under article 47 of the Labor Relations Commission's rules, whenever the commission is aware that one of its orders has been disobeyed, a conference of public members must be convened to determine whether a request for *kinkyu meirei* is to be filed with the court. As a practical matter, however, there generally must be notice of noncompliance with the order from the union that is affected before the commission will seek *kinkyu meirei*. In almost all cases, unions will notify the commission where a discharge or back pay is involved. What is interesting is that the percentage of cases in which *kinkyu meirei* is sought and obtained (and invariably it is obtained) is relatively small. For instance, from 1973 through 1977, all of the local Labor Relations Commissions throughout Japan submitted only 36 petitions for *kinkyu meirei*. Of these, the order was granted in 34 cases. During the same period of time the central Labor Relations Commission submitted 30 petitions, and *kinkyu meirei* was granted in 29 cases.

It appears that in most cases Japanese employers provide reinstatement, back pay, and other remedies in accordance with the Labor Relations Commission's order while a case is being appealed to the courts. Apparently, this is similar to the practice of Japanese litigants in other areas of law where orders—even those involving the payment of damages—are complied with while the case is pending. Great satisfaction is taken from the ultimate result even though a victorious party may not be able to recover that which has been paid as the result of a reversed lower court's order. Thus, while the term "emergency order" is an inaccurate translation, *kinkyu meirei* is an unusual order by virtue of the almost unanimous compliance by employers. This contrasts substantially with the American situation, where such provisions of NLRB orders as reinstatement and back pay are rarely provided while an appeal is pending.

Although *kinkyu meirei* is unknown to all other areas of Japanese law and is generally assumed to be borrowed from the Americans (it first appeared in Japanese law as part of the 1949 amendments to the Trade Union Law), the fact is that it differs fundamentally from temporary or preliminary injunctions. It is not a temporary or preliminary order pending some final relief. It stands on its own and is designed to provide for speedy and thus effective enforcement of the Labor Relations Commission's orders. However, no showing of irreparable harm or anything similar is necessary. The theory is that delay would undermine the effective implementation of the right to engage in collective bargaining protected by the Trade Union Law. And even though the courts do not examine the cases fully on their merits, nothing special need be evidenced. Only where there is a basis for denying the commission's order on the grounds that it constitutes clear and serious error and that circumstances have changed since the order can such relief be denied.

Generally, the district court will examine the documents submitted by the commission, and if there is a *prima facie* case based on the documents an order will be issued without any hearing. This is what happens in most cases. Infrequently, where the judges have some doubts about the matter, they will postpone the decision and neither grant nor deny relief. In most such cases, the court eventually reverses the order. Occasionally, a judge will postpone the case and then issue *kinkyu meirei* at a later date simultaneous with consideration of the case on its merits.

Reflecting the general Japanese attitude toward remedies, the Japanese courts will not hesitate to provide reinstatement and back pay as part of *kinkyu meirei*. They will treat orders involving notice posting or apologies with more care, however. Here it is thought that the loss an employer would suffer would be irreparable and unrecoverable in the event that *kinkyu meirei* was reversed by the court when it considered the case on its merits. In America the priorities are exactly the opposite. The result is one of comparative disadvantage for American unions and workers.

In the event of disobedience of *kinkyu meirei,* a fine may be imposed. Article 32 states that where an employer has violated a court order under article 27, the employer is liable to a fine not exceeding 100,000 yen, with the understanding that 100,000 yen may be multiplied by the number of days of noncompliance. In 1976, the Osaka District Court levied a fine of 1,500,000 yen for disobedience. There is no appeal from *kinkyu meirei* issued by a district court. This procedure makes relief all the more expeditious, and thus back pay is frequently small—although, as noted above, delays before the administrative agencies can be considerable.

Jokentsuki Kyusai Meirei

Jokentsuki kyusai (conditional relief) is made available only if the party seeking the relief adheres to conditions established by the Labor Relations Commissions and the courts. Because Japanese law deals only with unfair labor practices by employers, many of the conditional orders seem to be aimed primarily or exclusively at the unions, although this is not always the case and conditional relief can take a number of forms. Essentially, the view inherent in *jokentsuki kyusai* is that remedies are designed primarily to structure good industrial relations in the future rather than to recreate what would have been had there been no discrimination in the past. In this respect, the rationale for the remedy mirrors the back-pay and reinstatement cases in Japan. Both remedies are concerned with the creation of ongoing harmonious relationships. The view articulated in *jokentsuki kyusai* is that the unfair-labor-practice system is designed to further the collective bargaining process, and that, given the fact that the party that prevails can often not be considered blameless, a remedy should take this into account and bring the parties together. This is a kind of "no-fault" view of labor law and the unfair-labor-practice system, and it has no real analog in American labor law. The closest thing to such an analog is reflected in the NLRB's *Times Publishing Company* decision, issued shortly before the enactment of the Taft-Hartley amendments:

The test of good faith in bargaining that the [NLRA] requires of an employer is not a rigid but a fluctuating one, and is dependent in part upon how a reasonable man might be expected to react to the bargaining attitude displayed by those across the table. It follows that, although the Act imposes no affirmative duty to bargain upon labor organizations, a union's refusal to bargain in good faith may remove the possibility of negotiation and thus preclude the existence of a situation in which the employer's own good faith can be tested. If it cannot be tested, its absence can hardly be found.[69]

The opponents of *jokentsuki kyusai* take the view that it is an attempt to obtain the equivalent of Taft-Hartley amendments "through the back door." That is to say, *Times Publishing* notwithstanding, since there are no union unfair labor practices in Japan, any remedy that imposes obligations on the unions is opposed to the basic statutory policy. Moreover, runs the argument, conditional relief insofar as it imposes legal obligations on unions as in America is inconsistent with the constitutional protection given to unions in Japan. Revealingly, the opponents of conditional relief speak of the Trade Union Law as providing exclusively for adjudicative relief. Conditional relief, its opponents argue,[70] is inconsistent with the concept of adjudication and takes on characteristics of mediation and conciliation.

Illustrative of one line of Japanese cases that impose a kind of obligation on the unions as a condition for obtaining relief as the result of an employer's unfair labor practice is the *Nobeoka Post Office* case,[71] a 1965 decision of the Public Enterprise and National Corporations Labor Relations Commission (*Koroi*). In this case, the post office workers (*Zentei*) had disobeyed the management's order prohibiting entry into the offices of the postal building without permission. Apparently, the union executives had "carried on in loud voices and committed other indiscretions." Therefore, although the refusal to permit the union officials entry was itself unlawful and was an unfair labor practice by the employer, the union's behavior warranted a letter of regret and apology on their part. The *Koroi* conditioned the order against the employer's unfair labor practices on the union's apology. The Tokyo District Court reversed this, but the Tokyo High Court reversed the district court and affirmed the *Koroi*.

A second variation on this same theme is similar to the Japanese approach to back-pay proceedings and law generally. Here the example applies to orders against employers. Quite frequently, orders are framed in the most general and imprecise language; for example, a floor for benefits to be negotiated after consultation between the union and the employer.[72] The overriding considerations in both situations are the need to bring the parties together in the future and the view that the charging party is often blameworthy as well as the respondent.

Very much related to these concerns is the question of whether reinstatement and back pay should be an automatic part of the remedy once a violation has been found. American arbitrators frequently deny all or a portion of back pay, although where an employer has dismissed a worker in violation of a collective agreement the arbitrator does not believe that the employee is completely without fault.[73] Curiously, arbitrators have rarely denied reinstatement while awarding back pay where a violation has been found.[74] Ever faithful to the adjudicative model, the NLRB has generally awarded both reinstatement and back pay in discharge cases.[75] The exceptions only dramatize the rule. For instance, reinstatement has been denied where it is clear that the employee does not desire reinstatement,[76] and back pay has been denied where the amount was small[77] or where the employer had made an honest but mistaken interpretation of the collective agreement.[78] These exceptions demonstrate the uncritical automaticity of the awarding of back pay and reinstatement in the United States.

It may be that the lack of imagination in the remedy area in the United States has contributed to a tightening of standards relating to the circumstances under which a statutory violation can be made out. Specifically, the courts are more likely to be wary about finding statutory violations if such a finding would lead to automatic reinstatement of the employee involved.

Until 1981 the NLRB took the position that if a portion of the employer's motivation for dismissal or discipline of a worker was based on anti-union considerations, the employer conduct was unlawful. This so-called "in part" test created considerable confusion and was resisted by the circuit courts of appeals in many instances.[79] (The Japanese approach, which appears to be ultimately one of determining whether the "dominant motive" of the employer was for union activity or an "in part" test, similarly lacks precision.) In 1981 the NLRB, relying on the statutory language that requires the general counsel to establish a violation through a "preponderance of evidence" and on the portion of section 10(c) that states that the NLRB shall not order reinstatement or provide back pay where an individual was "suspended or discharged for cause," changed the rules and adopted the so-called "but for" test. In the important *Wright Line* case the NLRB said the following: "First, we shall require that the general counsel make a *prima facie* showing sufficient to support the inference that protected conduct was a 'motivating factor' in the employer's decision. Once this is established, the burden will shift to the employer to demonstrate that the same action would have taken place even in the absence of the protected conduct."[80]

The American approach is considerably more detailed and less vague than the Japanese. The Court of Appeals for the Third Circuit has taken the position that the employer's burden subsequent to the establishment of a *prima facie* case by the general counsel must not consist of a burden of proof inasmuch as that burden would be inconsistent with section 10's protection of employers against employees who have been dismissed for cause.[81] However, the Court of Appeals for the Ninth Circuit took the position that the *Wright Line* position is compatible with legislative history, which "shows that those who successfully advocated passage of the Taft-Hartley amendments over generally pro-labor opposition did so, in part, at least, on the strength of the argument that the burden of proving a good cause for discipline would remain on the employer."[82]

In 1983, the U.S. Supreme Court held unanimously that the NLRB could reasonably construe the NLRA to require an employer prove that a discharge would have occurred in any event despite the general counsel's *prima facie* case. Said Justice White, speaking for the court: "[Under the NLRB's holding,] proof that the discharge would have occurred in any event and for valid reasons amounted to an affirmative defense on which the employer carried the burden of proof by a preponderance of the evidence."[83]

Despite the burden that is thrust upon the employer, workers still must take care to maintain selectively unblemished records to prevail in an American unfair-labor-practice proceeding. Curiously, the Supreme Court observed that the NLRB's "in part" test as applied to mixed-motive discharges was also rational. This tighter standard, which now tolerates the dismissal of workers for both legitimate and illegitimate reasons, might have been less likely to emerge if the NLRB had exhibited more flexibility in the remedy area. If reinstatement is not automatic, a violation might be found with more ease.

The theme that cuts through the two countries' treatments of the remedy problem is that the American approach seems insufficiently attuned to the no-fault characteristics of industrial relations. The Japanese approach to deduction of interim earnings in back-pay cases, conditional relief, and notice posting is strong evidence of concern and care for a relationship that is designed to be lasting and harmonious.

Kinkyu meirei is responsive to the need for prompt enforcement—another problem that plagues Americans and one about which the unions, at least, have manifested concern in the debates on the Labor Reform Bill. Yet there are areas, such as two-union discrimination, in which the Japanese have been totally immobilized. Rejection of the *Phelps-Dodge* approach to the law's applicability to hiring discrimination, though arguably sensible in Japan, would be an enormous step backward in the United States. Even though there may be much to emulate in the Japanese concept of job security, it hardly seems to follow that prohibitions against discrimination in hiring should be eliminated. What is in order for the United States is a better blend of effective remedies, firmly in support of the public policy promoting self-organization, with a sensitivity toward formulating particularized orders that take account of the labor-management relationship.

5

Job Security

The prevailing attitude in the United States toward the relationship between labor and management in the collective bargaining process was expressed well by Justice William Brennan of the U.S. Supreme Court in the landmark *Insurance Agents* case:

It must be realized that collective bargaining, under a system where the government does not attempt to control the results of negotiations, cannot be equated with an academic collective search for truth—or even with what might be thought to be the ideal of one. The parties—even granting the modification of views that may come from a realization of economic interdependence—still proceed from contrary, and to an extent, antagonistic viewpoints and concepts of self interest. The system has not reached the ideal of the philosophic notion that perfect understanding among people would lead to perfect agreement among them on values. The presence of economic weapons in reserve, and their actual exercise on occasion by the parties, is part and parcel of the system that the Wagner [NLRA] and Taft-Hartley acts have recognized. Abstract logical analysis might find inconsistency between the command of the statute to negotiate toward an agreement in good faith and legitimacy of the use of economic weapons, frequently having the most serious effect upon individual workers and productive enterprises, to induce one party to come to the terms desired by the other. But the truth of the matter is that at the present statutory stage of our national labor relations policy, the two factors—necessity for good faith bargaining between parties, and the availability of economic pressure devices to each to make the other party inclined to agree on one's terms—exist side by side.[1]

This approach contrasts rather vividly with the cooperation model present in Japan as well as in Germany and some of the

Scandinavian countries. The differences emerge in a number of contexts, and the assumptions involved in Justice Brennan's commentary quoted above and its acceptance of an adversarial model manifest themselves in a variety of ways. It seems highly probable that the adversarial model includes distrust on both sides, which is hardly congenial to the development of procedures and rules enhancing job security.

Production Committees, Quality of Worklife Groups, Quality Circles, and Union Representation on Boards of Directors

The Japanese use of plant committees, "quality circles," and the like is thought to be responsible for the effective quality control and the harmonious labor-management relations in that country. A variety of mechanisms fall under the broad rubric of worker participation: more substantial involvement of unions and employees in decisions affecting jobs, sales, employment problems, and even investment. American attempts to emulate such behavior have run up against both union resistance and legal hurdles. The latter are found mostly in sections 2(5) and 8(a)(2) of the National Labor Relations Act.[2]

Section 2(5) defines labor organizations so broadly that groups such as production committees and "quality circles" in which employees' advice is received can easily be included. Under current interpretations of American labor law, it would seem as though most employee groups, given the functions designed for them, would be "dealing" with the employer. This satisfies a basic prerequisite for the definition of a labor organization confirmed in the Supreme Court's *Cabot Carbon* opinion.[3] Section 2(5) defines a labor organization as one that is involved in "dealing" with employers, and the supreme court interpreted the provision expansively so as to include within that definition practically any organization that puts forth grievances or complaints on behalf of employees.

Section 8(a)(2), which is designed to combat company formation or assistance of labor organizations, states that it shall be an unfair labor practice to "dominate or interfere with the formation or administration of any labor organization or contribute financial or other support to it."[4] The Japanese counterpart to this provision is broader, insofar as it protects the employer's "furnishing of office space" and does not scrutinize as carefully the kinds of funds to which employer contributions may be made. Moreover, the Japanese statute does not prohibit "other support" from management in addition to financial support. Japanese employers are so generous with unlawful as well as lawful support for their company unions that, as Hanami has noted,[5] litigation often arises over the discontinuance of benefits that were unlawfully provided—and such conduct has been held to be unlawful where an employer has changed its policy because it has changed its view about the value of a union.

A basic concern of the U.S. Supreme Court in cases involving section 8(a)(2) is that employee groups retain freedom to bargain collectively and to utilize economic pressure when there are disagreements with management. The vice in employer support is found in the impact on the group in question and in the likelihood that another, truly independent organization cannot be formed because of its disadvantage with respect to the employer-supported group. The willingness of the NLRB (and even the courts) to define violations in a majority of cases where office or clerical support has been provided by management would seem to create difficulties.[6] Between 1950 and 1974, in 136 cases in which unlawful company assistance was found, violations were based, in part, upon the employers' provision of facilities in 125.[7]

However, some American courts have rejected rigid application of the company-assistance prohibitions. The decision that is most representative of an approach that promotes cooperation rather than conflict is *Chicago Rawhide Manufacturing Company* v. *NLRB*.[8] In this case, the Seventh Circuit Court of Appeals fashioned three tests to determine whether the union was unlawfully dominated or assisted: an inquiry into whether there was domination in the perception of the employees, an examination of the kind of employer control involved and whether it constituted actual control of the labor organization and a distinction between actual and potential domination. (Potential domination was considered acceptable under the law.)

The *Chicago Rawhide* approach is a wise one, much sounder than some of the other decisions referred to above[9] and a step away from the adversarial relationship promoted by some of the Supreme Court's dicta in *Insurance Agents*. Although the NLRB and the courts often look to the history of labor relations in determining illegality, the NLRB does not appear to follow *Chicago Rawhide* faithfully when company facilities are provided by the employer, even in the context of a bona fide arm's-length relationship.[10] Another, even more sensible approach followed by a number of the circuits (most prominently the sixth) is reflected in *NLRB* v. *Scott & Fetzer Co.*, in which the court defined the term "labor organization" narrowly so as to avoid the section 8(a)(2) problem (an employer is only prohibited from providing assistance to a "labor organization" within the meaning of the NLRA) and stated

. . . communication between the committee and management does not itself bestow labor organization status upon a group. . . . Although we acknowledge the difference between communication of ideas and a course of dealings at times is seemingly indistinct, we believe, nevertheless, that it is vital here. . . . Whatever the reach of *Cabot Carbon* beyond the facts of that case, we do not think it applies here. We cannot accept the board's suggestion that *Cabot Carbon* should be read so broadly as to call any group discussing issues related to employment a labor organization.[11]

A similar problem has arisen in connection with union representation on boards of directors, the best known of which, in the United States, is the appointment of Douglas Fraser, former president of the United Automobile Workers, to Chrysler's board. This approach has not been undertaken in Japan, where worker involvement has been promoted at the plant level and where worker influence on boards of directors is expressed after a fashion through the appointment of former trade-union leaders. (In Germany and some other European countries, employee and trade-union involvement is mandated at both the enterprise level and the plant level through union representation on boards of directors as well as works councils at the plant level.) The Fraser appointment has been challenged before the National Relations Labor Board as unlawful coercion or a refusal to bargain by the union in the sense that a conflict of interest was present when the union represented other workers employed by corporations in competition with Chrysler. The general counsel has refused to issue a complaint, adhering to the NLRB precedent that there is no conflict of interest presented for a union where the union represents only a minority on a board of directors.

The NLRB has inquired into whether there was actually any

conflict or sacrifice of the employees' interests involved in the Fraser appointment. Said the general counsel:

> . . . there is no immediate danger of a conflict of interest based on the role of a union agent in management affairs. Indeed, such a conflict is far less likely than in [NLRB precedents] . . . where seven of 15 board members were union representatives and several other board members were representatives of employer-union trust funds. . . . There are no union loans to the employer and . . . Fraser himself owns no stock and has indicated that he will not personally accept any payments for his duties as a director. The union has no financial interest in the affairs of Chrysler, except to the extent that it, like any responsible union, has a vital interest in keeping the employer of representative employers [*sic*] financially healthy in order to preserve and promote jobs and job benefits. Further, Fraser has stressed publicly and in his proxy statement that his prime interest in being on the board of directors is to represent the interest of the employees he represents, particularly with respect to matters which affect terms and conditions of employments, e.g., plant closings. There is nothing in Fraser's conduct which suggests that he has behaved inconsistently with this prime interest in representing employees. Nor is there anything in the reputation of Fraser or of the union which would suggest that Fraser would use his position on the employer's board to compromise the interest of unit employees.
>
> Further, there is nothing to suggest that Fraser would utilize his twin roles to injure competitors of Chrysler and thereby injure the employees of such competitors. Although it is conceivable that the union would take "harsh" positions in bargaining with other auto manufacturers for the purpose of injuring them and benefiting Chrysler, there is no evidence to indicate that the union or Fraser has done that or plans to do that. Further, since the employees of such other manufacturers are also union-represented, and since an injury to these manufacturers would harm these employees, it is unlikely that the union or Fraser would pursue such a course. Finally, the whole relationship between the employer and the union has been free from infirmity. For many years, the employer and the union have been parties to an "arms-length" bona fide collective bargaining relationship.[12]

Again, the general counsel's position seems to be a sound one, devised to permit unions to bridge the difficult gap between their role as adversary and their need to be a cooperative partner with those on the other side of the bargaining table. If anything, the approach is too limited, insofar as it relies upon minority representation on the board as a factor weighing against conflict of interest. Parity on the board has long been a goal of the German unions, and there is no reason why legitimate trade unions in the United States may not emulate them. There should be no *per se* rule against union representation by the NLRB or other forms of cooperation unless subordination (or, in American parlance, domination) is in evidence. The Japanese style of cooperation may indeed take on some of the characteristics of subordination, a subordination that involves a paternalism culturally alien to America. That is not an argument against promoting cooperation as a more significant element in the labor-management relationship, however. While there are legal problems under the Landrum-Griffin Act, antitrust legislation, and corporate law, the better view is that union officials can serve on boards of directors without exposure to liability.

Chicago Rawhide and *Scott & Fetzer* notwithstanding, most of the American decisions seem to regard contact and representation between union and management as unlawful.[13] This view is anachronistic and should be disregarded by the Supreme Court when it next has the opportunity to consider the matter.

Confidential Information

West Germany and Sweden have been leaders in Europe in the statutory provision of union access to confidential information.[14] Their efforts have culminated in the Fifth Directive of the European Economic Community and the Vredling initiative or directive, which are designed to achieve the same basic objective at the EEC level. The underlying assumption is that workers ought to have information relating to sales, profits, future mergers, acquisitions, plant closures, and the like, inasmuch as these matters directly affect job security. In short, workers ought to know the economic facts of life. Such information, it is assumed, permits unions to bargain more intelligently about matters over which they have control or influence so as to alter circumstances (economic or otherwise) that might lead to job losses.

Although there is a potential for litigation, such matters are not handled through legal processes in Japan. The principal forum appears to be the joint consultation committees that exist

Table 5.1
Number of labor-management joint consultation committees and purposes for establishment.

Purpose	Total	Number of employees					
		≥1,000	500–999	200–499	100–199	30–99	≤29
Communication between labor and management	317 (29%)	142 (30%)	27 (27%)	49 (28%)	47 (30%)	43 (28%)	9 (25%)
Maintenance and improvement of working conditions	293 (27%)	143 (30%)	30 (31%)	41 (24%)	29 (19%)	38 (25%)	12 (33%)
Smoother and more amicable labor-management relations	260 (24%)	105 (22%)	20 (20%)	47 (27%)	38 (25%)	39 (25%)	11 (31%)
Increasing productivity	123 (11%)	35 (7%)	12 (12%)	26 (15%)	24 (15%)	23 (14%)	3 (8%)
Participation of labor in management	53 (5%)	28 (6%)	7 (7%)	6 (3%)	5 (3%)	6 (4%)	1 (3%)
Others	46 (4%)	20 (4%)	3 (3%)	5 (3%)	12 (8%)	6 (4%)	0
Total	1,092	473	99	174	155	155	36

in 60 percent of unionized companies and in over 70 percent of larger firms (table 5.1). The majority view in Japan seems to be that the system is a useful one. What precise purpose does it serve? The answer most often provided in Japan is that union leaders obtain information on a wide variety of matters—not only those set forth above, but also changes relating to automation, for instance—that could alter the job assignments of workers. However, the Ministry of Labor study set forth in table 5.1 highlights some of the ambiguity and diversity of objectives throughout Japan. The extremely low rating given to worker participation in management as an objective highlights the vagueness of the joint-consultation-committee concept. It seems to embrace both involvement in managerial decisions before they are implemented and subject matter that in the United States would be handled through the grievance-arbitration machinery.

The Trilateral Commission's report on this subject has stated the following:

Issues such as the rules concerning large-scale layoffs, transfers to other jobs, and the rules relating to discipline and discharge, if agreement is not readily reached, quickly become the subject of collective bargaining. Questions relating to recruitment methods, selection procedures, education and training, job analysis and job evaluation are usually treated as cases for communication and co-understanding, with a view to obtaining the opinions, understanding and, if possible, approval and support of the union. On production matters involving company plans and schedules relating to investment, equipment, measurement and control of productivity, and quality control, managements are expected to consult with trade unions, although they usually reserve the right to decide. Where executive policies, the financial status of the company and long-range plans for the future are concerned, decisions are often made items for communication, management taking the initiative to report on developments and progress. Where major decisions affect employment and working conditions, such as mergers and plant closures, discussions in consultative committees are treated by unions as prior discussions to collective bargaining.[15]

The same report notes that there are thus two methods for handling differences on potential problems: through consensus or through contract. But, as noted above, some of the subject matter is handled through the grievance-arbitration process in the United States, and some arises in the context of refusal-to-bargain charges involving access to information. Americans have been tardy in developing informal consensus mechanisms that might serve as an adjunct to collective bargaining. Insofar as union access to information is concerned, there are often before the NLRB and the courts disputes arising out of allegations that management has failed to bargain in good faith by not providing information. The leading case, *NLRB* v. *Truitt Manufacturing*,[16] dramatizes some of the difficulties involved in the American approach.

In the *Truitt* decision a majority of the Supreme Court indicated that an employer was obligated to open its books and verify its bargaining position only where it pleaded an inability to pay to the union. Thus, any well-advised employer, even though it may be prompted to take a certain bargaining stance by its economic troubles, does not rely on an inability-to-pay argument as a basis for its position. This would trigger an obligation to disclose under *Truitt,* and it can be simply avoided by not putting forward the defense that *Truitt* requires. Comparability or some variation on this theme is the position taken at the bargaining table by employers advised by competent counsel in the United States. Real problem solving is avoided by employers who view the firm simply as their own property and characterize its internal affairs as none of the concern of the union and the workers. Such antediluvian thinking hardly comports with what should constitute corporate responsibility to workers and the public. Even the argument put forward by publicly held corporations that premature disclosure will harm corporate stock should fail if labor is dealt with on a basis of trust, as in Japan, where at least the union's leaders are given information.

American employers undoubtedly would argue that company unions reduce the potential for disclosure of truly confidential information to competitors. However, union bargaining aimed more precisely at a company's peculiar financial situation ought to promote the role and the prestige of local union leadership. Swedish labor law provides that confidential information be afforded local leaders.[17] Although there is some doubt, they may be more appropriate recipients of information and better board of directors members than national union officials.

One additional and related problem in the United States is a 1981 decision of the Supreme Court, in *First National Maintenance Corp.* v. *NLRB*,[18] to the effect that an employer does not have a duty to bargain about a management decision to close one of its operations partially. The reasoning of the court reflected in the opinion written by Justice Harry Blackmun is complicated and sometimes contradictory,[19] but it appears to be based on a rationale that, while antithetical to the goals of Western European unions, would not be at literal variance with the attitudes on both sides of the bargaining table in Japan: that the NLRA does not contemplate equality or parity for labor with management. The difficulty here is that, if there is no duty to bargain, it is difficult to obtain information. One by-product of the decision in *First National Maintenance* (depending upon its breadth[20]) is that employers can bluff an intention to engage in an economic decision that may affect workers' jobs in order to reduce wages and fringe benefits. This is bound to create distrust and discord in collective bargaining relationships in the future.

Collective bargaining in some American industries (for example the automobile industry) has gone beyond the mandates of the Supreme Court. This has been triggered by concession bargaining in which a union has relinquished its contractual right to cost-of-living increases during the term of a collective bargaining agreement in order to make the employer more competitive. (Ironically, the difficulties for Americans in these industries were triggered by the superior Japanese productivity and product quality.) Part of the *quid pro quo* has been union representation on committees in which future management decisions affecting jobs are to be discussed. In a manner similar to that used by the Japanese, such committees are described as an "adjunct" to the collective bargaining process. Moreover, when substantial layoffs are about to take place,[21] national and local officials of the United Auto Workers have the contractual opportunity to discuss alternatives. In order to do this, they presumably need information about a wide variety of cost considerations.

In six plants of General Motors and Ford, the 1982 collective bargaining agreements provide for permanent employment for 80 percent of the workers. Although the income-maintenance approach, which provides that dismissed employees with at least 10–15 years' seniority will receive at least 60 percent of their wage until retirement, will indirectly discourage management from dismissing workers. To a lesser extent, supplemental unemployment compensation benefits accomplish the same objectives. This is the first major collective bargaining agreement that appears to emulate the Japanese *shushin koyo*. Its scope is limited, but one must recall the qualifications applicable to the Japanese system.

Moreover, subtle alternatives are frequently promoted and sometimes imposed by companies that adhere to the concept of permanent employment. Workers retire much earlier in Japan than in the United States, although a majority of Japanese companies now have a retirement age of 60. Nevertheless, inducements to retire early during periods of economic stress remain. The "tap on the shoulder" system of *katatataki* can extend down to age 45. The inducement to retire, aside from whatever social pressure may be employed, is a welfare benefit (in the form of a lump-sum payment (the *taishokukin*), the size of which is based on the employee's final salary and length of service), and appears to have been in existence before World War II.

During the 1970s, Japanese firms solicited large numbers of so-called voluntary retirees and attempted to get 10–20 percent of the total permanent work force to retire. For instance, in 1976, Yasukawa Electric Manufacturing Co., with 7,200 employees and five plants, announced a retrenchment scheme aimed at attracting 700 voluntary retirees. For workers who chose the voluntary retirement, Yasukawa offered a 15 percent supplement over the regular lump-sum retirement amount; an additional lump-sum payment of 100,000–500,000 yen (about $333–$717 at the time), depending upon age and length of service; extension of certain benefits normally reserved to retirees at age 60 to all retirees 50 and over; and a special allowance of 100,000 yen to retiring female workers.

Unless a Japanese employee retires at the age of 60, there is a hiatus between the time of retirement and the time of entitlement to social security benefits. In partial response to this problem, the government and some employers are promoting a switch from a lump sum to an annuity. Employers generally have an economic incentive to move toward an annuity because of the severe erosion of cash reserves if a substantial number of employees retire in the same year.

The method of computing the *taishokukin* is negotiated between management and the union, if there is a union. It is customary to multiply the worker's current monthly salary, excluding bonuses and allowances, by the number of years of service. A worker will receive less than the amount calculated under this formula if he leaves the company of his own accord before 20 years of service.

Japanese employers were able to respond in some measure to economic crises through attrition, also. Moreover, the *nenko* system of wage seniority came under more stress and modification, particularly when employers were not able to find other methods of shedding unnecessary labor. A 1978 Ministry of Labor survey found that only 1 percent of enterprises had a strict wage seniority system. Forty-six percent of the firms had a mixed system under which several factors were taken into consideration: age, length of service, past performance, and present performance in job potential. Other firms claimed to have a merit system only. Moreover, the shift is toward simply denying wage increases to workers who are beyond their mid-40s. In the United States this practice could produce age-discrimination litigation and serious potential liability; Japan, however, has no age-discrimination legislation. (Indeed, Japan has no fair-employment-practices legislation, although the constitution prohibits race and sex discrimination.)

Another system once utilized was that of *shukko*, the transfer of workers to a subsidiary. Since 1978, some companies have actually transferred or dispatched workers from one enterprise to another. Under this system, described by Koichiro Yamaguchi, workers can be dispatched to other enterprises (*haken*) when one company has a surplus and the other is seeking new labor. The company with the surplus, A, charges labor expenses to B. Often company A is a firm in the declining steel, shipbuilding, or textile industry and company B is in the automobile industry. Yamaguchi describes the system used by Isuzu Motors as follows:

A wage agreement is made in advance between the house company and the company which offers employees. Calculating wages of workers on loan, according to the wage system in Isuzu Motors, Isuzu gives the notice of wage rates to the dispatching company. When wages to be paid by Isuzu are less than wages which have been paid by the company which offers labor to Isuzu, the offering company usually pays the balance. This arrangement ensures the stability of the dispatched worker's earnings which is especially important because the wage level of the steel industry is higher than that of the automobile industry. An additional influence comes from the wage demands of the labor unions in the offering company.

Workers on loan are not entitled to take paid leave, because the special work rules for temporary workers are applied to them. If they take leave during the dispatch period, this would be regarded as absence. In such a case, however, wages are to be paid by the offering company, and it is arranged so that workers can actually take paid leave.[22]

It is unclear how significant this practice is likely to be, but the relocation and retraining of workers in depressed industries has been actively promoted by the Japanese government.[23] Undoubtedly, both government and private efforts in the United States must focus on the same kind of relocation of workers to areas of growth so as to provide some opportunities for workers from the "smokestack" industries.

Legal Limitations on Dismissals and Layoffs

In Japan, there are both procedural and substantive limitations on an employer's right to dismiss a worker. Two statutory provisions relate to the procedural aspect of the matter. Article 627 of the Civil Code of Japan addresses employment contracts and provides the following: "Under an employment contract with no fixed term, either party may at any time give a termination notice to the other. Upon the notice, the employment will terminate when a two-week period is passed." However, article 20 of the Labor Standards Law has amended the civil code so as to obligate an employer to provide 30 days' prior notice of dismissal or to pay the equivalent of 30 days' average wages.

Despite the absence of explicit statutory or constitutional authority, the courts have imposed a just-cause substantive limitation on employers' right to dismiss workers. If an employer does not have just cause for dismissing a worker, the dismissal will be regarded as invalid. In part, the courts have relied on article 27 of the Japanese constitution to support this position. The fact that the just-cause obligation applies to economic dismissals or layoffs attributable to a business decline as well as to disciplinary disputes makes the Japanese situation quite different from the American. In the United States, the seniority provisions that the unions have negotiated generally provide for the "last hired, first fired" concept and govern the criteria relating to the selection of the employees to be laid off. In Japan, there is a burden placed on management—similar to the burden utilized in American grievance-arbitration cases relating to disciplinary matters—to explain the reasons for a layoff that is attributable to economic considerations and to meet a just-cause test. A preliminary and important question relates to whether temporary as well as permanent employees have the right to challenge dismissals due to economic considerations. K. Hokao has summarized the state of the law relating temporary employees and disputes arising out of an employer's refusal to renew their contract in the following manner:

The employer keeps renewing the temporary worker's fixed period contract, then when business is bad, he simply refuses to renew the contract. This refusal to renew has been challenged in courts by temporary workers. In many courts, it has been judged unfair that a temporary worker who works at the same job as a permanent employee should be treated less favorably when it comes to the termination of employment, even though the nature of the contract differs from that of a regular employee. It has been widely acknowledged by the courts that a temporary worker whose contract has been renewed automatically can enjoy a degree of employment security. Some courts, applying the principle of the chain contract, have interpreted contracts as extending indefinitely from their inception. Other judgments have determined that a fixed period contract which has been repeatedly renewed has become, in effect, an indefinite period contract. However, the majority of the courts have held that no matter how often it has been renewed, a contract for a fixed period cannot be changed into one for an indefinite period; but, they have also concluded that the fact that it has been repeatedly renewed gives rise to a certain mutual trust relationship under which an employer is expected to not refuse renewal of the contract without a fair and just reason. In other words, as a result of repeated renewals and other factors, an employee has become entitled to expect the renewal of his contract, and therefore the employer's right to refuse renewal has become subject to the principle of good faith which prevents him from abusing his rights.[24]

Once the question of whether an employee is protected by the civil code is resolved, the Japanese courts generally require four prerequisites as indispensable to dismissal attributable to economic considerations. First, the employer must show that there simply is no economic alternative to the dismissal and that the dismissals are indeed the most effective way to remedy the employer's economic difficulties. In this connection, the bonuses and wage increases after layoffs have convinced courts that the first prerequisite has not been fulfilled. Second, the employer must show that there was no reasonable and suitable way other than dismissals to deal with the problem, once it has been established that the economic problem was indeed serious. Generally, the courts require that the employer make an effort to transfer the worker to another job or, in the case of large companies, to a subsidiary. Sometimes the courts have insisted that an employer first attempt to obtain voluntary resignations or to engage in *katatataki* before dismissing the complaining workers. Third, dismissals due to redundancy must be based on objective and reasonable criteria as to which employees are to be laid off. Here, the focus is similar to that of the subject matter addressed by seniority provisions in American collective bargaining agreements. Moreover, the approach is similar to the German requirement that dismissals be socially justified. Finally, the employer is obliged to give the employees complete information about planned dismissals or other measures and the necessity for them. The employer must consult with the union or with some other appropriate representative about the number of workers to be dismissed and the criteria on which the selection of those to be dismissed is based.

Disciplinary dismissals are similarly interdicted by the Japanese courts. Just as is the case with arbitration disputes in the United States and disputes relating to dismissals arising under legislation in Western Europe, it is frequently difficult to articulate the circumstances under which dismissals will be sustained in this area. Hakao writes:

The courts often consider the relative difference between the employer's interest in dismissing an employee and the damage incurred by the employee. It is therefore difficult to delineate specific criteria for just cause. For example, the falsification of one's personal history of qualifications, unsatisfactory work performance, laziness or chronic lateness, the absence from work without just cause, refusal to obey an employer's order, embezzlement or theft, violence or threats against other workers, intentionally causing damage to company properties, gross negligence, and so forth, have been approved as just cause.[25]

On the other side of the coin, certain grounds for discharge are explicitly prohibited by a statute. Dismissal for union activity is prohibited under the Trade Union Law, and dismissal for nationality, political or religious beliefs, or social status is prohibited under the Labor Standards Law. Similarly, various forms of sex discrimination that require women to resign when they marry or have children, and disparate retirement standards for male and female workers, are unlawful under the constitution. As a practical matter, however, many Japanese companies retain such practices. In the Anglo-American tradition *stare decisis* applies, binding courts to precedent.[26] To some extent, the absence of the *stare decisis* doctrine in the Japanese civil-law tradition has imposed a burden of seemingly endless rounds of litigation on female workers who challenge such practices.

As noted above, the underlying legal justification for the judicial activism displayed by the Japanese courts in the area of dismissal is to be found in the civil code and in the good-faith obligation the courts have derived from the code. This good-faith obligation appears to have been fashioned by the courts in light of the constitution, permanent employment, and the *nenko* system of wage payment. The courts have remarked about the difficulties dismissed Japanese employees are confronted with in obtaining alternative employment. The Supreme Court of Japan has not yet had an opportunity to review the above-mentioned criteria and the stringent standards imposed on an employer's right to dismiss workers by the lower courts, but at this writing it appears as though the decisions tend to reflect and mirror the practices involved in *shushin koyo* and *nenko*.

One practical upshot of the Japanese approach is that, when a dispute arises over the use of economic pressure by a union on an employer, the employer is not as likely to dismiss the employee as in the United States. Such disputes generally arise in the context of suits for civil damages or even criminal prosecutions. It may seem from the American perspective that resort to the courts is the most impractical method and that it is ill-suited to good industrial relations, yet the Japanese approach to employment security diminishes litigation. This is due both to the practices and to the legal standards enunciated in their wake. At the same time, it should be noted that if the dispute is volatile or violent the Japanese employer is in a better position to rely upon disciplinary sanctions, since the union officials with which he deals will be full-time employees far more often than in America. This means that union leaders are vulnerable to discharge and discipline.

In the United States, the development of law regarding job security for workers has been quite different. Although the United States purported to follow contract law that had developed in Great Britain relating to the employer-employee relationship, the fact is that long before the advent of modern labor legislation there the presumption was that a worker would be employed for a period of a year; the objective was to protect salaried workers.[27] The United States, which abandoned the British view more than a century ago and adopted a position that in the absence of explicit assent the employment contract is terminable at any time, has gone in an entirely different direction. Part of the rationale for this position has been that the worker, aside from his services, does not provide any consideration that is a prerequisite for a contract right of greater scope.

However, in recent years in the United States, the state courts have begun to limit the "terminable at will" doctrine. Twenty states have ruled that there are public-policy exceptions to the doctrine. Some of the early cases have dealt with dismissals attributed to the employee's insistence on performing a public obligation, such as serving on a jury or in the armed forces. Thirteen states have fashioned an implied contract through one of a number of approaches. For instance, the Supreme Court of California, speaking through Justice Tobriner, stated in the landmark *Tameny* decision that

In the last half century, the rights of employees have not only been proclaimed by a mass of legislation touching upon almost every aspect of the employer-employee relationship, but the courts have likewise evolved certain additional protections of common law. The courts have been sensitive to the need to protect the individual employee from discriminatory exclusion from the opportunity of employment, whether it be by the all-powerful union or employer. . . . This development of common law shows that the employer is not so absolute a sovereign of the job, that there are not limits to his prerogative. One such limit at least is the present case. The employer cannot condition employment upon required participation and unlawful conduct by the employee.[28]

Justice Tobriner was referring to statutes, such as the National Labor Relations Act, title VII of the Civil Rights Act of 1964, and related social and economic legislation, that have abrogated the "terminable at will" doctrine where employers impose dismissals for forbidden reasons. The modern cases began with those that, like *Tameny*, protected employees dismissed for reasons that were forbidden by law or were inconsistent with public policy.[29] Some jurisdictions have enacted legislation protecting employees who engage in "whistle blowing" against their employers (generally in the public sector). Moreover, the U.S. Supreme Court has recognized a property interest that public employees have in their jobs, at least insofar as to provide for some kind of minimal due-process protection for such employees.[30]

A second step has been the imposition of a so-called covenant of good faith and fair dealing obligation upon the employer. This concept appears to have been borrowed from the law of insurance contracts, the rationale for which is that such a covenant is appropriate because the contract is not a normal contract of law but rather one of adhesion between unequal parties, because the insurance company owes a fiduciary duty to those in the public with whom it contracts, and because the insurance industry performs public functions. It seems clear that not all of the underpinnings of this rationale are totally applicable to the employer-employee relationship, although the contract entered into (unless the worker possesses specific skills) is between unequal parties and thus is unlikely to provide for job security involving a guarantee of a contract of specific duration.

Finally, the courts—following the lead of the Supreme Court of Michigan—have attacked the "terminable at will" doctrine by implying contracts between an employer an employee under circumstances not recognized previously. For instance, a California court has said the following:

In determining whether there exists an implied—in fact—promise for some form of continued employment courts have considered a variety of factors in addition to the existence of independent consideration. These have included, for example, the personnel policies or practices of the employer, the employee's longevity of service, actions or communications by the employer reflecting the assurances of continued employment, and the practices of the industry in which the employee is engaged .[31]

Personnel manuals and policies, written or oral, have been relied on by the courts as a basis for implying a contract.[32] What standard is to be used in determining whether the contract has been violated? This answer has not been addressed in any detail in the United States, although the words "just cause" and "good cause" have been utilized. Whether the standards enunciated by arbitrators under so-called just-cause provisions of collective bargaining agreements will have applicability and will be used as expert evidence or testimony in such cases remains to be seen.

The above-mentioned cases deal only with individual relationships with employers in non-union situations. The larger percentage of unorganized workers in America compared with Japan and Europe and the lack of job security for such workers has prompted some scholars, such as Summers,[33] to advocate unfair-dismissal legislation for such workers. The practical difficulty here is that the labor movement has been indifferent, viewing job security as one of the main benefits that can be obtained through union representation in a collective bargaining agreement. Moreover, some unions have expressed opposition to Summers's proposals on the grounds that his proposed statute would interfere with the exclusive right of unions to process and to control the grievance procedure in established relationships—even though some of the same unions have noted that a number of cases cannot go to arbitration and be heard on their merits because the local unions involved simply do not have the financial resources.[34]

What of so-called collective dismissals or those that are attributable to economic decisions by management? Whereas managerial discretion in connection with such dismissals is carefully circumscribed in Japan, the situation is quite different in the United States. One aspect of the law in this area relates to the duty to bargain, which has been limited considerably by virtue of the U.S. Supreme Court's *First National Maintenance* decision. Two other avenues are open to unions seeking to limit or enjoin collective dismissals, however.

Recent NLRB decisions have held that relocations of jobs to other facilities deprive union-represented workers of jobs and wage rates provided for in the collective agreement and thus unilaterally modify the terms of such contracts in violation of the statutory duty to bargain.[35] Although the NLRB and the courts have not yet addressed the issue, the reasoning of these decisions would seem applicable to closures, mergers, and the like.

The second avenue is the method of obtaining preliminary injunction or orders pending the outcome of the case. Although the injunction is unknown to Japanese law, there is a judicial procedure (independent of the Trade Union law and *kinkyu meirei*) employed in connection with labor disputes in Japan which is remarkably similar. This is the provisional disposition system. Provisional disposition is relief that is temporary in nature and has gradually come to provide permanent relief.[36]

According to Yasuhiko Matsuda, the procedure for seeking provisional disposition contains four basic characteristics. The first is that the provisionary disposition procedure is a subordinate one in civil law for the purpose of preserving the enforceability of alleged rights in a dispute. Matsuda states that "in order to receive temporary relief, one must show proof that his future rights are endangered and *prima facie* evidence that there is a reasonable chance that his contested right in a dispute is likely to be confirmed through litigation."[37] Second, it must be practicable to resolve the issue in dispute expeditiously. Third, inasmuch as statutory law is involved and one is dealing with the civil-law aspect of the legal system (imported from Germany) rather than common law, there is no doctrine of *stare decisis*. Finally, such cases never go to the Supreme Court of Japan unless there is some issue of constitutionality. The supreme court takes the position that, since the relief is temporary in nature, a suit on the merits will follow which will provide an opportunity for review.

As in the United States, the system was first used in connection with strikes—particularly the "production control" method employed by Japanese labor just after World War II. Inasmuch as it involved seizure of company property along with an effort by the workers to continue production "production control" was ultimately viewed as unlawful trespass. According to Matsuda,

In view of various kinds of shortages and rampant inflation, many courts ruled that sit-down strikes which aimed at taking over the control of factory operations were illegal, going beyond the right to strike and invading the right of private property. The unions accused the courts of taking a reactionary step backwards by paving the way for "government by injunction," a notorious device used often in the history of the American labor movement.[38]

However, the Japanese courts soon began to use the provisional disposition order in the case of workers who had lost their jobs, on the theory that they would be unable to support themselves during the interim period on the job market in light of the very same stringent economic circumstances that had led to the use of the order in connection with strikes.

The prerequisites for obtaining a provisional disposition are similar, in some respects, to those for obtaining a preliminary injunction in the United States—i.e., the need to preserve one's future interest from interference by the other side. However, the case may be made out on the basis of *ex parte* testimony and *prima facie* evidence. This departs from the American standard to a considerable extent. Moreover, the relief is given for an indefinite period, again in contrast with the American system relating to temporary and preliminary injunctions.[39] Matsuda has maintained that the system has lost much of its original meaning inasmuch as it is no longer "expedient [expeditious], temporary or non-contentious."[40] One of the major objections put forward by Matsuda is that the courts are now involved in labor-management relations—in some instances, the interpretation of collective bargaining agreements—and that this is far beyond their expertise. Matsuda also contends that where provisional dispositions are obtained in connection with discharges (for instance, 90 percent of reinstated employees have left company within a year in Kamagawa Prefecture) and where unions seek relief, unfair-labor-practice jurisdiction, which is more appropriately that of the Labor Relations Commissions, is often involved.

To some extent, American labor law relating to preliminary injunctions in connection with no-strike-clause violations in labor disputes rings many of the same themes. In the first place, the jurisdiction of federal courts began with the *Boys Markets* v. *Retail Clerks* case,[41] in which the Supreme Court, by 5–2 vote, held that no-strike clauses could be enjoined. This was done, notwithstanding the Norris-LaGuardia Act's prohibition of injunctions in labor disputes, partly on the ground that expeditious relief was necessary or no effective alternative relief could be obtained. It did not take long for the courts to recognize that this reasoning has remarkable applicability to a wide variety of complaints brought by employees against employers.

The kinds of disputes that pose job-security threats to workers involve, for instance, bankruptcies or partial liquidations of businesses,[42] relocations of plants,[43] the contracting out of work previously done by employees of a bargaining unit, and the termination and sale of the business.[44] One of the principal difficulties with the *Boys Markets* decision involved the potential for judicial meddling in the merits of labor disputes, an evil the Supreme Court had been particularly concerned with in the early cases providing that collective bargaining agreements were enforceable in the federal and state courts. In a decision permeated with dubious reasoning, *Buffalo Forge Company* v. *United Steel Workers*,[45] the Supreme Court seems to extend the *Boys Markets* rationale to sympathy strikes that appear to violate the no-strike clauses of the collective bargaining agreement.

The unstated rationale in the *Buffalo Forge* decision may have been that contract interpretation was too complex. (Substantial disputes had taken place both in the NLRB[46] and, to a lesser extent, before arbitrators[47] over the question of whether such strikes violate no-strike clauses prohibiting strikes and picketing.) In any event, *Buffalo Forge,* which was decided by a 5–4 vote and has been challenged again by a number of the justices in the Supreme Court's 1982 term,[48] appears to be the law. A portion of its reasoning raises the question of whether the federal courts may enjoin decisions by employers that affect workers' job-security interests.

One of the basic problems confronting the courts here relates to the question of what showing must be made concerning the likelihood of arbitration's success and the potential for judicial examination of the merits "through the back door" at the stage at which the motion for preliminary injunction is granted or denied. The Court of Appeals for the Second Circuit has concluded that the union seeking a *status quo* injunction against an employer's decision that will provide irreparable harm to the employees' job status must show "some likelihood of success" not only in compelling arbitration but also in prevailing in the arbitration proceeding.[49] The Court of Appeals for the Seventh Circuit, in *IAM, Local Lodge 1266* v. *Panoramic,*[50] has taken the position that the union's arguments must not be "frivolous" and that arbitration should not be a "futile endeavor."[51] In this connection, the court has looked to the question of whether precedent in labor-management disputes involving similar issues supports the union. This approach provides for some inquiry into a union's potential for success, yet it also encourages judicial abstention regarding the merits of the dispute. This will never solve the dilemma, but it does address some of the concerns articulated by Matsuda in connection with the Japanese cases.

The principal issues in these cases involving contract disputes and the duty to bargain during a contract's term have not yet been addressed by the U.S. Supreme Court. The decided authority at this point is moving in a direction antithetical to that set forth in the *First National Maintenance* case.[52] These cases discussed, along with individual cases lodged in the state courts, suggest some convergence between American and Japanese approaches. However, the contrast between the two countries is rather great. Both countries' legal institutions, at this juncture, seem to reflect the practices of labor and management that have evolved principally without regard to the law. The Japanese have moved unabashedly toward the provision of job security and of the information on which managerial decisions are based. American labor law, on the other hand, has tended to genuflect to the concept of management prerogatives. Incursions into the realm of managerial autonomy are being made through both law and collective bargaining, but as of yet they are tentative and uncertain.

Unfair Labor Practices

Because the American and the Japanese unfair-labor-practice provisions that are applicable to employers are roughly comparable, the case law of the two countries offers an unusual opportunity to consider a number of issues that reflect the contrasting practices in the two societies.

Refusal to Bargain

In the United States, disputes about bargaining issues often turn on whether the item either labor or management demands to have negotiated is a mandatory subject of bargaining. In Japan, the issue generally emerges in a different form. The Trade Union Law states that an employer may refuse to bargain collectively for a proper reason. To refuse to bargain without a "proper reason" is an unfair labor practice.

Enterprise unions are dominant in Japan, and most labor-management relationships take place at that level. Nevertheless, at the national level the labor federations have infused themselves into negotiations from time to time (particularly through *shunto*) and have influenced or determined the time, the place, and the method of bargaining and strikes. Management resistance to this tactic has often taken the form of refusing to bargain with representatives of the national federations. There are two principal cases dealing with this problem in Japan. Both focus on the circumstances under which management has some kind of legitimate or proper reason for declining to bargain.

In a case concerning *Zenko* (the metal miners' union), the central Labor Relations Commission viewed the national federation's demand to be one of joint bargaining. However, where companies had entered into local agreements with enterprise unions, recognizing such unions as sole negotiators, the commission held that practices already in effect made such a demand impracticable. Accordingly, in the *Zenko* case, the commission was of the view that, where such agreements were in existence, management had a "proper reason" for refusing to bargain with the federation. Generally, such agreements may not be relied on by an employer to exclude or deny recognition to a second union. Although the union may extend the terms and conditions of its contract to other employees within the enterprise where three-fourths of the workers in the enterprise are members of the union, and management would not be obliged to bargain with the second union about the subject matter covered by the first union's agreement, sole bargaining agreements are generally regarded as unlawful or unconstitutional under the broad rights granted to workers under article 28 of the Japanese constitution. Thus, the apparent anomaly with respect to the treatment of sole negotiating agreements seems attributable to the deeply rooted practice of local negotiations and the preeminence accorded enterprise unions in Japan. However, by denying the "proper reason" defense to employers who did not have a sole-bargaining-agent agreement, the central commission seemed to indicate that an employer could not refuse to bargain with a federation simply because its representatives were not employees.

This issue was raised more clearly in the *Gokaroren* (chemical workers' union) case decided by the commission in 1960. In that case, the commission explicitly rejected the argument that the employer had a proper reason for refusing to bargain in that bargaining would give nonemployees access to confidential information. The commission stated the following:

The complainees also state as reasons for refusal the fact that heretofore the usual practice has been negotiation solely between the enterprise and the local union, the existence of provisions for a sole negotiating group in the former agreements, etc. Of course, the usual practice between labor and management must be valued, and the provisions for sole negotiating group in the labor agreements based on usual practices have great importance in actual fact in connection with the evaluation of the usual practice. However, in terms of the usual practice of negotiations between each enterprise and each local union, *Gokaroren,* especially in the 1959 spring wage increase dispute (*shunto*), although not able to implement its initially planned methods, played an important role in the solution of individual disputes by the participation in effect of individual *Gokaroren* leadership division members in negotiations with each company. From this, even discounting the general viewpoint that usual practice of provisions for a sole negotiating group cannot exclude overall group negotiations, it is difficult to see the defense of both practice and the sole negotiating contract provision as a legitimate reason for refusal.[1]

While rejecting the general concept of joint negotiations with both the *Gokaroren* federation and the enterprise unions present, the Labor Relations Commission took the view that the real objection to collective bargaining was the presence of *Gokaroren* officials and that therefore so-called joint negotiation could not be a proper reason for refusal to bargain under the circumstances. The commission noted that *Gokaroren*, under its own internal procedures, had the authority to determine timing and tactics. Accordingly, the commission predicated its decision to the effect that the employer had unlawfully refused to bargain on the "circumstances of labor-management relations in this case," the "situation of actual participation of officials of *Gokaroren* in the 1959 negotiations," and the "fact that *Gokaroren* has considerable, strong directive powers in the resolution of disputes as the overall organization."[2]

The limited nature of the *Zenko* and *Gokaroren* decisions reflects the generally agreed-upon exclusion of federations from enterprise bargaining. Generally, the federations simply advise, consult, and provide information for the enterprise unions, to the extent that they are involved at all. The demands of the enterprise unions may vary, depending on the economic situation with which each firm is confronted. At the other end of the spectrum, the seamen's union (*Kaiin*) is capable of independent bargaining at the industry level and is an industrial union in the Western sense of the word. Moreover, some of the industrial federations do engage in collective bargaining, jointly with negotiators from the affiliated unions. This is the case in coal mining, and privately owned railways, for example. But they are aberrations in the Japanese collective bargaining. Employers and workers prefer that outsiders be excluded from the "family" or "home" (*uchi*).

There are two lines of authority that present analogous issues in the United States. The first of them relates to the presence of representives of unions other than the union that has been certified or recognized in the appropriate bargaining unit. In *General Electric Co.* v. *NLRB*[3] the Court of Appeals for the Second Circuit upheld the NLRB's decision that a union may engage in "coalition bargaining" with representatives present from bargaining units other than the one certified in the International Union of Electrical, Radio and Machine Workers unit where the demand for bargaining was made and declined. The NLRB and the courts held that an employer could not refuse to bargain on the grounds that "outsiders" were present. The reasoning employed was similar to that present in the Japanese central Labor Relations Commission cases involving national-federation representatives, i.e., that the denial of such representation is inconsistent with the right of workers to freely choose their bargaining representatives. The specific purpose of the IUE in *General Electric* was to reduce the "ability of the company to play one [union] off against the other." "The plain facts," the decision continued, "are that the IUE proposed negotiating technique as a response to the company's past bargaining practices that is designed to strengthen the IUE's bargaining positions, and that both sides know it."[4]

The NLRB and the courts have concluded that an attempt by unions, through coalition bargaining or other vehicles, to subvert the board-certified appropriate unit (for instance) and expand it to a size more to the union's liking would be unlawful; indeed, the NLRB has concluded that insistence upon such a demand is a refusal to bargain in good faith.[5] However, in *General Electric* the court concluded that the company had not demonstrated a "clear and present danger to the bargaining process that is required to overcome the burden on one who objects to the representatives selected by the other party"[6] and that the policy of encouragement of free selection of bargaining representatives must therefore override the employer's insistence that the union was attempting to change the unit "through the back door."

A line of American cases that are somewhat analogous to the Japanese decisions are the so-called affiliation cases. These cases arise outside the NLRB's normal secret-ballot election process and occur where the certified or recognized union seeks to change its affiliation, sometimes by virtue of a merger or an affiliation on the part of a local or company union with an international union. The legal issue is raised by virtue of an employer's refusal to bargain or a union's attempt to amend its certification. The NLRB has held that the question of whether the employer is obliged to bargain or whether the certification may be amended depends on whether there has been an essential change in the identity of the bargaining representative. The NLRB has looked to whether the union is assured that it would be an "autonomous and separate" unit, whether the offices of the local would remain the same, whether there would be no change in the day-to-day relationship with the employer, and whether the newly affiliated local would honor all contractual commitments with the employer. The NLRB's view has been that the question of whether there has been substantial change in the internal union process is predicated on whether there has been change in union leadership, dues payments, or the obligations of employees, or whether a major official objects to the affiliation. If the answers are in the negative, the employer is obliged to bargain. Some of the courts of appeals, however, have taken a more cautious view of this matter. In particular, the Court of Appeals for the Third Circuit has denied a union's right to compel the employer to bargain with it where a 30-person local independent union affiliated with an international union that had a total membership of 200,000. In *Sun Oil Co. of Pennsylvania* v. *NLRB* the Third Circuit court stated the following:

The independent's constitution and by-laws were largely superceded by the international, which prescribed certain mandatory provisions for the constitution and by-laws of its locals, including inter alia: control by the international over the procedure for calling a strike and for granting strike benefits; required per capita tax payable to the International; authorization for the audit of the local's financial records by the international; and mandatory support by the local of any policy formulated by the national committee which is approved by 75 percent of the International's bargaining units. In addition, the company is now required to bargain with an international union which, with some 200,000 dues-paying members, has interests and positions of national scope not necessarily in harmony with the interests of the local union and which can also flex considerably more bargaining muscle than a 30-person local independent. This change in viewpoint because of national concerns, and the increase in the bargaining power combined with the transferral of the local independent's governing autonomy to the international indicate to us . . . that the OCAW locals were distinctive new bargaining representatives with which the company had no obligation to bargain until the locals were certified to the board.

. . . We hold that when a local independent union affiliates with and becomes a local unit of an international union and transfers control over the right to its members to the international whose constitutions and by-laws make substantial changes in the rights of employees to the contract, affects their obligations to management and links their concerns with thousands of other members of the international throughout the country, a change is affected in the bargaining agent of such employees.[7]

In recent years in the United States the advent of conglomerates has impelled local unions and independent company unions (in the Japanese sense of the term) to affiliate with internationals where they had not done so before. Corporate reorganizations have necessitated similar restructuring on the unions' side so that workers will not suffer an erosion of bargaining power and a lack of assistance and technical expertise. However, some of the NLRB's rules relating to the circumstances under which an employer is obliged to continue to bargain with a union that has affiliated with a new international have been niggardly and unsympathetic to the spread of effective collective bargaining.

Also troublesome is the *Amoco Production Company* case,[8] in which the NLRB concluded that an employer had no obligation to bargain where nonmembers as well as members of the union had not been afforded an opportunity to vote on the affiliation question in the internal union ballot—a ballot that is required by the NLRB as a matter of due process. The NLRB's reasoning was that to exclude nonmembers through "members only" affiliation votes would be inconsistent with the statutory protection of employees' free choice. The majority distinguished between the strike and ratification-vote procedures, which are not extended to nonmembers.

In *Amoco Production Company,* NLRB members Fanning and Zimmerman, in a persuasive dissent, took the position that the board ought not to intrude into internal union affairs, and that so long as a nonmember had the opportunity to become a member of the union and to vote in the affiliation election the procedure was consistent with the purposes of the NLRA. The dissent pointed out that strike and ratification votes affect nonmembers just as much as, if not more than, affiliation votes of the kind in question. Said the dissent:

Any tension between the right of members of the unit to a voice in their representation and the right of members of the union to decide for themselves the future of their union must be resolved in favor of the union membership. It is the union member who is most affected by union affiliation. In contrast, the effect of affiliation on the unit member who has elected not to join the labor organization which represents him is indirect. Nor is that unit member foreclosed from participation in a valid affiliation process should he feel vitally concerned; for, if he has not been given fair opportunity to join the union and to participate in its affairs, due process has not been satisfied. Lacking due process, we would not recognize the affiliation [and thus compel the employer to bargain].[9]

Yet the issue in the *Zenko* and *Gokaroren* cases, as well as in the *General Electric* decision on coalition bargaining, is really the same as that presented in most of the affiliation cases, such as *Sun Oil* and *Amoco,* where an independent local is affiliating with an international. A group of employees is attempting to obtain the benefits of what they perceive to be more efficient and expert technical and outside advice. In so doing, they may attempt to coordinate their bargaining power with that of other employees in other companies throughout the country. Whenever this happens, the focus on purely local or enterprise concerns may be diluted. The presumption should be in all of these cases that the freedom to bargain collectively and to select representatives ought to apply in the absence of some extraordinary circumstance that undermines another goal of the statute. *Sun Oil, Amoco, Zenko,* and some of the other circuit court decisions, particularly as they abhor enhanced bargaining strength for the union by virtue of its new affiliation, seem to be completely out of step with the purposes of both the National Labor Relations Act and the Trade Union Law insofar as they provide workers with the right to organize in the manner in which they deem to be most suitable to their self-interest. An irony here is that the leading American cases are more restrictive than their Japanese counterparts. A comparative view of the law does not reflect the differences in the two countries' union structures.

Refusal to Bargain because of Violent or Offensive Union Behavior
It has already been noted that the Japanese statute speaks in terms of proper reasons for declining to bargain with a union. In a sense, however, even though the NLRA does not contain similar language, the bargaining obligation will be excused under certain circumstances. The *Times Publishing* case provides a defense for an employer when it has declined to bargain: that the union is not bargaining in good faith. The NLRB's decision dramatizes the same kinds of problems with which Japanese agencies and courts are confronted.

Even though the statutes may be similar as a practical matter, there are major differences in the kinds of cases from which American and Japanese case law have developed. Violence or something close to it seems to be much more of a part of the bargaining process in Japan, at least in those cases that go to the commissions and the courts. Unions quite frequently engage in disorderly conduct similar to mass picketing and encircle the boss on plant premises. Curiously, Japanese authorities view power or might (*jitsuryoku*) as acceptable—in contrast with violence, which is not appropriate under the Trade Union Law.

K. Hokao has noted that "the union side can be held criminally liable if it forces long hours of negotiation by not allowing the employers time for rest and sleep, by cutting off their path of retreat, or by 'kangaroo court' type tactics, such as shutting the employers up in one room and keeping them under surveillance for long hours."[10] Such conduct is more widespread than even the cases reveal. Hokao reports a case where company negotiators were held in a factory for 35 hours, and another where employers were locked up in company offices for 17 hours, denied sleep and breakfast, and forced to accept a closed-shop proposal. States Hokao:

Court examples include a case in which during collective bargaining the fact that a "large number of union members collaborated in using threatening language to the company negotiators and, pressing persistently for acceptance of union demands, hit the table standing between the two parties and destroyed the table's plywood surface. They also obstructed the path of retreat by surrounding the company negotiators who halted the meeting and tried to leave the room. By acting in a manner which could result in physical harm to the company negotiators, they threatened and frightened them into formulating a written promise to accept the items demanded by the union." Similarly, there were situations where during negotiations violence was found where union members ". . . sang loudly, hit large drums and gongs very close to department and section chiefs, giving them a feeling of fuzzy headedness and dimmed consciousness to the extent of causing fainting spells and breathlessness."[11]

Frank Gibney has written:

Some of the most egregious *amaembo* (literally, "people who crave dependence") are found among Japanese trade unionists. Unlike unionists in the West, however, they rarely resort to open violence. That would bring prompt police intervention. But they regularly take advantage of the seasonal "joint struggle" periods to hold mass meetings during office hours, disrupting work by impromptu rallies and blockade executives in their offices. Sessions in the so-called *dantai kosho* ("group negotiations") often turn into improvised kangaroo courts. One or a handful of company representatives are surrounded by the entire membership of the union, or groups of unionists working in shifts, and held for hours on end, in the hope that they will finally break down, exhausted, and sign a favorable agreement. Even when one allows for Japan's prounion, postoccupation labor laws, the incidence of company representatives calling the police to break up such mob intimidation is remarkably small. Like the reluctance of Japanese professors to ask the police for protection against rioting students, this is, to the foreign mind, almost inexplicable. So, too, is the attitude of the union struggle committee members, who feel that such tactics are their right and expect, after the kangaroo courts are over, that everybody will end up smiling.

That, in fact, is what usually happens. The pattern of indulgence toward unruly behavior in Japanese life runs directly from the child breaking crockery unpunished to the struggle committee chairman's violent tactics being ignored, if not condoned, by those in authority. They are *amae*. In justice, it should also be said that most *amae* Japanese authority figures, whether parents, premiers, or company directors, tend to look with contempt on the views of children, citizens, or company employees; and they disregard them when making final decisions.[12]

The Japanese workers' sense of dependence is integral to the bargaining process. When expectations are not realized, particularly when dismissals are the subject of protest, the dispute can turn deeply violent. This may well account for the tolerance of violence as an "act of dispute" (*sogi koi*) under the Trade Union Law and the view that what Americans would characterize as mass picketing is "proper" or "appropriate" as a matter of labor law.

American unions also engage in violence. The case law before the NLRB and the courts (federal and state), as well as numerous congressional hearings (the McClellan hearings are among the best-known) provide testimony for this proposition. Generally, however, the violence does not take place during the collective bargaining process. Either it occurs in the context of strikes and picketing when negotiations have broken down or it involves intimidation of the opposing side through beatings, firebombings, and other actions away from the bargaining table. Under the *Thayer* doctrine the NLRB has permitted picketing and striking employees guilty of misconduct to be reinstated where the employer's unfair labor practices are serious enough to have been viewed as triggering the misconduct. Some of Japan's Labor Relations Commissions (the Tokyo and Osaka commissions in particular) seem to have a tolerance for similar behavior. A case that highlights this attitude in the context of a refusal to negotiate after the "breakdown of collective bargaining" (*Danko Ketsuretsu Gono Kosho Kyohi To Futo Rodo Koi*) is *Kotobuki Kenchiku Kenkyusho*.[13] In this case the company had indicated a willingness to engage in collective bargaining 2 months after a "stalemate" or impasse had been reached, and it had proposed that the negotiations take place for an hour and a half at the Meguro-ku Welfare Center with negotiators limited to seven per side. The union insisted that the company's offices be the site for collective bargaining and visited the offices 30 or 40 minutes before the negotiation session, demanding a change in the bargaining site. The company refused to agree, and then union members, including the employee whose discharge was the topic of the negotiations, "tussled" with the vice-manager and the planning-section chief. The union members encircled the vice-manager and closed in on him, demanding that the discharge be revoked. The section chief called the police, and the collective bargaining scheduled for that day was called off. Another "tussle" ensued when the union visited the company's offices for the purpose of resuming negotiations. The company then proceeded to refuse to bargain further, partly because of the union's conduct. In sustaining the unfair-labor-practice charge filed by the union, the Tokyo Labor Relations Commission, concluding that there had been a substantial lapse of time since the last collective bargaining session and arguing for the reconvening of collective bargaining on the ground that it would be "difficult" to say that a further session would be "meaningless," stated the following:

The conduct of the union on March 14 and 23, 1973 [the dates of the "tussles"], although done in order to propose collective bargaining, cannot be accepted. Judging from the development of such repeated strife, there are factors noted by the company's attitude of avoiding collective bargaining which cannot necessarily be termed groundless fears. However, one cause of the disorder on March 14 lies in the company's complete disregard of the union's desires concerning the time and place of collective bargaining. Moreover, it cannot be judged that on that day the company employed absolutely no force. It is natural to deny the use of force in any situation, and the union should strictly prohibit such action, so as not to be criticized by the company. Hitherto, the struggles accompanied by violence have occurred over the issue of whether the company would agree to reconvene collective bargaining. There has been no evidence that the union has used violence at collective bargaining sessions. Accordingly, although there is a problem in the union's persistence in its own view concerning the time and place of collective bargaining, there is no evidence to recognize that, should the company give up its persistent claim and collective bargaining be reconvened, there would be a probability of acts of violence occurring at the collective bargaining sessions. Should the unions act violently at the bargaining session, the company would be completely justified in refusing collective bargaining.[14]

The Tokyo District Court saw it differently and reversed the Tokyo Labor Relations Commission's order to bargain. The court concluded that the conduct of the union members at the first session could not be regarded as the seeking of a discussion on changing the location of the negotiations. The court stated that there was a legitimate reason for the company's refusal for collective bargaining that day, and concluded that it was "understandable" that the company would have a fear of the collective bargaining process in the future. (The court noted that one official had sustained an abrasion on the lower left thigh that required 5 days for complete recovery and that another had sustained a wound on the right side of his face requiring 4 days, although it stated that these facts did not influence its decision.) Accordingly, stated the court, there was a legitimate reason for declining collective bargaining under the circumstances.

American cases involving similar situations are infrequent, but they do occur. For instance, in *Fitzsimons Manufacturing Company*[15] the NLRB was confronted with the following facts. After a strike, the employer suspended members of the bargaining committee as the result of a petition requesting the termination of one of the company's supervisors. Unfair-labor-practice charges were filed with the NLRB alleging that the suspensions violated the NLRA. At a subsequent meeting between the company and the union, with federal and state mediators present, it was agreed that the suspensions could be resolved by giving full back pay to all members of the committee except the chairman, who would receive only partial back pay. This agreement was put in writing. At a subsequent grievance meeting, the company and union representatives (Foltz and Vogel for the company and Mastos for the union) became involved in a dispute about the use of a tape recorder at the meeting, and Foltz became aware that Mastos had not informed the bargaining committee of the agreement on back pay because he regarded the meeting as confidential. At a second meeting the same dispute took place, and when Vogel made reference to the settlement of the bargaining committee charges Mastos stopped the meeting, had the bargaining committee excused, and stated that the settlement meeting had been confidential. A dispute ensued about this. The NLRB described the facts as follows:

Mastos stated that he had called the state mediator who had indicated that he also felt the meeting had been confidential. Mastos then said that he would punch Vogel in the mouth and knock him on his ass if the subject was brought up again. The bargaining committee then re-entered the room, and Vogel said, "I have one comment to make about . . . ." Mastos interrupted Vogel, reached across the desk, grabbed Vogel by his tie and pulled upwards. Vogel came to his feet. Foltz then separated Mastos and Vogel, and Mastos challenged Vogel to come outside to the parking lot. The challenge was declined and the meeting broke up. Mastos had not engaged in any other physical altercation with any of the respondents in management prior to this incidence.[16]

On the basis of this conduct the company refused to bargain with Mastos, and, when the parties could not resolve their differences about this, new unfair-labor-practice charges were filed with the NLRB on this issue alleging refusal to bargain on the part of the company. The general counsel relied upon cases, such as the coalition-bargaining *General Electric* case, which stand for the proposition that an employer violates the statute when it refuses to bargain with the duly designated representatives of the employees. The position of the general counsel was that the facts did not contain persuasive evidence that Mastos's presence would make bargaining "impossible" and therefore did not justify the employer's refusal to bargain with Mastos. In this respect, the argument was quite similar to that employed by the Tokyo Labor Relations Commission. The general counsel contended that there had been no other physical altercation and that, in fact, Mastos did not strike or physically touch Vogel's person. The union argued not only that the incident was isolated and involved "only heated words and minor physical contact" but also that it arose out of a matter that management knew was of extreme sensitivity for the union representative. The employer stressed that it harbored no animosity toward the union and that all the evidence indicated that grievances were being processed by a union representative whose presence did not disrupt the grievance machinery. In resolving this matter, the NLRB took a fundamentally different tack than that taken by the Tokyo Labor Relations Commission:

. . . where the presence of a particular representative in negotiations makes collective bargaining impossible or futile, a party's right to choose its representative is limited, and the other party is relieved of its duty to deal with that particular representative. The test . . . is whether there is "persuasive evidence that the presence of the particular individual would create ill will and make good faith bargaining impossible."

In our view, Mastos's conduct was sufficiently egregious to make bargaining impossible under the above standard.[17]

Member Truesdale dissented on the ground that the evidence did not support the employer's argument that good-faith bargaining would be impossible, but the majority's view was sustained by the Court of Appeals for the Sixth Circuit.[18]

Thus, while the attitudes of the American and the Japanese courts appears to be in accord (although in *Fitzsimons* the court of appeals was simply sustaining the NLRB's decision under a substantial evidence test), the positions of the administrative agencies are remarkably different. The views of the latter institutions may well mirror the practices of the parties in each country in their own collective bargaining processes.

"Ribbon Struggle" (Ribbon Toso)

The wearing of armbands and headbands has been a favorite weapon of the Japanese unions when collective bargaining is proceeding and differences have not been resolved to the satisfaction of the union. The idea is to publicize the dispute and embarrass the employer without causing the economic losses and other harm to the enterprise that would flow from a strike.

Americans generally regard this form of activity as foreign and peculiar, yet there are rules of law that have emerged in the United States relating to roughly analogous problems. American unions are frequently involved in organizational disputes (issues arising out of employers' resistance to union organization) before the NLRB. Cases of this kind are not as common in Japan, and a union need not engage in any effort to obtain the allegiance of a majority of workers in an appropriate unit. In the United States, the need of unions to engage in such an effort leads to elaborate organizational campaigns in many instances, and one of the most frequent issues is the right of both employees and nonemployee union organizers to engage in union activity on company property.

In 1945 the U.S. Supreme Court approved an NLRB rule that provided that a union could engage in activities such as solicitation through the use of authorization cards and the distribution of literature during nonwork time on company property.[19] In the same case, *Republic Aviation* v. *NLRB*, the court also invalidated a company rule prohibiting union supporters from wearing union buttons on company property during work time. The employer's legitimate defense in all these cases, said the court and the NLRB, is its interest in production and discipline. Except under special circumstances, it has no interest in production and discipline outside of work time. The court also concluded that wearing of union insignia during work time is protected, again in the absence of special circumstances.

In Japan, by definition, the "ribbon struggle," or the wearing of armbands (and also the wearing of headbands, or *hajumake*), takes place on company property during and outside of work hours. The first case to be decided by the Japanese courts was heard and decided by the Kobe District Court in 1967.[20] The court stated that as a general proposition union activities during work hours could be prohibited, but that when workers exercised "fundamental labor rights" union activities could coexist with and not necessarily detract from the physical and mental concentration needed for production. Accordingly, said the court, inasmuch as employees would not be distracted, regulations promulgated by the employer prohibiting union activities during work hours were not violated.

The Japanese courts have been more cautious recently, and have sometimes referred to the size, color, and content of slogans and to the objective of the union wearing the ribbons as being determinative of whether they are a legitimate union activity and thus protected as an "act of dispute" or *sogi koi*. In a subsequent case[21] the Hakodate District Court concluded that, so long as employees gave a definite amount of physical and mental energy required by the employer, the wearing of ribbons as union activity was protected and did not violate the obligation to give undivided attention to work. Contrarily, the wearing of ribbons was held to be unlawful in the *Chunichi Hoso* decision of the Nagoya District Court[22] inasmuch as the employees involved had direct dealings with sponsors and others outside the company to conduct sales. The court concluded that ribbon wearing could not be considered a legitimate union activity inasmuch as it would interfere with effective salesmanship and greatly hinder the business operations of the company. The Nagoya High Court upheld this decision. Recent cases have all been against the labor movement's position and have generally denied the view that ribbon wearing is a protected act of dispute. This line of authority[23] has culminated in the *Hotel Okura* decision of the supreme court.[24]

In the *Hotel Okura* case, the union and the company were unable to resolve their differences about a wage increase. The union notified the company on October 3 as follows: "Should the company not present the sincere response by October 5, the union would implement ribbon wearing by 9:00 A.M. October 6."[25] The same day the company handed the union a written warning of its policy prohibiting the wearing of ribbons and of strict measures to be taken with all those who worked while wearing ribbons, and it posted the notice inside company facilities. On October 5 the company added 100,000 yen to its previous offer, but the union was still dissatisfied and engaged in ribbon wearing. The ribbons were a red and white flower approximately 6 cm in diameter, 6 cm long, and 2 cm wide, a white printed ribbon, or a pink and white flower approximately 5 cm in diameter, 6 cm long, and 6 cm wide. On the ribbon were the words "Fulfill demands" and "Hotel Union." The union members wore these ribbons underneath their nameplates on their jackets. Some of the union members wore the ribbons during the first two days of this conduct in front of guests of the hotel. The company instructed managers to persuade those wearing ribbons to take them off and to move union members who refused to comply with such orders into positions where guests would not see them. The majority of the union members took the ribbons off before they had contact with the guests; some refused to do so and wore them in front of the guests. The company reprimanded (but did not discharge) six union members who were regarded as the ringleaders in this activity. Charges were filed with the Tokyo Labor Relations Commission.

The commission took the view that employment regulations apply to employees in "normal times" and that, therefore, they could not apply to a union's acts of dispute undertaken in the midst of differences with the company. Said the commission: "As the 'ribbon struggle' in this case constitutes behavior obstructing the normal operations conducted by the unions for the purposes of displaying the solidarity of the union, of promoting and attaining the benefits of the claims made in collective bargaining, there is no question that this comes under one type of act of dispute. Therefore, it is incorrect to apply the employment regulations to this case."[26] Therefore, the commission's view was that the imposition of the rule against the union members in question was discriminatory treatment of the union's legitimate act of dispute.

On appeal, the central Labor Relations Commission took a decidedly different view of the matter. The commission's view was that during working hours, in the workplace, a worker must abide by the orders relating to his work. Accordingly, said the commission,

> . . . participation of workers in a union activity such as a "ribbon struggle" during working hours should be said to be an opportunistic conduct of the sort to benefit oneself at the expense of another (engaging in a *sumo* match using another's loincloth) and lacking in economic fairness. . . . Therefore, it is appropriate to interpret the participation of workers in union activities through "ribbon stuggle" while abiding by the duty to labor or work is a violation of the worker's obligations to discharge their duties. There is no reason that employers must submit to the development of union activities held during working hours by workers.[27]

The Labor Relations Commission also noted that the employer had no tactic it could utilize to counter the ribbon struggle. The lockout, said the commission, "has the regrettable quality of using a butcher knife, which is contrary to the principle of fairness between labor and management"; it was an inflexible and rigid weapon that could not be used with ease in response to the flexibility of the ribbon struggle. Finally, inasmuch as the rest, relaxation, and comfort of the guests in the hotel were at stake, the commission took the position that the union's tactic was particularly inappropriate. The commission said that "the reputation and prestige of the hotel would be degraded by the use of such weapons in a way which would be difficult to recoup."

The Supreme Court of Japan agreed with the central Labor Relations Commission. The court took the position that, as a general proposition, ribbon wearing is not an act of dispute during working hours. The court seems to have been influenced by the fact that the purpose of the ribbon wearing in this case was more to build solidarity or to "body build" the union than to engage in an act of dispute with the employer.

Although most of the American cases involve solicitation and the distribution of literature on company property, there are a number of cases involving insignia and buttons (and, indeed, ribbons). One of the cases was in the context of a dispute between labor and management in an established collective bargaining relationship. In the case in question, *Holladay Park Hospital,*[28] the employer had a written dress code that required nurses to "wear uniforms which meet professional standards of accountability." During collective bargaining, employees began to wear union buttons regularly on their uniforms at work. The buttons were about 1¾ inches in diameter, with a light background and blue letters stating

RN's* / ONA

*Represented Nurses

The employer did not object to the wearing of these buttons, but a dispute arose about the employees wearing yellow ribbons tied in a bow measuring 3½ by 2½ inches and pinned directly under their union buttons. An order went out ordering all nurses to remove the ribbons or to be sent home. All the employees complied, and thus no employee received any discipline as a result of wearing a ribbon.

The preliminary question posed in *Holladay Park Hospital* was one that would never arise in Japan. It was whether yellow ribbons were, in fact, a union insignia. The administrative law judge had held in the negative, but the NLRB reversed that, concluding that all the parties perceived the yellow ribbons to be an "indication of support for the union" and that employees had decided to wear the yellow ribbons as "symbols of their support for the union's bargaining position."[29]

Having identified the ribbons as a union insignia, the board noted its precedent and that of the courts to the effect that special circumstances could convert protected activity into unprotected conduct. The Court of Appeals for the Ninth Circuit has summarized the special circumstances relating to a union insignia as follows: ". . . cases where the insignia could exacerbate employee dissension, jeopardize employee safety, or damage machinery or products . . . distraction from work demanding great concentration, and a need to 'project a certain type of image to the public.' "[30] The NLRB stated that special circumstances could be found in a health-care institution where the employer was motivated by a "genuine concern for the health and welfare of its patients" and that "there was no evidence of discriminatory enforcement of the employer's long-standing rule against nurses wearing any attachments to their clothing."[31] The administrative law judge had found that special circumstances were present because the employer had a "proper and legitimate motive" of avoiding involvement of pa-

tients in collective bargaining negotiations. The administrative
law judge buttressed this conclusion by stating that the employer had not enforced its dress code in a discriminatory manner. The NLRB reversed this on the grounds that the dress
code had been enforced in a discriminatory manner and that
employees had been permitted to wear various objects on their
uniforms, including red ribbons and green ribbons, which were
presumably at least as conspicuous against their white or pastel
uniforms as the pastel yellow ribbons involved in this case. That
the employer had permitted other union buttons, which it had
characterized as more "professional," was deemed irrelevant by
the NLRB. The board concluded by noting that there was no
evidence of actual interference with patients here in any way,
and that therefore the employer's rule was implemented so as
to force employee involvement in concerted activities in support of the union's collective bargaining position. The board
also concluded that the rule altered the past practice of the
employer relating to dress code, and that therefore it was a
unilateral change instituted in violation of the employer's duty
to bargain.

The NLRB and the courts have indicated that more stringent
rules in connection with the distribution of literature, other
union activity, and the wearing of union insignia may be upheld as lawful where the employees have contact with the
public. Indeed, the U.S. Supreme Court has concluded that the
normal presumptions in favor of the illegality of rules prohibiting union activity during nonwork time may not have general
applicability in hospitals.[32] The Court of Appeals for the Ninth
Circuit stated in *NLRB* v. *Harrah's Club*[33] that the "appearance
of . . . uniformed employees" is sufficient justification for prohibiting buttons, even if wearing buttons is itself a protected
activity. Subsequently, however, the same court of appeals has
characterized that statement as dictum.[34] The courts have indicated that rules prohibiting union insignia may be lawful
where, for instance, a fashionable department store likes to
have its employees double as customers and models for its mer-
chandise and where the button is so large and blatant as to be
offensive to patrons of such establishments.[35]

Problems relating to the content of speech or slogans have
arisen in the United States (and in Japan, too). The discharge
of a worker wearing a t-shirt stating "Inland sucks" was held to

be unlawful where the reason for the discharge was not the wearing of the shirt.[36] On the other hand, the Court of Appeals for the Sixth Circuit reversed an NLRB decision and held that employees may not advertise a grievance by wearing a shirt with the slogan "I'm tired of bustin' my ass."[37] These cases represent exceptions to the basic rule that exists relating to the content of union insignia, i.e., that speech is protected in the interest of promoting speech which is wide open and robust.

One might ascribe the more solicitous attitude toward union insignia in America, as opposed to Japan, to the fact that in the United States such insignia are related to organizational activity. The U.S. Supreme Court has expressed particular solicitude for union activity that involves such fundamental rights.[38] *Holladay Park Hospital* moves the NLRB beyond the organizational stage into the collective bargaining process, however. At the same time, one cannot say with certainty that the courts will approve the NLRB's decision, given the Supreme Court's concern about the employer's legitimate concern for patients in health-care institutions. In both countries, the courts have shifted toward a concern for employees' attention during working hours. The Japanese now take the view that ribbon wearing is not an act of dispute. Thus, it may be a union activity for which, if it interferes with employees' attention during working hours, management has the right to discipline them. To the extent that it was otherwise before the *Hotel Okura* decision, the more permissive approach might be attributable to the idea of dependence in the union-employer bargaining relationship.

Union Posters and Notices on Company Property

Both in the United States and in Japan the question whether unions may have access to bulletin boards is often resolved through the negotiation of the collective bargaining agreement.

In Japan, it appears as though an employer is not obligated under the Trade Union Law to provide access to bulletin boards. On the other hand, denial of bulletin-board access simultaneous with denial of the right to post literature on other portions of company property is indeed a violation of law.[39] In any event, a company is obligated only to provide space. Who should provide the funds for the space is a matter to be resolved between the parties themselves. Hokao has noted that where bulletin-board space is agreed to by or imposed upon the employer the intent is to forbid notices and posters elsewhere.[40] However, in Hokao's view, this rule changes in the event of a *sogi koi,* or dispute between the parties: "During a dispute . . . agreements made to structure the order of labor-management relations during normal times cannot be applied, and even if the intent is that the affixing of posters on places other than the designed bulletin boards is prohibited during disputes as well, such agreements cannot help but be interpreted as improperly restricting union activities."[41] This view appears to be questionable in view of the general trend in this area manifested by some of the Japanese Supreme Court decisions alluded to above. Finally, in Japan employer censorship of the bulletin boards has generally been precluded by the Labor Relations Commissions and the courts once use of the bulletin board has been "recognized." This is so even when the material has been prepared by unions other than the one that has access to the bulletin board and despite the political content of the material.[42]

In the United States, the NLRB has held that the employer has no statutory obligation to provide a union with access to a bulletin board.[43] However, this rule is subject to a number of qualifications. If the bulletin board has been provided to other organizations of a similar kind, the rule excluding a union will be deemed discriminatory.[44] Where the employer is viewed to have singled out the union for special discriminatory treatment and where there have been no firm demarcation lines established for access to the bulletin board, again the rules excluding the union have been held unlawful.[45] In a recent and important decision by the Court of Appeals for the District of Columbia in *Helton* v. *NLRB,* Judge Wright, authoring the opinion, concluded that a dissident group (the Teamsters for Democratic Action) had a statutory right to a bulletin board that was provided for "official union business." The court compared this problem to the cases in which the courts and NLRB have held rules prohibiting the distribution of literature by rival unions during nonwork time to be unlawful.[46]

The affixing of posters to company property is a more common tactic where disputes arise in Japan than in the United States. Hokao has concluded that the right to affix posters to company property is generally protected by the Trade Union Law,[47] but in a 1982 ruling the Supreme Court of Japan appears to have taken a contrary position.[48]

Generally, the same considerations apply to the posting of notices on company property that apply to "ribbon struggle" problems and to the distribution of union literature. For instance, posters affixed on company property in a hospital in a place where outpatients would readily see them were viewed as having an "irritating effect inviting the unease of patients generally, and creating improper obstacles to the normal operations of the hospital."[49] Similarly, affixing posters to and writing graffiti on company cars go beyond normal propaganda measures and were considered to be illegal dispute activities interfering with the company's right to manage. The affixing of posters whose contents included personal attacks on individuals by the teacher's union at a private girls' high school where students could readily notice them was said to hinder the school's educational function, but inasmuch as the action was undertaken to resist "improper dismissals and propaganda activity involving the display and distribution of literature by school authorities," and inasmuch as the posters were placed not in classrooms and hallways, but on bulletin boards at the main entrance, the activity was regarded as a permissible act of dispute.[50]

The manner of affixing posters has caused great problems in Japan. Hokao states that

... the affixing of posters has been ruled legal when "vinyl tape was used to affix the posters, so as not to damage or dirty company buildings," or even when the posters were pasted on but "could easily be removed without leaving marks." However, the affixing of posters was held to exceed the bounds of justification when "marks remained, dirtying the white wall, even after the posters were removed," and when the "posters were affixed with glue strong enough for cast materials," such that the posters could not easily be removed.[51]

Hokao describes the kinds of situations in which criminal responsibility can arise in relation to the affixing of posters. He has noted precedent in which there was actual physical damage to a structure, including a case where there was damage to the building and facilities of an employer's private residence when well over 100 posters made of newspapers cut into fourths were pasted on the entranceway, nameplate, traditional doors (made out of branches and usually found in gardens), fence, veranda, pillars, windows, paper doors, earthen wall, and white wall of the main building. In another case, 950 posters the size of newspapers, pasted indiscriminately to the ceilings, walls, wall moldings, windows, counters, desks, and other places in a company's general offices and in the president's office, dirtied the facilities and interfered with their basic functions. In yet another case, a train station master's office windows were completely covered with posters so that no light could come through them, even at noontime, and a bucket of glue was dumped onto the station master's desk and posters were affixed to it, making it impossible to work. Hokao states that the critical questions, in terms of the exemption from criminal action given by the Trade Union Law, concern the number of posters, the number of times they are affixed, their location, the manner of affixing, the employer's reaction and attitude, and other circumstances. However, Hokao stressed the difference between the question whether an activity is protected under the Trade Union Law as an act of dispute and the question whether it can be the subject of criminal liability. The absence of protection in Japan, as in the United States, does not mean that the subject matter is outside the scope of the statute and therefore within the jurisdiction of the criminal courts. According to Hokao,

The affixing of posters [in cases involving] . . . a private residence, president's office, manager's office, station master's office, etc. . . . cannot be judged as justifiable union activity in principle, even though they were part of overall dispute activities. Even in these cases, however, whether the actions constitute criminal damage to the structures of the facilities is a separate problem that must be investigated individually. . . . The affixing of posters to the extent that company property of no exceptional cultural value can be restored to its original state with a simple washing must be viewed as not constituting criminal damage to structures or facilities.[52]

In other words, in Hokao's view, in order for there to be criminal liability, ordinary property must be destroyed completely or irreparably.

In addition to the manner in which posters are affixed, their content must be examined. "Insulting expressions" that harm the character and reputation of other people and untrue facts that invade the privileges of a company or a particular individual are considered beyond the bounds of justification. For instance, posters with statements such as "The crematorium's waiting for you, president," "Die, you stupid old bastard," and "President, we're going to send you to Hell" were considered beyond common sensibilities and not protected conduct. Where, in the midst of layoffs, telegrams were sent to a company with such messages as "We dare you to fire us—be warned," "Stop the firings—you'd better watch out," and "This betrayal won't end here," it was held to constitute criminal intimidation. Said the court, "Such telegrams which were sent to private homes and appeared to include the threat of physical harm must be seen as invading the average citizen's sense of security and as having the nature of an intimidating threat."[53] On the other hand, a union poster saying "President . . . We'll kill you" was held not to indicate an intention to intimidate the president but rather was characterized as a manifestation of dissatisfaction with the company's response to a demand put forward in a mischievous and black-humored manner. Since the poster did not expose the executive's private life or make false statements, the action was held not to be greatly malicious or illegal. In one case, employees wrote slogans with India ink on paper the size of a sheet of a newspaper disparaging the company president with statements such as "Entrance for dogs and presidents," "Bloodsucking hag," "You can't eat carp," and "The more you watch, the sicker you get." Many of these signs were stuck on the company's doors and windows. The supreme court held that these acts "decreased the usefulness of the . . . window glass and doors" and were "inappropriate as a tactic for acts of dispute."[54] The volatility of such behavior and the inflammatory nature of these statements—both those that are protected as acts of disputes and those that are not—indicate the extent to which labor disputes can raise the deepest passions. It would be a rare and extraordinary situation where language of this kind would be seen in union literature, let alone posters, in the United States.

In the United States the use of posters is much less frequent. The NLRB has taken the position that employees may drive their cars onto company property with signs urging consumers and employees not to buy the employer's product,[55] and has said that it does not "regard the rights of employees under the [NLRA] to engage in union activities at an employer's premises . . . to include the right to post union stickers on the employer's wall and property."[56] However, with regard to "stickers" on company equipment the NLRB has simply stated that the policy must be applied in a nondiscriminatory, uniform manner.[57] That is, an employer cannot allow certain stickers to be placed on plant equipment and then prohibit union posters. Moreover, in a case involving public employees where the first amendment to the constitution (protecting free speech) was directly applicable, the Court of Appeals for the Tenth Circuit has held that the Veterans' Administration's prohibition of union posters is not unconstitutional. Said the court: "The government has a legitimate interest in promoting the efficiency and productivity of its employees at their workplaces. The district court found that because of the work nature of the areas where posting was prohibited, and the alternate means available for expression, the union and its members had been denied no First Amendment right. We agree."[58]

The affixing of posters to company property is peculiarly Japanese. Curiously, the American decisions seem to provide more protection by virtue of their insistence upon nondiscriminatory employer practices.

Political Activity

This issue, as well as that of disloyalty, cuts across a wide variety of problems relating to union expression on company property: the distribution of literature, the wearing of insignia, the posting of notices, and so on. On political issues, the American and the Japanese courts seem to share the position that political activity is not a part of union activity to the extent that it may not be engaged in on company property. The problem is in defining what is political. The U.S. Supreme Court held in *Eastex Inc.* v. *NLRB*[59] that employees had engaged in concerted activities for the purpose of mutual aid of protection under section 7 when, on company property during nonwork time, they distributed literature relating to legislative issues that could affect their working conditions. On the other hand, the NLRB and the courts have said that "purely political tracts" supporting particular campaigns and candidates are not protected where the union attempts to distribute them on private property, even though the election of a particular candidate might have a very substantial impact on the employees' working conditions.[60] The Supreme Court of Japan appears to have taken an almost identical position.[61]

Disloyalty

The other major issue that arises in connection with all forms of union communication is disloyalty. The American cases are somewhat confusing, owing to the Supreme Court's *Jefferson Standard* decision[62] (against which Justices Frankfurter, Black, and Douglas vigorously dissented). In *Jefferson Standard,* the court held that nonstriking employees' distribution of handbills containing a "vitriolic attack on the quality of the company's television broadcast," and not referring to the labor-management controversy between the union and the employer, was unprotected activity, thus subjecting the employees to dismissal or discipline. The NLRB subsequently extended this rule so that disparagement was unprotected even where the employees were on strike,[63] despite the fact that the nonstriking Jefferson Standard employees seemed to have influenced the court's conclusion that the striking employees were disguising the labor-management controversy. However, in general, the NLRB seems to have mitigated the apparent harshness of this rule by defining what constitutes disparagement of the product in a narrow fashion; it concluded that the *Jefferson Standard* case means that there must be direct reference in the handbills or literature to the labor dispute. The combination of these two approaches has meant that *Jefferson Standard* is less troublesome for unions and employees than would have first appeared.

The Japanese do not seem to have had cases involving the disparagement of companies and their products. This seems to run against the grain of Japanese labor-management and employer-employee relationships, which gives some support to the view that loyalty to the firm has a good deal to do with the success of the three pillars of the Japanese system (enterprise unionism, permanent employment, and *nenko*).

When boycotts themselves do occur in Japan, although they are protected generally, they go beyond the limits of justifiability where, for instance, in a department store the boycott causes "severe discomfort to the customers," and exerts "unreasonable pressure on customers," and "destroys customer good will." Such acts are "obstruction of business" (*gyomu bogai*).[64]

Supervisory and Managerial Personnel

The National Labor Relations Act excludes supervisors from its coverage.[65] The Trade Union Law contains similar provisions, yet the demarcation line between supervisor and employee in Japan is vague. There is a hierarchical split between upper and lower management. Only the section chief (*kacho*) is clearly excluded as a supervisor under Japanese labor law. Those just below the *kacho* level, although they are supervisors or managerial employees and thus excluded in the United States, are protected by the Trade Union Law. Frequently they compose the union leadership. The significance of the exclusion in Japan is that the union may not be a "judicial person" and avail itself of the remedies under the Trade Union Law if it admits supervisors to membership. However, in the United States supervisory or managerial unions may use the NLRA so long as they do not admit their own supervisors.

The American law is clearly more adversarial in nature. Justice Douglas's dissent in *Packard Motor,* in which he concluded that supervisory employees are properly excluded from the NLRA, won the day at the Taft-Hartley amendments' enactment in 1947. The theory was that—because supervisors and their working conditions were not a focal point of the NLRA debates, and because supervisors were properly representatives of management and involvement in unions would pose a conflict of interest for them—the statute ought not to be concerned with their grievances against management. In an effort at consistency (which is superficial, in my view), a majority of the NLRB has taken the position that the discharge of supervisors for union activity is not addressed by the NLRA, even where such conduct is part of a pattern of unlawful conduct against employees.[66]

Strikes, Picketing, and Other Forms of Economic Pressure

Japanese scholars tend to view the strike weapon as less useful in that country because of the organizational framework of unions. Being organized along enterprise lines, unions are unable to exert control over labor beyond the enterprise, and thus management finds it easier to employ strikebreakers. Craft unions in the United States, on the other hand, are able to bring secondary pressure or solidarity to bear beyond corporate lines through control of the apprenticeship programs, the *de facto* closed shop (actually unlawful in the United States), and the exclusive hiring hall, through which the union controls or influences the labor that is available to the employer.[67] However, among the industrial unions, which must employ secondary picketing and thus run afoul of the secondary-boycott prohibitions in the United States, the difference between the two countries is less exaggerated than it might seem.

In Japan, after World War II when the trade-union movement had the upper hand, picket lines were infrequently used because they simply were not needed. The trade-union movement at that time was an "irresistible force" that struggled against the "capitalist camp" as it recovered its position. This recovery restructured the balance of power between labor and management and, thus, the use of the picketing weapon.

Though both the Japanese and the American supreme courts have recognized that a union's obvious objective through picketing is to bring the enterprise to a halt and to dissuade employees and customers from entering or doing business with the company,[68] both courts have condemned violent behavior in the context of the picket line.[69] When one union picket lay down in front of a bus driven by a non-union member, forcing it to stop, and another union member put a bamboo pole through the window to the steering wheel, preventing it from being driven,[70] the Supreme Court of Japan ruled that it was an illegal, forcible obstruction of operations. There are a number of other cases similar to this, and Japan's Supreme Court has not hesitated to condemn what Americans would characterize as mass picketing and disorder, which interferes with entrance to and exit from plant premises.[71] However, there are precedents in the Japanese courts that seem to vary from this standard. For instance, according to one district court, "Since it is impossible to expect the union members to stand back idly and only watch non-union members trying to break through the picket line, giving no chance for peaceful persuasion," the stopping of a bus driven by non-union members by lying in front of the bus "should be permitted as an inevitable action to avoid the danger [presented by the bus] to the picket line," and the forcible action was ruled lawful as an emergency measure.[72] Similarly, the Japanese courts have concluded there is no illegality when union members "hold the way" of individuals who are attempting to split the union. The permissibility of such conduct was established on the grounds that the object was "persuasion" and that the detention of the workers involved was over a comparably short period of time (about 30 minutes), during which there was no violence as such. Moreover, the attitude toward "scrum lines," in which what Americans would call mass picketing is sometimes tolerated, seems to make the Japanese approach considerably different from that employed in the United States.[73]

Again, the question in Japan is whether or not the conduct is proper and therefore an act of dispute within the meaning of the Trade Union Law. If the answer is in the affirmative, there is no civil or criminal liability; otherwise there is liability. In the United States, the question whether union conduct or tactics are protected determines whether management may engage in self-help such as discharge or discipline. Only where the conduct is violent, a threat to peace and order (as is mass picketing), an unlawful restraint of trade under antitrust law, or the like is the union subject to liability in damages in federal or state court.

In addition to the question whether conduct is violent or not, there are limitations on union economic pressure. Partial strikes are unprotected in the United States (that is, when employees refuse to perform some of their duties the employer may dismiss or discipline them), but there is no prohibition against such conduct independent of a violation of the collective bargaining agreement negotiated between labor and management. However, in Japan, the refusal to carry out one part of one's duties is lawful as an act of dispute.[74] At the same time, some of the courts have said that the refusal to accept orders or to follow the employer's directions, the incorrect delivery of goods, or similar kinds of action can constitute illegal dispute tactics.[75] The slowdown, or "soldiering," is regarded as "sabotage," and therefore not an act of dispute. The concept of sabotage in Japan applies to three kinds of situations: the actual or attempted destruction of machinery or property, "open-mouth sabotage" (the disclosure of the employer's secrets or the making of defaming statements about the employer to a company or client), and the slowdown or "intentional lowering of work efficiency."[76]

It seems that the taking of machinery or plant property can

be lawful in Japan where the action is carried out peacefully. Some of the sabotage cases are similar to the disloyalty cases referred to above. For instance, in the *Iwataya* incident decided by the Fukuoka District Court, the employees on the picket line called out to customers "Iwataya foods are expensive" or "Iwataya stuff is full of dysentery germs," and the tactics were held to be appropriate to dispute actions, inasmuch as these were legal techniques undertaken to "smoothly move toward the realization of collective bargaining.[77] In light of the *Jefferson Standard* decision, the American courts would hardly permit more inflammatory language and perhaps would not sanction less.[78]

Two problems arise in Japan that do not appear in the United States. The first is the "payment strike" (*nokin*), a dispute in which collections of bills from a firm's customers is carried out as usual but the transference of funds to the firm is not permitted. The collected funds are retained in the union's custody. The action constitutes a partial withholding of service and has been characterized as a "go-slow action" or as a "go-slow strike" or sabotage. The critical question is whether the tactic involves on-the-job misappropriation of funds. The degree and type of custodial action taken relates to the propriety of the act. One question relates to whether the intention of the union was to actually misappropriate funds for the purpose of obtaining profit or to use *nokin* as a tactic. Where a union deposited electric utility fares in a bank, notified the bank of the conditions relating to the deposit, and stated that after the resolution of the dispute the deposit would be immediately turned over to the company and that nothing would be withdrawn during the strike, the action was appropriate. In this case, however, the deposit was made at a bank that was involved in transactions with the company at which the payment strike was aimed. The company issued an order that the payment strike be immediately halted, and thereupon the entire amount of the deposit was turned over intact to the company's account. The supreme court has determined that in a situation where a bank other than the bank designated by the company to handle moneys opens an account in the union's name before or after a *nokin* incident without notifying the company, or if the bank does not expeditiously turn the collected moneys over to the company when requested to do so, the conduct manifests illegal intent.

The second of the two tactics peculiar to Japan is that of "production-management stoppage," where the employees take over an entire plant and its machinery or some part thereof and attempt to operate the plant itself. Again, income is taken into custody, supposedly for the employer's ultimate benefit. This tactic was used frequently in the wake of World War II,[79] just as sitdowns were used during the Great Depression in the United States. The view in Japan is that, if the company's property or material is sold, the crime of theft has been committed, and the crime of unlawful entry into a building is also present. Although no clear response (at least none as clear as that provided by the U.S. Supreme Court in the sitdown cases) has been provided, it appears as though production control is an impermissible action.

Most of the Japanese unions provide advance notice to an employer before engaging in a protected act of dispute. The Trade Union Law requires a secret ballot on the strike before it takes place. In the United States (except in the health-care industry, in which 10-day strike notices are required) there is no obligation on a union to provide notice of a strike. Nevertheless, where a collective bargaining agreement is in effect, notices must be served on the federal and state mediation agencies beginning 60 days before the expiration of a contract. With the exception of national emergency strikes,[80] there is no statutory ballot provided. Many American unions have established internal procedures for strike ballots at their own initiative.

The mere fact that specific demands have not been formulated before a walkout by workers does not render the activity unprotected under the National Labor Relations Act.[81] However, work stoppages called sporadically or without announcement are regarded as unprotected.[82] The Japanese authorities seem to take a more narrow view of this matter for act-of-dispute purposes. For instance, the Yokohama District Court held that a union's immediate engagement in an act of dispute without participating in any negotiation or presenting demands to the employer was inappropriate.[83] Nevertheless, the prevailing view seems to be that the legitimacy of an act of dispute is based not on the basis of whether there was formal collective bargaining, but on whether the urgency and importance of the demands required prompt action, and also on the attitude of the employer.[84] The majority of academics in Japan appear to support judicial decisions that there is no general obligation for a union to give warning.[85]

Article 37 of Japan's Labor Relations Adjustment Law provides that the parties in a dispute involving public utilities must, before they resort to any act of dispute, notify the Labor Relations Commission and the Ministry of Labor or the prefectural governor at least 10 days before the act of dispute is to be commenced.[86] So long as the 10-day notice is complied with, it is clear that any further warning is not a prerequisite to a legitimate or justifiable act of dispute.[87]

American courts and the NLRB have developed a wide variety of rules to enforce the no-strike clause which is contained in most collective bargaining agreements and which is viewed as the *quid pro quo* for a broad arbitration clause compelling the parties to resolve most disputes during the term of the agreement through the use of a neutral third party. Japanese courts have dealt with the question of whether the "peace obligation" of the agreement has been violated. The Japanese Supreme Court's first consideration of this matter was in the *Konan Bus Employees* case in 1968. The court stated

. . . whether the peace obligation is the so-called relative peace obligation determined in the labor agreement, or whether the peace obligation is that based upon the so-called absolute peace obligation provisions, . . . an act of dispute in violation of the peace obligation is merely a nonfulfillment of contractual obligations. It cannot be considered to be an infringement upon the order of the company. Furthermore, it is appropriate to interpret the participation in this act of dispute by individual union members as being nothing more than a nonfulfillment of contractual obligations.

Therefore, it must be said that the employer cannot subject said worker to disciplinary action for the sole reason that the worker performed or participated in an act of dispute in violation of the peace obligation.[88]

Along similar lines, the Sendai High Court has stated: "The dispute in this case which violates . . . the absolute peace obligation provision is confined to giving rise to the union's responsibility for nonfulfillment of the obligation. It is not something that would cause the deprivation of legitimacy of acts of dispute of individual union members. Therefore, the respondents . . . cannot be charged as responsible for their participation in this dispute. . . ." In the United States, the law is quite clear. The U.S. Supreme Court has held that union officials may not be individually liable for no-strike breaches committed by the labor organization, and that where a union has not authorized an unlawful strike the individual employees may not be sued in damages.[89]

Perhaps the most important issue relates to preliminary injunctions (in the United States) and provisional disposition (in Japan). In the landmark *Boys Markets* v. *Retail Clerks* decision,[90] a 5–2 majority of the U.S. Supreme Court held that—notwithstanding the Norris-LaGuardia Act's provision for a ban on federal court injunctions in labor disputes—an injunction may issue against a strike and a violation of the no-strike clause where the underlying grievance that triggered the strike is subject to the arbitration process. (Subsequently, the court has held that the reasoning of the *Boys Markets* decision is not applicable to sympathy strikes[91] and political strikes.[92])

The Tokyo District Court concluded in the *Pan American World Airways* case that a petition for provisional disposition where an act of dispute is in violation of the peace agreement is appropriate.[93] In the *Northwest Orient Airlines* case, a petition for provisional disposition aimed at a stoppage over a wage increase in violation of the peace agreement was denied by the Tokyo District Court on the grounds that an increase in prices could not have been anticipated at the time that the agreement was entered into and that the employer had not shown that "irreversible damage" would flow from the act of dispute in question.[94] Such a narrow view of the no-strike clause is not generally found in the United States.[95] Repeated violations of the peace obligation by the union, however, would serve to cancel the contract in Japan. For the purpose of compelling arbitration in the United States, the same result does not follow where there have been violations of the no-strike clause. However, where employers have canceled a contract in response to no-strike violations they have successfully defended themselves against refusal-to-bargain charges filed with the National Labor Relations Board by the union.[96]

The question whether an employer has the right to engage in economic pressure has arisen in both the United States and Japan. The U.S. Supreme Court has attempted to distinguish between "offensive" and "defensive" lockouts, the former being an unfair labor practice and the latter being perfectly lawful.

The first of the Supreme Court's decisions on this subject was in the *Buffalo Linen* case.[97] The court held that employers in a multiemployer association could lock out the union members when confronted with a "whipsaw" tactic, that is, the attempt to strike one of the association's members so as to pick them off or isolate them, and to go then to the others one by one. The theory was that the tactic employed by the union necessarily eroded the unity the employers had legitimately sought to achieve through their association. Accordingly, a lockout against this tactic was considered defensive. Similarly, the court held in the *American Shipbuilding* case that the union was attempting to time a strike so that it would occur when the order books were full. A lockout in anticipation of such a tactic was considered allowable.[98]

The Supreme Court of Japan has similarly distinguished between offensive and defensive lockouts by justifying an employer's lockout in response to union slowdowns and other tactics of *sogi koi*, such as union posters, demonstration marches with "loud voices," and the singing of union songs on company property when it interferes with the execution of other workers' duties. The closest American analog to this decision is *Johns-Manville* v. *NLRB*,[99] in which the Fifth Circuit Court held (despite the strong dissent of Judge Wisdom) that an employer was justified in locking employees out where the employees were engaged in an in-plant strike or in concerted improper conduct that warranted such a reaction. Said the court: "The employees' conduct was so severe that we cannot help but find that their behavior was such that it forced the company to lock them out. . . . This history of the relationship between the parties revealed the company's continuing desire to negotiate in full recognition and acceptance of the union, notwithstanding numerous incidents of prior sabotage by the employees."

Sometimes the unfair labor practices described in this chapter produce issues and answers that exhibit cultural dissimilarities, and sometimes they do not. Representative of the latter category are the case of national-federation involvement at the enterprise level of bargaining in Japan and the case of affiliation of unions in the United States. Japanese labor law makes it possible to circumvent the enterprise environment. American labor law, which operates in a society with important national unions, makes it difficult in cases other than those involving coalition bargaining for workers to enhance their position through affiliation with the same national unions. It is difficult to observe cultural or societal differences in these cases. Indeed, if anything, the cases obscure the industrial-relations realities in both countries.

Other cases present the contrasts vividly. Illustrative of this group are the refusal-to-bargain disputes in which the Japanese agencies are responding to behavior problems (which arise more frequently in Japan than in the United States) with more tolerance for physical contact than the Americans generally show. Some elements of this attitude spill over into the strike area. The "ribbon struggle" cases, however, demonstrate a common concern by the Americans and the Japanese for a balance between union activity and protection of business. In short, no common theme emerges here, but the cases make clear that the Japanese can be more rambunctious than it frequently appears from afar.

7

The Public Sector

The growth of public-employee unionism has been substantial in both the United States and Japan. In Japan, however, militant trade unionism developed in the public sector before it did in the private sector. This was the result of the pro-labor policies of the MacArthur occupation. The offensive undertaken against both government and management in 1946 was led by public-sector unions (in cooperation with the Japanese Communist party). Some of the most powerful unions were the National Railway Workers, the Communications Workers, the Teachers, and the Postal Workers. These efforts in late 1946 culminated in the calling of a general strike scheduled for February 1, 1947. The intent was to involve 2.5 million government employees as well as tens of thousands of private workers. Ultimately, General MacArthur ordered that the strike be called off in light of the dire straits in which the Japanese economy found itself at that time. This confrontation was the turning point in the MacArthur occupation's relationship with the Japanese trade-union movement, and changed the Allies' attitude toward Japanese public-sector trade unionism. Accordingly, on July 22, 1948, General MacArthur sent a letter to Prime Minister Oshida ordering that legislation be enacted that would preclude access to the collective bargaining process for public employees and would remove their coverage under the Trade Union Law. The government's response to this letter was the issuance of ordinance 201, which prohibited collective bargaining and "acts of disruption" in all sectors of public employment and provided for one year's imprisonment or a fine of $16 for those who disobeyed. Individuals who violated the law could be summarily discharged or disciplined. Subsequently, the National Civil Service Law was amended to conform to both General MacArthur's letter and the government ordinance. A new Public Corporation and National Enterprise Labor Relations Law[1] (hereinafter referred to as the PCNELR Law) was enacted to address labor-management relationships in the so-called public corporations (among them railway, tobacco, and salt monopolies), which had been also encouraged by General MacArthur. In 1950 the Local Civil Service Law, covering employees of local governments, was enacted, and in 1952 the Local Government Enterprise Labor Relations Law was enacted. Subsequently, telephone and telegraph workers were brought within the coverage of the PCNELR Law.

These statutes prohibited the right to strike for public employees entirely. They followed an approach that has come to be associated with the Taylor Report (which formed the basis for the New York Taylor Law of 1967[2]) in the United States. The theory of the Taylor Report and of the Japanese laws is that governmental functions cannot be subjected to inordinate pressure by those who are not duly elected and responsible officials. This theory has proceeded upon the assumption that the right to strike, and sometimes collective bargaining itself, would distort what would otherwise be a democratic model and would interfere with the ability of officials to discharge their democratic functions. Accordingly, whereas the private sector is within the jurisdiction of the Trade Union Law, the public sector and its employees and the employees of the public corporations are under the jurisdiction of the statutes referred to above. However, where the Trade Union Law is not specifically modified by the PCNELR Law, the Trade Union Law applies to public employees.

Employees covered by the PCNELR have the right, under article 4, to organize and to select representatives and unions. However, unlike private sector employees (as noted above) they (along with other employees) are precluded from using industrial action or economic pressure under article 17. The PCNELR Law resembles the Trade Union Law more than it resembles other statutes addressing labor-management relations in the public sector in Japan, but there are differences between the PCNELR Law and the Trade Union Law beyond the strike issue.

One of the most important differences (ultimately eliminated as a result of intervention by the International Labor Organization) relates to eligibility for membership and leadership in the union. Because union officials in the public corporations were often dismissed because of their involvement in illegal stoppages, they lost their union offices. As a result of this, public employers frequently refused to bargain with such unions when they insisted on the involvement of such officials. However, when the Japanese government ratified ILO convention 87, which provides for the right of freedom of association, in 1965, subsequent to the landmark Dreyer Report, this provision of the statute was repealed.

A second basic difference between the Trade Union Law and the PCNELR Law relates to the question of union shop. The Trade Union Law provides that a union shop may exist if a majority of the workers employed at a particular establishment are organized into one union. Article 3 of the PCNELR Law specifically excludes the right of workers to negotiate a union shop under the principles contained in the Trade Union Law. Indeed, the PCNELR Law, like the American Taft-Hartley amendments, provides that workers have the right to refrain from organizing into unions as well as the right to organize and join unions.

A source of considerable controversy under the PCNELR Law rests with article 8. This article provides that the parties may bargain about wages and other forms of pay, hours of work, rest time, holidays, vacations, promotions, demotions, transfers, discharges, suspension, seniority, principles for disciplinary action, safety and sanitation procedures, and other conditions of employment. Though the list is a long one, the question of what affects conditions of employment and what does not, and how far management prerogative cuts into the former, has been vigorously debated.

Finally, inasmuch as the strikes or other forms of industrial actions are prohibited, the assumption is that the parties will resolve their differences through third-party procedures, including arbitration. The difficulty with arbitration is that article 16 of the Trade Union Law explicitly states that a public employer is not bound to abide by the award when the award involves the expenditure of funds not available from the appropriate public corporation funds. This led to several major confrontations between governments and the unions in the 1950s. The statute has since been revised so as to oblige government to exert as much pressure as possible to implement the award through the allocation of moneys, if necessary, from the Diet.

Additionally, an award from the Public Corporation and National Enterprise Labor Relations Commission (*Koroi*) enables the employer to divert money for wage increases from other sources of funds; thus, a negotiated agreement between parties is often put forward in the form of an arbitration award. This practice appears to be followed more often in Japan than in the United States.

The PCNELR Law establishes *Koroi* for the public corporations and national enterprises—an agency similar to the central and local Labor Relations Commissions that operate under the Trade Union Law. *Koroi* consists of 17 commissioners: seven representing the public interest, five representing the public corporations and national enterprises and thus the employer, and five representing the employees or unions. *Koroi,* like its counterparts under the Trade Union Law, has authority to involve itself in mediation, arbitration, and conciliation, as well as to exercise jurisdiction over unfair labor practices.

The problem of the right to strike in the public sector has been a continuing one in Japan, as it has in the United States. No small part of the dispute between the governments and the unions has been triggered by the above-mentioned provisions relating to the dismissal of union leaders involved in the calling of stoppages. Hundreds of union leaders have been dismissed as a result of such incidents.

The public-sector unions spearheaded the *shunto* in its early days, the mid-1960s. Strike issues are thus likely to arise frequently in the public sector, because in April and May, at the climax of negotiations over *shunto*, a substantial number of public-employee unions engage in strikes of short duration, generally several hours or one to two days. Both the central Labor Relations Commission and *Koroi* conduct mediation, which sometimes culminates in arbitration. A few months after *shunto* is completed, the public personnel authority makes a recommendation for pay increases for national civil servants. States Kazuo Sugeno:

A basic strategy of the recent spring offensive has been to create large-scale emergency situations with nationwide joint strikes in the important public services. The offensive has thereby been successful in pressing the government and Labor Relations Commissions to intervene in the disputes and award high wage increases. Thus, the Public Corporation and National Enterprise unions, which have under their control essential public services, such as the national railways and communication services, have become the major forces to promote this strategy, along with the private railway workers. In this way, for good or ill, strikes by public employees to back up their wage demands have been firmly institutionalized in the mechanism of the annual spring offensive, in spite of the legal prohibition.[3]

Before the emergence of *shunto* and before public employees participated in it, the public-employee unions utilized a number of tactics as an alternative to the strike because of a fear of governmental enforcement of the broad strike ban. "Work to rule," slowdowns, and refusals to work overtime were utilized. However, Sugeno notes, escalation to frequent paralyzing strikes began to occur in 1972. According to Sugeno, this move toward militancy was encouraged both by liberal judicial interpretations of the strike prohibition from 1966 onward, and also by the deterioration of labor relations at Japan National Railways as a result of its disciplining of strikers and of other problems related to labor relations.[4] The pattern was repeated in 1973. On April 24 of that year—a joint strike day called by the Public Corporation and National Enterprise unions during *shunto*—thousands of angry passengers rioted at 38 stations in the Tokyo metropolitan area. Sugeno states

The unions were shocked by this explosion of anger. They began to reconsider their techniques of causing the greatest inconvenience to the public with the least legal sanctions for the members. But, instead of curbing their militancy, they began to replace disruptive work to rules with less irritative regular strikes. The public employers still maintained the inflexible policy of punishing every illegal act. On the other hand, the unions had to fight hard for wage demands to protect their members from mounting inflation. Thus, while work to rule tactics decreased considerably in the latter half of 1973 and in the whole of 1974, the Public Corporation and National Enterprise unions escalated the number and magnitude of regular strikes, both for their wage demands and for protesting against the massive disciplines.

In this way, by the end of 1974, the frequent paralyzing national railways strikes and the "vicious circle" of the illegal strikes and disciplines became urgent nationwide problems. The prohibitive law had not only been totally disregarded by the public employee unions, but also the disparate enforcement of the law aggravated the strike situation. It became clear to many people that the law had to be reformed.[5]

In the United States, although the right to picket has been read by the Supreme Court as protected by the free-speech provisions of the first amendment,[6] the court has never taken the position that the right to strike is protected by the constitution. In contrast, it is generally accepted by scholars and judges in Japan that the right to "act collectively" set forth in article 28 of the constitution includes the right to strike. Accordingly, the question arises as to how the broad strike bans referred to above are constitutionally compatible in Japan.

In a trilogy of cases in the 1950s, the Supreme Court of Japan simply took the position that, because of provisions in the constitution referring to the welfare of the community[7] and the obligations of public servants,[8] a ban on strikes was constitutional. These decisions quickly came under attack because their broad prohibitions against strike activity and economic pressure applied to all public employees regardless of the kind of work in which they are engaged, and also because they held out the possibility of 3 years' imprisonment, which seemed to make them akin to oppressive statutes that had existed before World War II. Accordingly, the same debate that has arisen in the United States over the question whether the ban on public-sector strikes should be limited to particular kinds of employees whose services are essential arose in Japan. Ultimately, as previously noted, the Japanese government came under pressure from the International Labor Organization, and the Dreyer Committee in 1965 stressed the excessive breadth of the strike prohibition.

In the *Hiyamamaru* case, the Supreme Court concluded that the provision of the Trade Union Law exempting appropriate activities of strikers from criminal prosecution applied to public employees covered by the PCNELR Law even though, for other purposes, employees covered by the latter are not governed by the former statute. Although the decision did not rest upon article 28 of the constitution, the court stated that, inasmuch as the constitution covers public as well as private employees, both the Diet and the judiciary should be cautious in restricting the rights guaranteed to both groups. The court interpreted article 17 of the PCNELR Law as providing for criminal punishment only in the case of political strikes, where there was violence, or where the "people's daily life" was jeopardized by a stoppage. Subsequently, this decision of the court was applied by lower courts to cases involving disciplinary action taken by public employers as well as those involving criminal punishment, even though the Supreme Court precedent addressed only the latter. In strikes involving public education, the Tokyo District Court took the position that if the educational program could be made up by the end of the academic year without difficulty, the people's daily life was not endangered and therefore the strike did not interfere with the government's obligation to give children an adequate education. In a case involving the Japan National Railways, the same court held that article 17 of the PCNELR Law prohibited strikes that obstructed the movement of many trains or inconvenienced many passengers, obstructed the movement of long-distance trains, or obstructed the movement of trains by violence. The vagueness of the terms gave rise to disputes and further litigation. Labor lawyers and trade unionists could not predict with certainty whether a strike would be lawful or unlawful.

After seven of the fifteen Japanese Supreme Court justices were replaced by conservatives, the court became more cautious. (The appointments reflected the more conservative Sato government of the early 1970s.) In the 1973 *All Agricultural Ministry Workers Union* case, the court reversed the doctrine that the courts and the Diet should minimally restrict the right to strike in the public sector. The court in this case stressed the basic difference between the functions of public and private employees, reiterating the basic views set forth by the Taylor Report as well as by some American academics.[9] Accordingly, the court stated that the right to strike in the public sector would erode the democratic process and make it impossible for public officials to respond to the electorate rather than to employees:

In private enterprises, except some special ones highly related to public interest, generally the employers have the counter measures against the acts of dispute, such as what is called closure of workshop (lockout), and, besides, to comply with the excessive demands of the workers would bring them serious results of worsening the management of the enterprise and endangering the existence of the enterprise itself, and further, of incurring the unemployment of the workers themselves. Consequently, the demand of the workers naturally cannot escape from the restrictions resulting from these factors. This fact, too, gives one of the reasons why it is impossible to consider the acts of dispute of the private enterprise workers and those of public officials in an equal and the same manner. Furthermore, in ordinary private enterprises, what is called [the] checking function of the market necessarily works on the acts of dispute, because the demand of the supply for the goods and services which they produce and offer cannot escape from the influence of the pressure of the market. In cases of public officials, on the other hand, the fact that the function of the market does not work on their acts of disputes at all, sometimes makes the acts of dispute one-sided strong pressure, resulting in distorting the process for the termination of working conditions of public officials.[10]

In the wake of the supreme court decision, the railway workers have called a series of strikes over the right to strike and Japan National Railways has responded with discipline. The postal workers have raised the strike issue with the International Labor Organization, but it has taken the position (as it did with the air traffic controllers in their 1981 strike in the United States) that ILO conventions 87 and 98, which assure workers of the right to organize and to bargain collectively, do not necessarily provide the right to strike so long as some kind of adequate substitute for the strike is available. In the public sector, the International Labor Organization has noted the propriety of mediation and arbitration under the public-sector statutes as a substitute for the strike weapon.

In the United States, the federal government and most of the states prohibit striking by common law or statute. However, an increasing number of jurisdictions (Hawaii, Pennsylvania, Vermont, Alaska, and Minnesota are among the leaders) have permitted a limited right to strike to be incorporated into their statutes. The state laws that take such an approach usually attempt to distinguish between essential and nonessential employees and sometimes permit the strike to be used only after the impasse procedures, such as mediation or fact finding, have failed to resolve disputes over new contract terms.

A majority of jurisdictions—39 states—have fairly comprehensive legislation providing for the right of public employees to organize and bargain collectively. The U.S. Supreme Court, while recognizing a constitutional right to organize for public employees, has rejected the idea that there is a constitutional obligation upon public employers to bargain collectively with public-employee unions, or even to permit workers to have representatives of their own choosing process grievances for them.[11] At the federal level, employees may not negotiate wages. The principal statute there is the Civil Service Reform Act of 1978. The U.S. Postal Service is covered by a separate statute, the Postal Reorganization Act of 1970, which also prohibits striking, even though the service is an independent establishment within the executive branch. Postal employees are covered by the National Labor Relations Act and the Landrum-Griffin Act, but the prohibitions against federal strikes apply to them. The Postal Reorganization Act contains its own dispute-resolution procedures. Striking is banned for federal employees, and striking federal employees can be punished with felony charges and dismissal.

The American influence in Japan has clearly been more pervasive in the public sector than in the private. The United States and Japan are somewhat out of step with other industrialized countries in their insistence on a prohibition of the strike weapon for all employees in the public sector. In recent years the Japanese government appears to be more unyielding, despite proposals by academics such as Ishikawa for substitutes for the strike as well as a limited right to strike for public employees.

In sum, there is a similarity in response to public-employee unions by the Japanese and Americans. Yet, while public-sector unions in both countries have had more than their share of troubles with the law, this may be more attributable to the law than to the unions. Japan's public-sector unions have shown militant, Marxist tendencies ever since their initial post–World War II confrontation with the SCAP. Disproportionately congregated in *Sohyo*, these unions have adopted a more unyielding political and economic posture than their private-sector counterparts. Until recent years, their leftist stance produced an estrangement from the AFL-CIO.

There is no comparable ideological demarcation line between public- and private-sector unions in the United States. Indeed, unions representing federal employees have been relatively quiet under the Civil Service Reform Act of 1978, the 1981 air controllers' strike notwithstanding. However, one problem is shared by both countries' public-sector labor movements: the taxpayers' revolt. This has reduced budgets and threatened job security in both nations, and the result has been a more beleaguered public-employee labor movement.

8

Conclusion

The Japanese culture is unique in many respects. So too is Japan's system of industrial relations and labor. Beneath the superficial similarities, Japan's labor law and industrial-relations system stand in vivid contrast with those of the United States. It is, therefore, obvious that the United States cannot emulate or transfer Japanese practices and institutions. For instance, the concept of *amae* (dependency) is alien to Western labor-management relations. American unions or workers, regardless of their bargaining strength, would find such formal subordination or paternalism extremely difficult to tolerate.

Yet it is quite obvious that labor practices (as well as different management practices unrelated to labor considerations[1]) have contributed mightily to Japan's spectacular productivity—particularly in the automobile industry, where workers produce more and exercise their own responsibility for quality control. The Japanese have been masters at examining foreign technology and institutional practices and adapting them to their own needs. Within limits, there is no earthly reason why Americans cannot do the same thing just as selectively as the Japanese. Vogel, deliberately one-sided and propagandistic, was the first to make this point emphatically. This path is likely to yield results far more constructive than those that will flow from "local content" legislation and other protectionist barriers, which would inherently jeopardize international trade. The agenda for American labor and management can focus upon private collective bargaining, the modification or reversal of existing Supreme Court precedent, and the Congress and the state legislatures.

For Japan, this has been the lesson of the imposition of American labor law. The central and prefectural Labor Relations Commissions only vaguely resemble the American National Labor Relations Board. Japan's remedies (prime examples are deductions from back pay for interim earnings and conditional relief), statutory coverage (lack of protection against hiring discrimination and the defining of supervisors), and national-federation involvement in local bargaining are vivid testimony for the proposition that her laws are quite different from those of the United States. The joint-consultation system has emerged without legal protection. The Japanese have had to shape the unfair-labor-practice system and concept of acts of dispute to their system's peculiarities, such as "ribbon struggles" and the greater acceptance of company involvement in union matters. For Americans to show some of the same flexibility might be both sensible and invigorating.

The Japanese are the prime exponents of what might be characterized as the cooperation model. The Americans, while lagging considerably behind the class-ridden British in this respect, have operated under the assumptions of the adversarial model, as Justice Brennan's opinion in the *Insurance Agents* case notes. That adversarial model will not be abandoned in the forseeable future. For starters, the existence of craft unions and the exclusion of supervisors from statutory coverage in the private sector make that clear. However, Japan's success cannot be ignored. The Japanese approach with the greatest potential for adaptation to the United States is the use of company facilities by unions. Though the Trade Union Law does not specifically address the issue, the unions utilize plant premises for a variety of purposes, including union meetings. Americans view this with suspicion as an attempt to undercut the union and ultimately rid the company of it. However, depending on the facts, such gestures by employers can be viewed as an attempt to produce more cooperation and not thwart unionism. After all, the workplace is the best venue for unions to communicate with workers. American unions have sought access to it in a variety of contexts.

Where the plant is unorganized, why should the law condemn employee groups, which enhance communication, to be defined as "labor organizations," and thus prohibit the company to assist them? Again, the question of illegal conduct ought to be determined on all the facts. With almost 80 percent of American workers unorganized, it is inevitable that worker participation programs will be developed with or without unionism. The unions ought to try to build on such committees or employee groups which are fostered by management so that their inadequacies will be highlighted, just as they should take advantage of the same opportunities in connection with the new, NLRB-bestowed right of representation for unorganized workers in disciplinary interviews.[2]

As noted above, the administrative processes are fundamentally different in the two countries. The frequent tension between collective and individual rights in the United States (duty-of-fair-representation, job-discrimination, and Landrum-Griffin cases are representative of the types) will continue; the individual is often in conflict with the union and the company. Although American society and American workers need to develop a greater sense of the group and a consequent sense of solidarity, the fact is that a tripartite NLRB bringing together labor, management, and the public would not suit American needs. There are too many divisions within groups to make the tripartite idea useful here. In Japan, tensions can surface (perhaps because of the absence of the exclusivity doctrine) at the top, and seats on the Labor Relations Commissions can be allocated between *Sohyo* and *Domei*.

However, there is no reason why the NLRB's rules could not provide for conciliation and even, under some circumstances, recommendations by a third party (such as an administrative law judge) after the conclusion of a hearing. We have enough difficulty with our delays without emulating the Japanese penchant for delay, but we can temper our very legitimate concerns with expediting the administrative process through enactment of reforms along the lines of the Labor Reform Bill, coupled with the adaptation of a buffer and the opportunity to review and think again before review is sought with the NLRB board in Washington.

Moreover, the NLRB would be well advised to follow the opinions of members Pennello, Walther, and Murphy and be cautious about interfering with private settlements and imaginative in developing remedies likely to result in collective bargaining agreements.

Unions and workers must be in a position to know the economic facts of life and to thus bargain intelligently. The Japanese have been more successful than the Americans in accomplishing this through their system of joint consultation. The Germans have provided for co-determination at both the company level and the plant level. (In Germany, "works councils" at the plant level receive financial assistance from companies—something that would raise legal problems in the United States.) The Swedes have attempted to build co-determination into collective bargaining. The European Economic Community through the Vredling initiative has taken steps to promote dialogue and access to information. Yet American labor law is counterproductive in this respect. In the first place, the U.S. Supreme Court's *Truitt* decision limits union inspection of financial records to situations where the employer pleads poverty or an inability to pay. Accordingly, well-advised management does not generally articulate such reasons, even if they are the basis for its posture at the bargaining table. How can unions bargain intelligently if they do not have access to information? Similarly, the U.S. Supreme Court's *First National Maintenance* decision rejecting the concept of partnership and parity between labor and management is also designed to keep the unions in the dark. How can society expect the unions to be trustworthy and loyal when it seems unalterably opposed to union involvement? How can a union be convinced to negotiate reverse cost-of-living adjustments (admittedly geared to the national price index) or profit sharing whereby wages will rise or fall depending on the company's viability when it is not involved in acquisition decisions in a new industry? It is in this critical area of trust and confidence that the Japanese, concerned as they are with relationships, have been able to focus on the peculiarities of firms and inspire loyalty.

Finally, the United States—so out of step with industrialized countries in the area of job security—should amend the NLRA to protect all workers, organized and unorganized, against unfair dismissals. The rise of state court decisions limiting or modifying the "terminable at will" doctrine may assist the process if employers seek immunization against large damage awards. In the absence of federal legislation, the states might enact laws of their own. California might be a prime candidate because of the considerable litigation and liability for employers there.

Of course, in the United States there are very real constraints that do not exist in Japan. One major feature not present in Japan is the presence of craft unions as well as industrial unions. Craft unions inhibit job mobility. Moreover, the fact that low-level supervisors are not represented by American unions strengthens the unions' resistance to the employment of supervisors and other employees not in the bargaining unit on work normally performed by union members. Job-security guarantees could, through law or collective agreement, remedy the situation to some extent among the industrial unions. In any event, unions might be accommodative depending upon the guarantees given to the employees in the unit.

American unions, unlike the Japanese, are unlikely to welcome or applaud the promotion of union leaders to top management. One can find support for this in the contract clauses that limit or preclude foremen from retaining seniority accumulated in the bargaining unit in the event they should return to the rank and file.

Moreover, the sense of inequity is not as substantial in Japan, owing to the smaller gap between manager and worker in that country. This is attributable not only to the comparative immobility of Japanese managers (which depresses salaries) but also to the way in which Japanese companies raise money for investment (through banks rather than the stock market). In Japan there is less of an immediate need to show a profit than in the United States, and this permits other considerations, such as employee morale, to be taken into account. However, the increasing reliance on the Japanese stock market in new industries and the advent of concession or crisis bargaining and job and income guarantees in industries in the United States may be harbingers of convergence between the two countries.

The law has limits. Industrial-relations practices emerge and are retained despite the law. But in this unique situation where two countries possess what is, on the surface, the same basic legal framework, one can see the law reshaped for specific objectives. Some of those objectives pursued by the Japanese have served them well and should be of interest to Americans. We had best discard as soon as possible the idea that wisdom ends at the shores of California or Hawaii.

Notes

Introduction

1. H. Kahn and T. Pepper, *The Japanese Challenge* (Crowell, 1978), p. 146.

2. W. Safire, "Questionable Protection," *New York Times*, January 19, 1978, p. A19. However, see "Getting Tough with Japan," *New York Times*, December 27, 1977, p. 36.

3. J. Tokuyama, "The Law as a Family Sword," *Newsweek*, September 8, 1975, p. 54.

4. T. Ariizumi, "The Legal Framework," in *Workers and Employers in Japan*, ed. K. Okochi, B. Karsh, and S. Levine (University of Tokyo Press, 1973), p. 114.

5. My own observations in this respect are buttressed by studies and polls— see "Young Japanese Want a More Carefree Life," *Times* (London), August 3, 1978, p. 6; "Life Employment Under Fire," *Asahi Evening News*, March 13, 1978, p. 2; "Over-Employment Poses Problem," *Japan Times*, February 6, 1978, p. 4; "The Sting in Japan: A Backlash of Success," *Japan Times*, February 5, 1978, sec. 17; "Workers Untouched by Japan's Magic Wand," *New York Times*, July 4, 1982, p. 4E; "Japan Struggling with Itself," *New York Times*, June 6, 1982, business section, p. 1.

Chapter 1

1. E. Vogel, *Japan as Number One: Lessons for America* (Harvard University Press, 1979), p. 98.

2. S. Levine, *Industrial Relations in Postwar Japan* (University of Illinois Press, 1958), pp. 117–118.

3. The Development of Industrial Relations Systems, OCED study group report, 1975, pp. 11–13.

4. The percentages of workers organized in trade unions are 30.8 percent in Japan (down from 31.6 percent in 1979 and 35.4 percent in 1970) and approximately 20 percent in the United States (also down). See T. Hanami, *Labor Relations in Japan Today* (Kodansha International, 1979), pp. 88–93 (especially the chart on p. 93).

5. H. Scott-Stokes, "Workers Untouched by Japan's Magic Wand," *New York Times,* July 4, 1982, p. 4E.

6. Id.

7. NLRA §9(b)(2), 29 U.S.C., §159(b)(2). See *Mallinckrodt Chemical Works,* 162 NLRB 387 (1966).

8. NLRA §8(b)4(D), 29 U.S.C., §158(b)4(D). See generally *NLRB* v. *Plasterers Local 79,* 404 U.S. 116 (1971); *NLRB* v. *Radio & Television Broadcast Engineers Union, Local 212,* 364 U.S. 593 (1961).

9. R. Clark, *The Japanese Company* (Yale University Press, 1979), p. 191.

10. Ibid., p. 109, n. 12.

11. Shirai, "A Theory of Enterprise Unionism," in *Contemporary Industrial Relations in Japan,* ed. T. Shirai (University of Wisconsin Press, 1983), p. 117.

12. Vogel, *Japan as Number One,* p. 141.

13. *Packard Motor Co.* v. *NLRB,* 330 U.S. 485, 496–497 (1947).

14. NLRA §2(11), 29 U.S.C. §152(11) (1970).

15. *Parker-Robb Chevrolet, Inc.,* 262 NLRB 58 (1981). See also D. Barney, "Bell Aerospace and the Status of Managerial Employees Under the NLRA," 1 *Indus. Rel. L. S.* 346 (1976).

16. "Work on a Pay Cut," *The Economist* (London), November 27, 1982, pp. 11–12.

17. R. Crabbe, "Japan's Steel Industry Suffers From Glut," *Japan Times,* February 6, 1978, p. 1.

18. J. Goulden, *Meany: The Unchallenged Strongman of American Labor* (Atheneum, 1972). For a scholarly examination of the general subject from the European vantage point, see R. Flanagan, D. Soskice, and L. Ulman, *Unionism, Economic Stabilization, and Incomes Policies: European Experience* (Brookings Institution, 1983).

19. R. Cole, *Japanese Blue Collar: The Changing Tradition* (University of California Press, 1971), pp. 227–228.

20. Ibid, pp. 81–82, 85. See also R. Cole, *Work, Mobility, & Participation* (University of California Press, 1979), p. 120.

21. N. Funahashi, "The Industrial Reward System," in *Workers and Employers in Japan,* ed. K. Okochi, B. Karsh, and S. Levine (University of Tokyo Press, 1973), p. 395.

22. Kahn and Pepper, *The Japanese Challenge,* pp. 53–54.

23. 29 U.S.C. §621 et seq. (1976).

24. Vogel, *Japan as Number One,* p. 133.

25. See, for instance, *Tameny* v. *Atlantic Richfield Company,* 164 *Cal. Rptr.* 839 (1980); *Toussaint* v. *Blue Cross and Blue Shield,* 408 Mich. 579 (1980). See generally "Glendon and Lev, Changes in the Bonding of the Employment Relationship: An Essay on the New Property," 20 *Boston College L. Rev.* 457 (1979); Summers, "Individual Protection Against Unjust Dismissal: Time for a Statute," 62 *Va. L. Rev.* 481 (1976); note, "Protecting At Will Employees Against Wrongful Discharge: The Duty to Terminate Only in Good Faith," 93 *Harv. L. Rev.* 1816 (1980); note, "Implied Contract Rights to Job Security," 26 *Stan. L. Rev.* 335 (1974).

26. OCED study group report, n. 3 supra, p. 25.

27. *Labor Standards Law,* chapter IX: Rule of Employment. See specifically article 90, reprinted in *Labour Laws of Japan* (Ministry of Labour, 1980).

28. "General Motors–UAW Contract Settlement," *Labor Relations Reporter News and Background Information,* 109 L.R.R.M. 261, 264 (1982).

29. See *European Community News,* February 14, 1983.

30. W. Gould, "Taft-Hartley Comes to Great Britain," 81 *Yale L. J.* 1421 (1972).

31. S. Levine and K. Taira, "The Industrial Conflict: The Case of Japan," in *Labor Relations in Advanced Industrial Societies,* ed. Martin and Kassalow (Carnegie Endowment for International Peace, 1980), p. 66.

32. Ibid. pp. 65–66.

33. Hanami, *Labor Relations in Japan Today,* pp. 122–123.

34. T. Hanami, "The Characteristics of Labor Disputes and Their Settlement in Japan," in *Social and Cultural Background of Labor-Management Relations in Asian Countries,* proceedings of the 1971 Asian Regional Conference on Industrial Relations (Japan Institute of Labor, 1971), p. 209.

35. The imbalance remains even when one takes into account the relatively large number of unfair-labor-practice cases in which the courts assert overlapping jurisdiction. See T. Hanami, "The Function of the Law in Japanese Industrial Relations," in *Contemporary Industrial Relations in Japan,* ed. T. Shirai (University of Wisconsin Press, 1983), p. 177.

36. K. Koshiba, "Annual Shunto Movement Losing Steam," *Japan Times,* April 18, 1978, p. 5; " '78 Spring Pay Increases Reflect Trend in Economy," *Japan Times,* April 28, 1978, p. B2.

37. K. Ishikawa, "The Regulation of the Employer-Employee Relationship: Japanese Labor Relations Law," in *Law In Japan,* ed. T. von Mehren (Harvard University Press, 1963), p. 439. See n. 35 supra.

Chapter 2

1. I. Ayusawa, *A History of Labor in Modern Japan* (East-West Center Press, 1966), p. 246.

2. W. Manchester, *American Caesar* (Little, Brown, 1978), p. 448.

3. T. Cohen, *Labor Democratization in Japan: The First Years in The Occupation of Japan Economic Policy and Reform* (MacArthur Memorial, 1980), p. 161.

4. See generally H. Tanaka, *The Japanese Legal System* (University of Tokyo Press, 1976).

5. Ayusawa, *A History of Labor in Modern Japan,* p. 250.

6. See Cohen, *Labor Democratization in Japan.*

7. Manchester, *American Caesar,* p. 498.

8. Ayusawa, p. 245.

9. Ayusawa, pp. 219–222.

10. J. Gross, *The Reshaping of the National Labor Relations Board* (State University of New York Press, 1981), pp. 42–48.

11. 208 U.S. 274 (1908).

12. *Duplex Printing Co.* v. *Deering,* 254 U.S. 443 (1921). See also W. Gould, *A Primer on American Labor Law* (MIT Press, 1982), p. 18.

13. F. Frankfurter and N. Greene, *The Labor Injunction* (Macmillan, 1930; Peter Smith, 1963).

14. 312 U.S. 219, 231 (1941).

15. *R.C.A. Mfg. Co.,* 2 NLRB 168 (1936); *New York Handkerchief Mfg. Co.* v. *NLRB,* 114 F.2d 144 (7th Cir. 1940); *cert. denied,* 311 U.S. 704.

16. NLRA §9(b)(2) 29 U.S.C. (b)(2). See generally *NLRB 23rd Annual Report* (1958), pp. 36–37; *NLRB* v. *Truck Drivers Local 449,* 353 U.S. 87 (1957); *NLRB* v. *Brown,* 380 U.S. 278 (1965).

17. *NLRA* §8(a)(2), 29 U.S.C. §158(a)(2) (1970).

18. *NLRA* §8(a)(3), 29 U.S.C. §158 (a)(3) (1970). See also *NLRB* v. *Great Dane Trailers, Inc.,* 388 U.S. 26 (1967) and *Molders Local 155* v. *NLRB,* 442 F.2d 742 (D.C. Cir. 1971).

19. *NLRA* §8(a)(4), 29 U.S.C. §158(a)(4) (1970).

20. *NLRA* §8(a)(5), 29 U.S.C. §158(a)(5) (1970).

21. K. Ishikawa, "The Regulation of the Employer-Employee Relationship: Japanese Labor Relations Law," in *Law in Japan,* ed. von Mehren (Harvard University Press, 1963), p. 439. See generally E. Takamae, *The U.S. Labor Policies for Japan* (Nihon Hyoron-sha, 1970); E. Takamae, *The Postwar Labor Reform in Japan* (Tokyo University Press, 1982).

22. T. Hanami, *Labour Law and Industrial Relations in Japan* (Kluwer, 1979), p. 128, paragraph 253.

23. See generally R. Smith, H. Edwards, and R. Clark, "The Right to Join and Form Unions," in *Labor Relations in the Public Sector* (Bobbs-Merrill, 1974), pp. 89–150.

24. NLRA §2(5), 29 U.S.C. §152(5) (1970).

25. See *Hill* v. *Florida,* 325 U.S. 538 (1945).

26. Pub. L. 86–257, Sept. 14, 1959, 73 Stat. 519, 29 U.S.C., §§401 et seq. (1976).

27. F. Bartosic and I. Lanoff, "Escalating The Struggle against Taft-Hartley," 39 *U. Chi. L. Rev.* 255 (1972).

28. *Critique of the Trade Union Law and Ordinances,* prepared by Leonard Appel of the Labor Advisory Committee, July, 1946, p. 1.

29. Ibid, p. 1.

30. Id.

31. Ibid., p. 2.

32. Id.

33. Ibid., p. 3 (section on outlawing employer- or company-dominated unions).

34. Id.

35. Ibid., p. 6 (section on rights of employees).

36. Ayusawa, *A History of Labor in Modern Japan,* p. 257.

37. *Critique of the Trade Union Law and Ordinances,* p. 4 (section on ensuring collective bargaining).

38. Ibid., p. 5.

39. Id.

40. Ibid., pp. 7–8 (section on enforcement procedures and safeguards).

41. Id.

42. Ibid., p. 11 (section on involuntary disqualification or dissolution of trade unions).

43. Ibid., p. 13 (section on recommended SCAP policy in revision of the law).

44. Constitution of Japan, chapter III, article 28, reprinted in *Labour Laws of Japan* (Ministry of Labour, 1980), p. 11. The 1949 statute is discussed in E. Takamae Revision of Japanese Labor Legislation in 1949 (unpublished).

45. Freedom of association under the first amendment protects union activity. See *Thomas* v. *Collins*, 323 U.S. 516 (1945); *Staub* v. *City of Baxley*, 355 U.S. 313 (1958). The American cases involving picketing have provided some constitutional protection of union activity. See *Thornhill* v. *Alabama*, 310 U.S. 88 (1940); *AFL* v. *Swing*, 312 U.S. 321 (1941). However, see *International Brotherhood of Teamsters* v. *Vogt*, 354 U.S. 284 (1957). This protection has not been extended to the strike and similar economic pressures. See *Dorchy* v. *Kansas*, 272 U.S. 306 (1926); *UAW* v. *Wisconsin Employment Relations Board*, 336 U.S. 245 (1949); *United Federation of Postal Clerks* v. *Blount*, 325 F. Supp. 879 (D.D.C.), Aff'd 404 U.S. 802 (1971); 304 U.S. 333 (1938).

46. 44 Stat. 577 (1926), as amended, 45 U.S.C. §151 et seq.

47. W. Gould, *A Primer on American Labor Law* (MIT Press, 1982), pp. 35–39.

48. 29 U.S.C. §20 et seq.

49. *Labour Standards Law*, chapter II, article 20, reprinted in *Labour Laws of Japan*, p. 74.

50. See generally O. Kahn-Freund, *Labour and the Law*, second edition (Stevens, 1977).

51. See generally E. Sykes and H. Glasbeek, *Labour Law in Australia* (Butterworths, 1972).

52. *Trade Union and Labor Relations Act of 1974*, International Labour Office, Legislative Series, no. 31 (1975).

53. *San Diego Building Trades Council* v. *Garmon*, 359 U.S. 236 (1959); *Sears, Roebuck & Co.* v. *San Diego County District Council of Carpenters*, 436 U.S. 180, 198–207 (1978).

54. *Trade Union Laws*, chapter I, article 2, subsection 2, reprinted in *Labour Laws of Japan*, p. 22.

55. See note, "New Standards for Domination and Support Under Section 8(a)(2)," 82 *Yale L. J.* 510 (1973).

56. NLRA §8(a)(2), 29 U.S.C. §158(a)(2); LMRA §302(c)(2); 29 U.S.C. §186(c)(2); 61 Stat. 136 (1947), as amended in 1976.

57. R. Kesselring and P. Brinker, "Employer Domination Under §8(a)(2)," *Labor L. J.* 340 (1979).

58. See the original proviso from 29 U.S.C. §159(e) (1941):
(1) Upon the filing with the board, by 30 per centum or more of the employees in a bargaining unit covered by an agreement between their employer and a labor organization made pursuant to section 158 (a)(3) of this title, of a

petition alleging they desire that such authority be rescinded, the board shall take a secret ballot of the employees in such unit and certify the results thereof to such labor organization and to the employer; (2) No election shall be conducted pursuant to this subsection in any bargaining unit or any subdivision within which, in the preceding twelve-month period, a valid election shall have been held.

This was amended by act on October 22, 1951, by striking out subdivisions (1) and renumbering subdivisions (2) and (3) to be (1) and (2).

59. NLRA §14(b) 29 U.S.C. §164(b) (1976).

60. *Linden Lumber Division, Summer Co.* v. *NLRB,* 419 U.S. 301 (1974); *NLRB* v. *Gissel Packing Co., Inc.,* 395 U.S. 575 (1969).

61. Theodore Cohen, personal communication, September 27, 1978.

62. Ishikawa, n. 21 supra, p. 447.

63. R. Cole [*Japanese Blue Collar* (University of California Press, 1971)] disputes the existence of such a difference between Japan and the West.

64. T. Hanami, *Labor Relations in Japan Today* (Kodansha International, 1979), pp. 80–81.

65. J. Gross, *The Reshaping of the National Labor Relations Board* (State University of New York Press, 1981), pp. 331, 227.

Chapter 3

1. 359 U.S. 236 (1959).

2. The doctrine is not applied to "merely peripheral" concerns of the NLRA or to tortious activities. See, e. g., *International Union, United Automobile Workers* v. *Russell,* 356 U.S. 634 (1958) (mass picketing and threats of violence); *International Association of Machinists* v. *Gonzales,* 356 U.S. 617 (1958) (wrongful expulsion from union membership); *Linn* v. *Plant Guard Workers,* 383 U.S. 53 (1966) (malicious libel), *Farmer* v. *United Brotherhood of Carpenters Local 25,* 430 U.S. 290 (1977) (intentional infliction of emotional distress), *Sears, Roebuck & Co.* v. *San Diego County District Council of Carpenters,* 436 U.S. 180 (1978) (trespass for an arguably prohibited purpose; *Belknap, Inc.* v. *Hale,* — U.S. — (1983) (suits by strikebreakers for breach of contract).

3. Section 301 provides that "suits for violation of contracts between an employer and a labor organization representing employees in an industry affecting commerce as defined in this chapter, or between any such labor organizations, may be brought in any district court of the United States having jurisdiction of the parties, without respect to the amount in controversy or without regard to the citizenship of the parties."

4. Section 10(e) of the NLRA provides, in relevant part, that "the findings of the board with respect to questions of fact if supported by substantial evidence on the record considered as a whole shall be conclusive." See *Universal Camera Corp.* v. *NLRB,* 340 U.S. 474 (1951).

5. K. Ishikawa, "Proposals for Expediting Examinations of Unfair Labor Practices," in *Law in Japan: An Annual,* vol. 4, no. 17 (1970), p. 18.

6. Ibid., pp. 18–19.

7. Ibid., p. 21.

8. Study Group on Labor Management Relations Laws, Report to the Minister of Labor (May 22, 1982): Promotion of Rapid Examination in Unfair Labor Practice Cases, Etc. (English translation provided by Ministry of Labor).

9. *Leeds & Northrup Co.* v. *NLRB,* 357 F.2d 527 (3d Cir. 1966).

10. In 1975, only 20 percent.

11. 236 NLRB No. 102 (1978) (referred to also as *Clear Haven*).

12. Ibid., p. 855.

13. Id.

14. See "Report on Case-Handling Developments at NLRB," *Labor Relations Reporter News and Background Information* (BNA), 110 L.R.R. 247 (1982).

15. *1976 Interim Report and Recommendations of the Chairman's Task Force on the NLRB,* reprinted in *Labor Relations Yearbook 1976;* Final Report and Recommendations of the Chairman's Task Force on the NLRB (January 1978) See *Labor Relations Reporter News and Background Information* (BNA), April 25, 1977.

16. Tokyo High Court decision, May 28, 1975, *Rominshu,* vol. 26, no. 3, p. 451.

17. *Sawanomachi Motor Pool* case, supreme court decision, May 24, 1962, *Shomugeppo,* vol. 8, no. 5, p. 926.

18. K. Ishikawa, "The Regulation of the Employer-Employee Relationship: Japanese Labor Relations Law," in *Law in Japan,* ed. T. von Mehren (Harvard University Press, 1963), pp. 466–467.

Chapter 4

1. NLRA §10(c).

2. *Trade Union Law,* chapter IV, article 27(4), reprinted in *Labour Laws of Japan* (Ministry of Labour, 1980), p. 31.

3. *Universal Camera Corp.* v. *NLRB,* 340 U.S. 474 (1951).

4. See, e. g., *NLRB* v. *Erie Resistor Corp.* 373 U.S. 221 (1963); *NLRB* v. *Weingarten, Inc.,* 420 U.S. 251 (1975).

5. *American Shipbuilding* v. *NLRB,* 380 U.S. 300 (1965); *Textile Workers Union* v. *Darlington Manufacturing Co.,* 380 U.S. 263 (1965); *First National Maintenance Corp.* v. *NLRB,* 49 U.S.L.W. 4769 (1981).

6. *Republic Steel Corp.* v. *NLRB,* 311 U.S. 7 (1940). See generally "NLRB Power to Award Damages in Unfair Labor Practice Cases," 84 *Harvard L. Rev.* 1670 (1971).

7. Labor Reform Act of 1977, H.R. 8410, 95th Cong., 1st Session (1977).

8. *Ex-Cello Corporation,* 185 NLRB 107 (1970).

9. See note, "NLRB Power to Award Damages in Unfair Labor Practice Cases," 84 *Harvard L. Rev.* 1670, 1684 (1971).

10. *Phelps Dodge* v. *NLRB,* 313 U.S. 177 (1941).

11. It should be noted that article 27 of the Trade Union Law speaks of "relief

sought," and that there is no similar limitation contained in section 10(c). Though the NLRB and the courts take the view that remedies in the United States may be fashioned by the agency or the courts *sua sponte,* on their own initiative, the opposite assumption appears to apply in Japan because of the statutory language. However, in the view of Japanese scholars, the matter is by no means resolved.

12. 312 U.S. 426 (1941).

13. 312 U.S. 426, 433 (1941).

14. Ibid., p. 435.

15. Ibid., pp. 436–437.

16. L. Jaffe, "The Judicial Enforcement of Administrative Orders," 76 *Harvard L. Rev.* 865, 866 (1963).

17. *Hicknott Foods, Inc.,* 242 NLRB 1357 (1979).

18. *Tochigi Kasei* (chemical workers) case, Supreme Court, III petty bench, October 9, 1961, O. no. 255 (1960).

19. See generally F. Bartosic and I. Lanoff, "Escalating the Struggle against Taft-Hartley Contemnors," 39 *U. Chi. L. Rev.* 255 (1972).

20. *NLRB Second Annual Report,* p. 15.

21. See *J. P. Stevens Co.,* 668 F.2d 767 (4th Cir. 1982).

22. Cf. *J. P. Stevens Co.* v. *NLRB,* 380 F.2d 292 (2d Cir. 1967), *cert. denied,* 389 U.S. 1005 (1967).

23. *Churyugun Tachikawa Kichi* (U.S. forces stationed at Tachikawa Base), Tokyo District Court, February 8, 1960, GYO no. 78 (1960).

24. 44 Stat. 577 (1926), *as amended,* 45 U.S.C. §§151 et seq.

25. *Texas & New Orleans Railroad Company* v. *Brotherhood of Railway and Steamship Clerks,* 281 U.S. 548 (1930).

26. *Phelps-Dodge* v. *NLRB,* 313 U.S. 177 (1941).

27. NLRA §2(3), 29 U.S.C. §162(3). See 313 U.S. 177, 178.

28. *Manza Io* (Manza Sulfur) case, central Labor Relations Commission, order of October 15, 1952, Fu sai no. 8; *Iwano Mokukosho* (Iwano Sawmill) case, Saitama District Labor Relations Commission, order of July 26, 1962, Fu no. 3.

29. 313 U.S. 177, 187 and 188 (1941).

30. National Labor Relations Act Remedies: The Unfulfilled Promise, report of Special Subcommittee on Labor, Committee on Education and Labor, House of Representatives, December 1968, pp. 24–27.

31. *St. Clair* v. *Local Union No. 515, International Brotherhood of Teamsters,* 422 F.2d 128, 132 (6th Cir. 1969).

32. *Nihon Kamotsu Kensu Kyokai Kobe* (Kobe, Japan, Freight Inspection Cooperative) case, Hyogo District Labor Relations Commission, order of March 18, 1952, Fu no. 14–16; *Sawa Taxi* case, Tottori District Labor Commission, order of August 19, 1961, Fu no. 2; *Shin Nihon Kotsu* (New Japan Transportation) case, Wakayama District Labor Commission, Fu no. 4 (1973).

33. *In re Maritime Union,* 78 NLRB 971, *enforced,* 175 F.2d 686 (C.A. 2d Cir. 1949).

34. 422 F.2d 128, 132 (6th Cir. 1969).

35. 313 U.S. 197, 198 (1941).

36. 313 U.S. 208 (1941).

37. *NLRB* v. *Gullet Gin Co.*, 340 U.S. 361 (1951).

38. "Dai Ni Hato Taxi case," *Jurist*, April 15, 1977, pp. 105–111; Yuhikaku, Tokyo (1977).

39. Ibid., p. 294.

40. Ibid., p. 317.

41. Ibid., p. 315.

42. K. Hiraga, "Why Back Pay?" (part I), on the supreme court decision of February 23, 1977, *Hanrei Jiho*, no. 863, Hanrei Jihosha, Tokyo (1977), p. 3.

43. *NLRB* v. *Seven-up Co.*, 344 U.S. 344 (1952).

44. *AFL* v. *NLRB*, 308 U.S. 401 (1940).

45. *NLRB* v. *Gissell Packing Co.*, 395 U.S. 575 (1965).

46. *Ex-Cello*, 185 NLRB 107 (1970).

47. *H. K. Poster* v. *NLRB*, 397 U.S. 99 (1970).

48. W. Gould, "Prospects for Labor Law Reform: The Unions and Carter," *The Nation*, April 16, 1977, pp. 466–467.

49. D. Nolan, "Improving NLRB Unfair Labor Practice Procedure," 57 *Texas L. Rev.* 47 (1978).

50. *Atlas Tack Corporation*, 226 NLRB 222–224 (1976).

51. Id.

52. Ibid., no. 38 (Justice Kishi dissenting), pp. 320–328.

53. *Midwest Piping and Supply Co., Inc.*, 63 NLRB 1060 (1945).

54. *Bruckner Nursing Home and Local 1115, Nursing Home and Hospital Employees Division*, 262 NLRB 115 (1982); *RCA Del Caribe, Inc. and Rafael Cuevas Kuinlam and Local 2333 Int'l Brotherhood of Electrical Workers*, 262 NLRB 116 (1982).

55. *RCA Del Caribe*, p. 124.

56. Y. Matsuda, "Wage Discrimination and 'Continuing Practice,' " in *Theoretical Problems of the Labor Union Law*, Essays in Honor of the 60th Commemoration of Dr. Kubo (Sekai Shisosha, 1980), p. 264.

57. See *Carpenter Steel Co.*, 76 NLRB 670 (1948).

58. *NLRB* v. *Pennsylvania Greyhound Lines*, 303 U.S. 261 (1938); *NLRB* v. *Pacific Greyhound Lines*, 303 U.S. 272 (1937).

59. *Ringin Shiki Insatsu* (Ringin Paper Article Printing) case, Osaka District Labor Relations Commission, order of May 21, 1954, Fu no. 17; *Showa Seisaku Sho* (Showa Factory) case, Saitama District Labor Relations Commission, Fu no. 6 (1961).

60. Labor Reform Act of 1977, H.R. 8410, 95th Cong., 1st Session (1977).

61. See *Angle* v. *Sachs*, 382 F.2d 655 (10th Cir. 1967). Here the court contended the "reasonable cause" requirement as to whether an injunction was necessary to prevent a frustration of the purposes of the National Labor Relations Act.

62. LMRA 29 U.S.C. §160(5): "The board shall have power, upon issuance of

a complaint . . . charging that any person has engaged in or is engaging in an unfair labor practice, to petition any United States district court within any district wherein the unfair labor practice in question is alleged to have occurred or wherein such person resides or transacts business, for appropriate temporary relief or restraining order. Upon the filing of any such petition the court . . . shall have jurisdiction to grant to the board such temporary relief or restraining order as it deems just and proper."

63. *Kaynard* v. *Meso Corp.,* 484 F. Supp. 167 (E.D. New York 1980). Cf. *McLeod* v. *General Electric Company,* 366 F.2d 847 (2d Cir. 1966). See also *Masan, etc.* v. *Universidad Interamericana De Puerto Rico,* 559 F. Supp. 255 (D. Puerto Rico 1983).

64. See, e. g., *Retired Persons Pharmacy* v. *NLRB,* 519 F.2d 486 (2d Cir. 1975); *Seeler* v. *Trading Post,* 517 F.2d 33 (2d Cir. 1975).

65. *Seeler* v. *Trading Post,* p. 38; *De Prospero* v. *The House of the Good Samaritan Keep Nursing Home,* 474 F. Supp. 552 (N.D. New York 1978).

66. See *Westinghouse Electric Corp.* v. *Free Sewing Machine Co,* 256 F.2d 806 (7th Cir. 1958); *Minnesota Mining Co.* v. *Meter,* 385 F.2d 265 (8th Cir. 1967).

67. *Automated Business Systems* v. *NLRB,* 497 F.2d 262 (6th Cir. 1974).

68. Section 10(e) of the American statute mandates temporary relief against union unfair labor practices.

69. *Times Publishing Co.,* 72 NLRB 676, 682–683 (1947).

70. For a view against conditional relief, see *Themes and Prospects On Labor Suits, Bessatu Hanrei Times,* no. 5; K. Tanaka, "Various Views on Conditional Relief, 'Hiteisetsu's' (Negative Theories)" (unpublished).

71. *Nobeoka Post Office* case, Tokyo district court, August 6, 1971, 670 v. no. 742.

72. See generally *Mainichi Shimbun* case, Tokyo District Labor Relations Commission, order of July 7, 1970, Fu no. 73 (1970); *Hochi Shimbun-Hochi Insatsu* (Hochi Newspaper–Hochi Printing) case, Tokyo District Labor Relations Commission, order of August 1, 1972, Fu no. 52–3.

73. F. Elkouri and E. Elkouri, *How Arbitration Works* (BNA, 1981), pp. 357, 359, 648.

74. *Safeway Stores, Inc.,* 64 L.A. 563 (1973).

75. For examples, *see Essex International Inc. and International Union of Electrical, Radio and Machine Workers,* 222 NLRB 121 (1976); *Logan Equipment Corp. and Local 4, International Union of Operating Engineers, AFL-CIO,* 199 NLRB 384 (1972).

76. *NLRB* v. *Biscayne Television Corp.,* 337 F.2d 267 (1964); *Baxter Bros.,* 91 NLRB 1480 (1950); *Sellers Mfg. Corp.,* 92 NLRB 279 (1950); *Happ Bros. Co.,* 90 NLRB 1513 (1950); *Burnette Castings Co.,* 79 NLRB 398 (1948).

77. *Jim Thomas Produce,* 1962 CCH NLRB, para. 11,304, case no. 13, CA-4539, May 1, 1962.

78. *McKesson* v. *Robbins, Inc.,* 17 NLRB 778 (1940); *Jefferson Co.,* 110 NLRB 157 (1954).

79. *NLRB* v. *New York University Medical Center,* 702 F.2d 284 (2d Cir. 1983);

NLRB v. *Webb Ford,* 689 F.2d 733 (7th Cir. 1982); *Royal Development Co* v. *NLRB,* 703 F.2d 363 (9th Cir. 1983).

80. *Wright Line,* 251 NLRB 1083, 1089 (1980).

81. *Behring International, Inc.* v. *NLRB,* 675 F.2d 83 (3d Cir. 1982).

82. *Wright Line,* n. 80 supra, p. 1088.

83. *NLRB* v. *Transportation Management Corp.,* 51 U.S.L.W. 4761, 4763 (June 15, 1983).

Chapter 5

1. *NLRB* v. *Insurance Agents,* 361 U.S. 477, at 488–489 (1959).

2. See *NLRA* §2(5), 29 U.S.C. §152 (5) (1970); *NLRA* §8(a)(2), 29 U.S.C. §158 (a)(2) (1970).

3. *NLRB* v. *Cabot Carbon,* 360 U.S. 203 (1959).

4. *NLRA* §8(a)(2), 29 U.S.C. §158(a)(2) (1976).

5. T. Hanami, *Labor Relations in Japan Today* (Kodansha International, 1979), pp. 54–64. Hanami recalls "arbitrating a case where a firm was forced to rent rooms to hold a high-level company meeting because their conference room was being used by the union." Hanami has also noted the following:
The unions are . . . dependent on the privileges granted them by management, in the form of office space in company buildings, meeting rooms, telephones, furniture, stationery, and sometimes even photocopy services. These facilities, provided free of charge by the companies, symbolize the intimacy of their relationship with the unions. It is also by no means unusual to find full-time union officials being paid, at least in part, by company management, not to mention the common practice of granting employees leave of absence for union activities and providing a free payroll deduction system for union dues. Such extensive privileges are more frequently to be found in the larger enterprises, where it may be said without exaggeration that the unions function at the company's expense. . . . In adjudicating unfair labor practice cases, it has been my experience that unions sometimes take it for granted that the company will grant paid leave to employees attending the hearings either as witnesses or observers for the union. The unions perceive their dependence on the company either financially or in other ways as a routine matter and one by no means inconsistent with fighting a legal battle with the same company.
In an essay that has been roundly criticized by the Japanese, Walter Galenson has taken the view that the Japanese trade union movement lacks the strength and independence to establish itself as a substantial political and economic force; see "The Japanese Labor Market," in *Asia's New Giant: How the Japanese Economy Works,* ed. H. Patrick and H. Rosovsky (Brookings Institution, 1976), p. 587. A graphic Japanese account, which in some respects supports Galenson's analysis, is S. Kamata's *Japan in the Passing Lane: An Insider's Account of Life in a Japanese Auto Factory* (Pantheon, 1982).

6. See *Bethlehem Steel Co.* v. *NLRB,* 120 F.2d 641 (D.C. Cir. 1941); *Pacific Manifolding Book Co.,* 17 L.R.R.M. 176 (1945). As noted above, a different approach was taken in *Chicago Rawhide Mfg. Co.* v. *NLRB,* 221 F.2d 165 (7th Cir. 1955), in which the court noted "neither mere cooperation and patience nor possibility of control constitutes unfair practices."

7. R. Kesselring and P. Brinker, "Employer Domination Under Section 8(a)(2)," 30 *Labor L. J.* 340 (1979). The authors further note: "Ultimately, the company was found guilty of an 8(a)(2) violation in 118 (91.5 percent) of these cases. In only 11 cases (8.5 percent of the total) did the outcome result in a no-violation finding. Eventually, 52 of these cases were appealed to the appropriate circuit court. Board orders involving 8(a)(2) violations were enforced in 45 (86.5 percent of the total appealed) instances. Only on 7 occasions did a circuit court reverse a violation finding by the board." More recent cases following these cases include *Homemaker Shops Inc. and Retail Store Employees Union, Local 876*, 261 NLRB 50 (1982); *Classic Industries and AFL-CIO, District Lodge 63*, 254 NLRB 1149 (1981); *Kaiser Foundation Hospitals, Inc. and American Federation of Nurses, Local 535*, 223 NLRB 322 (1976); *Hy-Grain Electronics*, 96 L.R.R.M. 1254 (1977); *Sportspot Inc.*, 88 L.R.R.M. 1533 (1974).

8. *Chicago Rawhide Manufacturing Company* v. *NLRB*, 221 F.2d 165 (6th Cir. 1955).

9. See note, "Domination and Support Under Section 8(a)(2)," 82 *Yale L. J.* 510 (1973).

10. For example, *American Tara*, 242 NLRB 1230 (1979).

11. *NLRB* v. *Scott & Fetzer*, 691 F.2d 288 (6th Cir. 1982). The positions taken by sixth and seventh circuit courts has been criticized in the note "Collective Bargaining as an Industrial System: An Argument Against Judicial Revision of Section 8(a)(2) of the National Labor Relations Act," 96 *Harv. L. Rev.* 1664 (1983).

12. Case 7-CB-4815, advice memorandum of general counsel, October 22, 1980. Other cases dealing with issues of this kind are cited in the memorandum. Generally they arise under section 8(a)(2) of the NLRA.

13. See n. 7 supra.

14. See, e. g., F. Schmidt, *Law and Industrial Relations in Sweden* (Rothman, 1977).

15. Collective Bargaining and Employee Participation in Western Europe, North America, and Japan, report of Trilateral Task Force on Industrial Relations, 1979, p. 78.

16. *NLRB* v. *Truitt Mfg. Co.*, 351 U.S. 149 (1956).

17. Schmidt, n. 15 supra.

18. *First National Maintenance Corp.* v. *NLRB*, 452 U.S. 666 (1981).

19. W. Gould, "The Supreme Court's Labor and Employment Docket in the 1980 Term: Justice Brennan's Term," 53 *U. of Colo. L. Rev.* 1, 9–11 (1981).

20. Ibid., p. 18.

21. See "Ratification of UAW-GM Agreement," *News and Background Information of the Labor Relations Reporter*, April 19, 1982, p. 32; "American Motors–UAW Agreement," ibid., April 26, 1982, p. 357; "UAW Organizing of White-Collar Workers," ibid., May 31, 1982, p. 82.

22. K. Yamaguchi, "Employment Adjustment and the System of Loaned Employees," *Japan Labor Bulletin*, May 1978, p. 9.

23. Id.

24. K. Hokao, Employer Initiative in Employment Termination and the Income Security of the Worker Concerned, National Report—Japan, p. 4.

25. Ibid., p. 3. For instances when the employer can dismiss for reasons of economic depression, see Y. Suwa, "Recent Cases on Dismissals By Reason of Redundancy: Economic Depression and Labor Law in Japan," *Japan Labor Bulletin* 18, no. 2 (1979), p. 5.

26. W. Gould, "On Labor Injunctions, Unions, and the Judges: The Boys Market Case," 1970 *Sup. Ct. Rev.* 215.

27. S. Jacoby, The Origins of Internal Labor Markets in Japan, University of California, Berkeley, Institute of Industrial Relations reprint 428 (1979), pp. 164–196.

28. *Tameny* v. *Atlantic Richfield Co.*, 27 Cal. 3d 167 (1980), p. 178.

29. Mich. Stat. Ann. (Callaghan 1982), §17.428(2) (the Whistle-Blowers Protection Act).

30. *See Board of Regents* v. *Ruth*, 408 U.S. 564 (1972); *Perry* v. *Sindermann*, 408 U.S. 593 (1972); *Arnett* v. *Kennedy*, 416 U.S. 134 (1974).

31. *Pugh* v. *See's Candies, Inc.*, 116 Cal. App. 3d. 311 (1981).

32. *Toussaint* v. *Blue Cross & Blue Shield of Michigan*, 408 Mich. 579 (1980).

33. C. Summers, "Individual Protection Against Unjust Dismissal: Time for a Statute," 62 *Vir. L. Rev.* 481 (1976).

34. Brief for UAW and its Local 509, p. 14, n. 11 (presented by UAW in regard to *Clayton* v. *International Union, UAW*). See also Gould, n. 19 supra, pp. 28–37.

35. *Los Angeles Marine Hardware Co.*, 235 NLRB 720 (1978), *aff'd*, 602 F.2d 1302 (9th Cir. 1979); *Milwaukee Spring Division*, 265 NLRB no. 28 (1982).

36. Y. Matsuda, "Judicial Procedure in Labor Disputes in Japan," *Japan Labor Bulletin*, May 1973, p. 8.

37. Id.

38. Ibid., p. 9.

39. Y. Matsuda, "Judicial Procedure in Labor Disputes in Japan," *Japan Labor Bulletin*, June 1973, p. 5.

40. Id.

41. *Boys Markets* v. *Retail Clerks*, 398 U.S. 235 (1970).

42. *Crowe & Associates, Inc.* v. *Bricklayers and Masons Union Local No. 2*, 112 L.R.R.M. 2080 (1982).

43. *Lever Brothers Co.* v. *International Chemical Workers Union*, 554 F.2d 115 (4th Cir. 1976). See also *Int'l Union, United Automobile, Aerospace, Agricultural and Implement Workers of America* v. *Dana Corporation*, 697 F.2d 718 (6th Cir. 1983); *Oakland Local, American Postal Workers Union, AFL-CIO* v. *United States Postal Service*, 107 L.R.R.M. 2943 (1981).

44. *Local Lodge No. 1266, Int'l Ass'n of Machinists and Aerospace Workers, AFL-CIO* v. *Panoramic Corporation*, 668 F.2d 276 (7th Cir. 1981).

45. *Buffalo Forge* v. *United Steelworkers*, 428 U.S. 397 (1976).

46. W. Gould, "On Labor Injunctions Pending Arbitration: Recasting Buffalo Forge," 30 *Stanford L. Rev.* 533 (1978).

47. Ibid., pp. 551, 560.

48. *Jacksonville Bulk Terminals* v. *International Longshoremen's Association*, 456 U.S. 212 (1982).

49. *Hoh* v. *Pepsico, Inc.*, 491 F.2d 556 (2d Cir. 1974).

50. See n. 44 supra.

51. See n. 44 supra, p. 285.

52. *First National Maintenance Corp.* v. *NLRB*, 452 U.S. 666 (1981).

Chapter 6

1. *Gokaroren* (chemical workers' union), central Labor Relations Commission (unfair labor practice, initial hearing), April 1960.

2. Ibid., p. 97.

3. *General Electric* v. *NLRB*, 412 F.2d 512 (2d Cir. 1969).

4. Ibid., p. 519.

5. *AFL-CIO Joint Negotiating Committee* v. *NLRB*, 459 F.2d 374 (3d Cir. 1972); *cert. denied*, 409 U.S. 1059 (1972).

6. See n. 3 supra, p. 520.

7. *Sun Oil Co. of Pennsylvania* v. *NLRB*, 576 F.2d 553, 557 (3d Cir. 1976), p. 558.

8. *Amoco Production Company*, 262 NLRB 160 (1982). See generally comment, "Union Affiliations and Collective Bargaining," 128 *U. Pa. L. Rev.* 430 (1979).

9. Ibid., slip opinion, p. 11.

10. K. Hokao, *Rodo Dantai Ho* (Labor Organization Law), Gendai Hogaku Zenshu (Contemporary Legal Studies Series) (Chikuma Shobo, 1975), pp. 380–385.

11. Ibid., p. 9 of manuscript, translated into English.

12. F. Gibney, *Japan, The Fragile Super Power* (Norton, 1975), pp. 125–126.

13. *Kotobuki Kenchiku Kenkyusho* (Kotobuki Architectural Research Company) case, Tokyo High Court of Judgment, June 29, 1977, Rominshu 28.3.223; taken from *Jurist*, special edition, Rodoho no Hanrei (Labor Law Casebook), vol. 2, *Kihon Hanrei Kaisetsu* series (Basic Case Interpretations series, no. 5), ed. K. Ishikawa and K. Yamaguchi (Yuhikaku Tokyo, 1978), pp. 160–161.

14. *Ibid.*

15. *Fitzsimons Manufacturing Company, West Branch Tube Division* v. *International Union, United Automobile, Aerospace and Agricultural Implement Workers of America, UAW, Local 1874*, 251 NLRB 375 (1980), *enforcement granted*, 109 L.R.R.M. 2810 (6th Cir. 1982).

16. Ibid., p. 376.

17. Ibid., p. 379.

18. 109 L.R.R.M. 2810 (6th Cir. 1982).

19. *Republic Aviation* v. *NLRB*, 324 U.S. 793 (1945).

20. Kobe District Court judgment, April 6, 1967, Rominshu 18.2.302, taken from *Bessatu Hanrei Times*, no. 5, IV *Hanrei Tenbo* (overview of cases) 55, *Sogi Koi* (acts of dispute), pp. 354–355.

21. Ibid., Hakodate District Court judgment, May 19, 1972, Rominshu 23.3.347.

22. Ibid., Nagoya High Court judgment, January 31, 1969, Rominshu 20.1.58.

23. See n. 20 supra.

24. *Taisei Kanko* (Hotel Okura) case (Tokyo Local LRC, 1971 Unfair Labor Practice 2, Decision September 19, 1972), pp. 348–352.

25. Ibid., p. 9 of author's unpublished transcript, translated into English.

26. Ibid., p. 5 of author's unpublished transcript, translated into English.

27. *Taisei Kanko* (Hotel Okura) case, Tokyo District Court, 1972 no. 45; judgment March 11, 1975; *Rodo Hanrei* no. 221, May 15, 1975, pp. 32–41.

28. *Holladay Park Hospital and Oregon Nurses Association, Inc.,* 262 NLRB 26 (1982)

29. Ibid., slip opinion, p. 4.

30. *Pay 'n Save Corp.* v. *NLRB,* 641 F.2d 697 (9th Cir. 1981).

31. *Holladay Park Hospital and Oregon Nurses Association, Inc.,* n. 28 supra, slip opinion, p. 5.

32. *NLRB* v. *Baptist Hospital, Inc.,* 442 U.S. 773 (1979).

33. *NLRB* v. *Harrah's Club,* 337 F.2d 177 (9th Cir. 1964).

34. *Pay 'n Save Corp.* v. *NLRB,* n. 30 supra, p. 701.

35. *Davison-Paxon Co.* v. *NLRB,* 462 F.2d 364 (5th Cir. 1972).

36. *Inland Steel Co.,* 257 NLRB 65 (1981).

37. *Borman's, Inc.* v. *NLRB,* 676 F.2d 1138 (6th Cir. 1982).

38. *NLRB* v. *Magnavox Co. of Tennessee,* 415 U.S. 322 (1974). See also *Eastex, Inc.* v. *NLRB,* 437 U.S. 556 (1978); *The Firestone Tire and Rubber Co. and Amalgamated Local Union No. 336, United Rubber, Cork, Linoleum and Plastic Workers of America, AFL-CIO-CLC,* 238 NLRB 1323 (1978).

39. *Roadway Express, Inc. and Lehigh Valley Chapter Teamsters for a Democratic Union,* 260 NLRB 78 (1981); *enforcement denied sub. nom., Helton* v. *NLRB,* 656 F.2d 883 (D.C. Cir. 1981). See *Professional Air Traffic Controllers' Organization and PATCO Employees Union,* 261 NLRB 132 (1981); *Shultz Foods Co., Inc. and Chocolate Workers Local Union No. 464,* 260 NLRB 162 (1981).

40. K. Hokao, *Rodo Dantai Ho* (Labor Organizations Law) Gendai Hogako Zenshu (Contemporary Legal Studies Series) (Chikuma Shobo, 1970), chapter 4.

41. Ibid., p. 7 of author's unpublished transcript, translated into English.

42. Ibid., pp. 10–11 of author's unpublished transcript, translated into English.

43. *Vincent's Steakhouse,* 216 NLRB 647 (1975); *Union Carbide* v. *NLRB* 114 LRRM 2129 (6th Cir. 1983).

44. *Vincent's Steakhouse,* p. 653.

45. *Cashway Lumber Inc.,* 202 NLRB 380 (1973); *Container Corporation of America,* 244 NLRB no. 53 (1979); enforcement granted 649 F.2d 1213 (6th Cir. 1981).

46. *Helton* v. *NLRB,* 656 F.2d 883 (D.C. Cir. 1981).

47. Hokao, n. 40 supra.

48. Showa Mizuho Post Office, Supreme Court, First Petty Bench, Oct. 7, 1982, *Rodokeizai* Hanrei Soroho, Vol. 1115, p. 3.

49. *Tokyo Kosei Nenkin Byoin* case, Tokyo District Court, September 20, 1966, Rominshu vol. 17, no. 5, p. 1134). In the *Nishi-Fukuoka Byoin* case (Fukuoka District Court, December 25, 1965, Rominshu vol. 16, no. 6, p. 1179), the affixing of posters to a hospital's reception area, entrance, and hallways was ruled illegal for the same reason. In the *Juntendo Byoin* case (Tokyo District Court, November 10, 1965, Rominshu vol. 16, no. 6, p. 909), "the affixing of posters was limited to the hospital's outer walls and its vicinity," and the action was "not taken as causing particular unease to patients beyond the sense of inviting general patient unease due to there being a dispute action" and was ruled legal.

50. *Jissen Joshi Gakuen* case, Tokyo District Court, April 16, 1964, Rominshu vol. 15, no. 2, p. 308.

51. Hokao, n. 40 supra. See also *Kochi Newspaper* case, Kochi District Court, December 28, 1956, Rominshu, vol. 6, p. 1018; *Mainichi Broadcasting* case, Osaka Mediation Commission, December 27, 1967, Reishu no. 37, p. 88; *Kunimitsu Denki* case, Tokyo District Court, March 29, 1966, Rominshu vol. 17, no. 2, p. 273.

52. Hokao, n. 40 supra. See also T. Kumakura, "The Affixing of Posters and Criminal Damage to Facilities," in *The Theory of Labor Law and Economic Law,* Essays in Honor of the 60th Commemoration of Mr. Kikuchi (Yuhikaku, 1960), p. 382.

53. *Japan National Railways Akita Bunkai* case, Sendai High Court, Akita Branch, April 19, 1950, Rokeishi no. 3, p. 351.

54. *Heiwa Taxi,* Supreme Court No. 3, Petty Bench Decision No. 876(a), 1969 (trespass upon structures, violent acts, etc.); Penal Law Violation Appellate Case, 1973.

55. *Firestone Tire and Rubber Co. and Amalgamated Local Union No. 336,* 238 NLRB 1323 (1978).

56. Ibid. See also *Cashway Lumber and Local Union 135, Teamsters,* 202 NLRB 380 (1973).

57. *Vincent's Steakhouse,* n. 43 supra.

58. *McGurran* v. *Veterans Administration,* 665 F.2d 321 (10th Cir. 1981).

59. *Eastex Inc.* v. *NLRB,* 437 U.S. 556 (1978).

60. Local 174 International Union, *UAW* v. *NLRB,* 106 L.R.R.M. 2561 (D.C. Cir. 198).

61. *Sawanomachi Motor Pool* case, Supreme Court, First Petty Bench, May 24, 1962, Shomu Geppo, Vol. 8, p. 926.

62. *NLRB* v. *Local No. 1229, IBW,* 346 U.S. 464 (1953).

63. *The Patterson Sargent Company,* 115 NLRB 1627 (1956).

64. Another problem that arises in connection with loyalty relates to the propriety of discharge or discipline for conduct off the job. Both American arbitrators and Japanese courts have had considerable difficulty with these kinds of cases. Although it may be that the standard used by Japanese com-

panies is a stricter one insofar as behavior away from the job is concerned, the judicial attitude of the Japanese courts relating to job security seems to carry over into this area.

For instance, in a case involving the Yokohama Rubber Company the Supreme Court of Japan held invalid under the Civil Code a discharge of a worker who, when intoxicated late at night, loitered around the streets, opened the door to a bathhouse and came face to face with someone, fled, and was apprehended. He was charged by the court with trespassing and intruding on a private dwelling and was fined 2,500 yen. The company maintained that the individual in question had violated employment regulations and that this justified dismissal inasmuch as the employee had "severely cast discredit upon the company through committing a deed of immoral impropriety." However, the court's reasoning was that the impropriety occurred in private life and had nothing to do with the company's business. The court was influenced by the fact that the employee was a rank-and-file production worker and that he had no leadership position in the company. On the other hand, the supreme court has taken the position that where the maintenance of honor and trust are betrayed by the employee and the employee's actions have a serious and unfavorable influence upon the company's social reputation, the employer may take action to discipline and discharge the worker. Similarly, the court has upheld a discharge imposed by the Japan National Railways. An important portion of the rationale was that, inasmuch as the railroad is a publicly owned corporation with "a high degree of public character," "the preservation of probity is required, so that . . . even the off-duty actions of an employee of such an enterprise" are "subject to more severe and more comprehensive and restrictive regulation" than those of an employee of the typical private corporation.

However, the general rule appears to be that the dismissal will not be upheld unless there has been a considerable degree of loss and damage done to corporate discipline and order, or honor and reputation, or some other substantial company interest, such as loss of profit. The Supreme Court of Japan in the *Nippon Kokan* decision reiterated the above-mentioned considerations, and also pointed out that another relevant one was where penal servitude had the result of prohibiting the worker from working for the employer. On balance, it would seem as though the Japanese courts have fashioned a more liberal rule that is more favorable to workers than that articulated by American arbitrators, despite what may be an even greater concern with the employee's behavior and loyalty to the firm.

American arbitrators have generally taken the position that an employee's personal conduct that has no direct effect on employment is not a basis for discharge unless it reflects a general lack of fitness to perform the job, or unless the employee's conduct will reflect negatively on the employer in some significant way, or unless other employees are reluctant to work with the grievant as a result of the conduct. Off-duty sexual conduct has presented particular difficulties. In one 1960 case concerning an employee who was fired upon being convicted of immoral behavior with his 14-year-old daughter, the arbitrator upheld the discharge because the small town was appalled by the employee's conduct and this would have adversely affected the employer's business and reputation. On the other hand, in another case around the same time, an arbitrator ordered reinstatement of an employee who was discharged because of absences occasioned by an illegal abortion, despite the fact that there was a possibility of negative effects on the employer's business and reputation. Arbitrators have generally held that violent conduct that is not work-related is not a basis for discharge unless it is clear that the employees are in fear of the grievant as the result of such conduct.

One particularly difficult area is that of immoral behavior by teachers, who are in a position to influence their pupils. One would expect the approach to differ with the age or grade level of the students involved, but this factor does not appear to have been given much weight by the arbitrators or the courts. Similarly, in the civil service, the Court of Appeals for the District of Columbia justified the dismissal of an employee who publicly flaunted and broadcast his homosexuality on the ground that the dismissal promoted the efficiency of the public service.

Labor-law cases involving off-duty use of drugs and alcohol, which can, in fact, have a bearing upon employment, do not appear to arise in Japan. Though arbitrators have upheld the right of employers to proscribe off-duty possession of drugs, if the rule is not properly enforced arbitrators may refuse to apply it. Recently, however, arbitrators have begun to recognize drug abuse as a disease and to require greater tolerance by employers. Alcoholics have received even more sympathy from arbitrators than drug abusers. It would appear as though the consensus is that an employer cannot discipline or dismiss an employee who is undergoing treatment and who is absent because of participation in a rehabilitation program, and that such absences must be tolerated.

65. *NLRA* §2(11), 29 U.S.C. §152(11) (1970). See also "The NLRB and Supervisory Status: An Explanation of Inconsistent Results," 94 *Harvard L. Rev.* 1713 (1981).

66. *Parker-Robb Chevrolet, Inc.*, 262 NLRB No. 58 (1981). For some of the background to this case see "Member Truesdale on Significant NLRB Decisions," in *1982 Labor Relations Yearbook* (BNA, 1982), pp. 66–73.

67. *Local 357 Teamsters* v. *NLRB*, 365 U.S. 667 (1961).

68. *Asahi Shimbun Ogura Branch* case, Supreme Court, October 22, 1952, Minshu , vol. 6, no. 9, p. 857, Rominshu, vol. 3, no. 5, p. 382; *Mitsutomo Tanko* case, Supreme Court, December 11, 1956, Keishu, vol. 10, no. 12, p. 1605; compare *NLRB* v. *Retail Store Employees*, 447 U.S. 607 (1980). *International Rice Milling Co.* v. *NLRB*, 341 U.S. 665 (1951).

69. *Asahi Shimbun Ogura Branch* case, Supreme Court, October 22, 1952, Minshu, vol. 6, no. 9, p. 857; Rominshu, vol. 3, no. 5, at 382; *Mitsutomo Tanko* case, Supreme Court, December 11, 1956, Keishu, vol. 10, no. 12, p. 1605; *Milk Wagon Drivers, Local 753* v. *Meadowmoor Dairies, Inc.*, 312 U.S. 287 (1941).

70. *Churyugun Yokohama Ground Transport Group* case, Keishu, vol. 12, no. 10 (1978), p. 2250.

71. See generally *Tohoku Denryoku Otani Generating Plant*, December 25, 1958, Keishu, vol. 12, no. 16, p. 3555; *Shikoku Denryoku Zaita Substation*, December 25, 1958, Keishu, vol. 14, no. 7, p. 3627; *Yoshiho Kogyo*, May 26, 1960, Keishu, vol. 14, no. 7, p. 868; *Mitsui Chemical Miike Senryo*, October 18, 1960, Minshu, vol. 4, no. 12, p. 2528.

72. *Churyugun Yokohama Rikujo Transport Group* case, Yokohama District Court, December 24, 1953, Rokeishu, no. 5, p. 599.

73. *Steelworkers Union, Local 3887* and *Stephenson Brick & Tile Co.*, 129 NLRB (1960).

74. *Densan Kyoto Incident*, Kyoto District, Rominshu 21.3.1052, March 17, 1955.

75. *Meijiya Incident*, Nagoya District, Rominshu 14.5.1081, May 6, 1973.

76. *Tokyo Daigaku Rodoho Kenkyukai* (Tokyo University Labor Law Study Group), *Chushaku Rodo Kumiai Ho* (Annotated Labor Union Law) (Yuhikaku, 1980), pp. 102–105.

77. *Iwataya Incident*, Fukuoka District, Rominshu 12.3.347, May 5, 1961.

78. *International Brotherhood of Teamsters, Local 695* v. *Vogt, Inc.*, 354 U.S. 284 (1957). See most recently *NLRB* v. *Retail Store Employees' Union*, 100 S. Ct. 2372, 2378 (1980).

79. K. Ishikawa, "The Regulation of the Employer-Employee Relations: Japanese Labor Relations Law," in *The Law and the Economy*, ed. T. von Mehren (Harvard University Press, 1963).

80. See generally the National Emergency Strike Provisions of the Taft-Hartley Act, 29 U.S.C. §§176–180.

81. NLRA §13, 29 U.S.C. §163.

82. *Local 232 et al.* [Briggs & Stratton Corp.] v. *Wisconsin Employment Relations Board*, 336 U.S. 245 (1949).

83. The Case of Nihon Shokuen petition for provisional disposition for status maintenance and wage payment (Rominshu 15.2.393, April 27, 1964).

84. Kubota and Hashimoto, *Rodo Saidan/Han no Riron to Jitsmu* (The Theory and Practice of Labor Hearings/Cases), p. 225. See also O. Tomoaki, *Bessatu Hanrei Times*, no. 5, IV, Hanrei Tenbo (overview of cases) 46 [*Sogi Koi* (acts of dispute)] without completion of collective bargaining and strikes without warning, pp. 314–315.

85. Tomoaki, pp. 314–315.

86. Labour Relations Adjustment Law, chapter V, article 37, reprinted in *Labour Laws of Japan* (Ministry of Labour, 1980), p. 42.

87. See generally Tomoaki, n. 84 supra, p. 314; M. Kawaguchi, "Nukiuchi Suto—Fuji Bunka Kogyo Jiken" (Strikes Without Warning—*Fuji Bunka Kogyo* case), *Jurist Bessatsu Rodo Hanrei Hyakushan Dai Sai Han*, p. 234; J. Honda et al., eds., *Hanrei Commentary, Rodo Ho* (Law Cases Commentary, Labor Law) (Sanseido, 1980), p. 42.

88. *Konan Bus Employees* case, Supreme Court Third Petty Court Judgment, December 24, 1968, Minshu 22.13.3194.

89. *Atkinson* v. *Sinclair Refining Co.*, 370 U.S. 238 (1962); *Complete Auto Transit, Inc.* v. *Reis*, 101 S.Ct. 1836 (1981).

90. *Boys Markets* v. *Retail Clerks*, 398 U.S. 235 (1970).

91. *Buffalo Forge Co.* v. *United Steelworkers*, 428 U.S. 397 (1976); W. Gould, "On Labor Injunctions Pending Arbitration: Recasting Buffalo Forge," 30 *Stanford L. Rev.* 533 (1978). See also W. Gould, "On Labor Injunctions, Unions and the Judges: The Boys Market Case," 1970 *Sup. Ct. Rev.* 215.

92. *Jacksonville Bulk Terminal* v. *International Longshoremen's Association,* 50 U.S.L.W. 4789 (1982).

93. *Pan American World Airways,* Tokyo District Court Rulings, Rominshu 24.6.669, 1973.

94. *Northwest Orient Airlines,* Tokyo District Court Rulings, Rominshu 24.6.666, 1973.

95. See generally W. Gould, "Recent Developments Under the National Labor Relations Act: The Board and the Circuit Courts," 14 *Univ. of Calif L. Rev.* 497 (1981).

96. *Marathon Electric Mfg. Corp.,* 106 NLRB 1171 (1955); *enforced,* 223 F.2d 338 (D.C. Cir.); *cert. denied,* 350 U.S. 981 (1956); *Dow Chemical Co.,* 212 NLRB 330, 340–341 (1974).

97. *NLRB* v. *Truck Drivers (Buffalo Linen),* 353 U.S. 87 (1957).

98. *NLRB* v. *American Shipbuilding,* 380 U.S. 300 (1965).

99. *Johns-Manville Products Corp.* v. *NLRB,* 557 F.2d 1126 (5th Cir. 1977), *cert. denied,* 436 U.S. 956.

Chapter 7

1. Public Corporation and National Enterprise Labor Relations Law, reprinted in *Labour Laws of Japan* (Ministry of Labor, 1980), pp. 44–65. For some of the background see J. Moore, *Japanese Workers and the Struggle for Power, 1945–1947* (University of Wisconsin Press, 1983).

2. Governor's Committee on Public Employee Relations, State of New York, Final Report, March 31, 1966; GERR, no. 135, April 11, 1966, B-1, D-1.

3. K. Sugeno, Public Employee Strike Problem and Its Legal Regulation in Japan (unpublished), p. 16. Cf. A. Cook, *Japanese Trade Unionism* (NYSILR, 1966).

4. "Work to rule" and other tactics were carried on in protest against rationalization plans and over political issues such as the proposed Okinawa treaty during the Vietnam War.

5. Ibid., p. 21.

6. The seminal case is *Thornhill* v. *Alabama,* 310 U.S. 88 (1940).

7. *National Railways Hirosaki Engine-District* case, Sup. C., Grand C., Tokyo Supreme Court, April 8, 1953; *National Railways Mitaka Engine-District case,* Sup. C., Grand C., June 22, 1955; *National Railways Hiyamamru case,* Sup. C., 2nd C., March 15, 1963; Constitution of Japan, chapter III, article 12, reprinted in *Labour Laws of Japan* (Ministry of Labour, 1980), p. 9. See also Sugeno, n. 3 supra, pp. 23–24.

8. Constitution of Japan, chapter III, article 15, reprinted in *Labour Laws of Japan,* p. 10.

9. *All Agricultural Ministry Workers Union* case, Keisho, vol. 27, no. 4 (1973), p. 547. See also Sugeno, n. 3 supra, pp. 30–31. A more detailed and up-to-date treatment is provided by K. Koshiro, "Labor Relations in Public Enterprises" and by K. Yamaguchi in *The Public Sector: Civil Servants in Contemporary Industrial Relations in Japan,* ed. T. Shirai (University of Wisconsin Press, 1983).

10. *All Agricultural Ministry Workers Union* case.

11. *Smith* v. *Arkansas State Highway Employees,* 441 U.S. 463 (1979).

Conclusion

1. A controversial treatment of this subject is contained in W. Ouchi's *Theory Z: How American Business Can Meet the Japanese Challenge* (Addison-Wesley, 1981). Earlier critiques of Japan by Americans have been similarly controversial; See J. Abegglen, *Management and the Worker: The Japanese Solution* (Kodansha International, 1973).

2. *Universal Research Corp.,* 262 NLRB no. 122 (1982).

Index